TEACHING AND
CHRISTIAN IMAGINATION

TEACHING AND CHRISTIAN IMAGINATION

David I. Smith and Susan M. Felch

With Barbara M. Carvill, Kurt C. Schaefer,
Timothy H. Steele, & John D. Witvliet

WILLIAM B. EERDMANS PUBLISHING COMPANY
GRAND RAPIDS, MICHIGAN / CAMBRIDGE, U.K.

Published 2016 by
Wm. B. Eerdmans Publishing Co.
2140 Oak Industrial Drive N.E., Grand Rapids, Michigan 49505 /
P.O. Box 163, Cambridge CB3 9PU U.K.

www.eerdmans.com

Printed in the United States of America

22 21 20 19 18 17 16   7 6 5 4 3 2

Library of Congress Cataloging-in-Publication Data

Smith, David I.
Teaching and Christian imagination / David I. Smith and Susan M. Felch ;
with Barbara M. Carvill, Kurt C. Schaefer, Timothy H. Steele, & John D. Witvliet.
pages   cm
Includes bibliographical references.
ISBN 978-0-8028-7323-1 (pbk. : alk. paper)
1. Teachers — Religious life. 2. Teaching — Religious aspects — Christianity. 3. Education —
Philosophy. 4. Imagination — Religious aspects — Christianity.   I. Title.
BV4596.T43S65   2016
248.8′8 — dc23

2015032350

**The authors and publisher acknowledge permission
to use Scripture quotations from the following sources:**

New American Standard Bible (NASB), Copyright © 1960, 1962, 1963, 1968, 1971, 1972, 1973, 1975, 1977,
1995 by The Lockman Foundation.

New Revised Standard Version Bible, copyright © 1989 the Division of Christian Education of the
National Council of the Churches of Christ in the United States of America. Used by permission.
All rights reserved.

Revised Standard Version of the Bible, copyright © 1946, 1952, and 1971 the Division of Christian
Education of the National Council of the Churches of Christ in the United States of America.
Used by permission. All rights reserved.

Scripture taken from the Holy Bible, Today's New International® Version TNIV®. Copyright 2001, 2005
by International Bible Society®. Used by permission of International Bible Society®. All rights reserved
worldwide. "TNIV" and "Today's New International Version" are trademarks registered in the United
States Patent and Trademark Office by International Bible Society®.

Contents

Acknowledgments

No book is written without gifts received from others; how much more so for a book that tries to draw widely on the imaginations of saints past and present. The debts incurred in the writing of this book are many, and what follows is but a partial list of some that specially require naming.

We are grateful to Calvin College and Seminary and our colleagues there (including members of a 2006-7 study group that sowed some seeds) for providing the kind of environment where conversations like those informing this book are possible. We are grateful to the Kuyers Institute for Christian Teaching and Learning for funding this project through to completion. We are also grateful to Jon Pott, Mary Hietbrink, and the staff at Eerdmans for remaining patiently invested in this project even as it took us rather longer to bring to fruition than we had first fondly imagined. It has been a great blessing to be allowed to converse richly about what it means to teach and learn outside of the pressure of immediate outcomes.

Several individuals helped us make the manuscript a better potential experience for others. Chris Smit offered valuable feedback on substantial sections of the book at an early stage. Debra Buursma read the whole and saved us from many a stylistic infelicity. Our thanks go to them, and also to Jeff Bouman, James Bradley, Matt Phelps, Doug Vander Griend, and Scott Waalkes, whose stories made their way into these pages alongside those of the larger cloud of witnesses enumerated in the endnotes.

Numerous others have given feedback or simply provided a sounding board for particular sections, either in their written form or as they were road tested at conferences and teacher education events in many times and places over the past few years. Thank you to everyone who has graciously allowed us to try out our ideas in public. This includes, of course, our various students who have enthusiastically embraced (or patiently endured) many of the ideas and practices that emerged out of our discussions.

Barbara M. Carvill
Susan M. Felch
Kurt C. Schaefer
David I. Smith
Timothy H. Steele
John D. Witvliet

April 2015

Introduction

WHY READ THIS BOOK?

Imagine this: it is Friday afternoon, and you are sitting at your computer. Classes have not gone well today — not badly, but not well. They've seemed a little dull, pedantic. You only barely resisted haranguing the student in the back row who obviously had not read the assignment; you were impatient with the eager but socially-challenged young man with his hand in the air. Somehow you managed to take a topic about which you are really passionate and make it boring. Worst of all, as you trudged through the minutes, you recalled the question you'd been asked when you were hired: "How will teaching here, at a Christian institution, be different from teaching elsewhere?" And you recalled your enthusiastic response: "Teaching here will really make a difference in students' lives; they will grow in love for God and his world as I help them understand not just my subject area but also their vocation as learners." You wince, not because you no longer believe in your answer but because today's class session seemed such a long way from questions about how to teach in ways that are deeply and authentically Christian. Fleetingly, you wonder if you should register for another educational seminar, read a how-to book, learn a new computer program, add more technology to your classroom, resign.

This book is an invitation to take a deep breath, slow down, and allow your weary soul to recover. The constant pressure we experience to tackle the next task and check the next box can leave our pedagogical imaginations eroded and threadbare. We need vision, not just beliefs and techniques. And that vision, if it is to sustain us, must be deeply Christian. Although our work may be framed by clear and well-intentioned statements of belief, the sources that mold how we actually imagine teaching and learning often end up being pragmatic and secular, and these sources will not nourish us as Christian teachers and scholars.

What might happen, however, if teaching and learning and classrooms and all that belongs to education simply began to look different to us, to inhabit a different space in our imaginations? What if the arduous march through the semester were transformed into a pilgrimage? What if planning for what will be "covered" came to seem more like building a cathedral than completing a chart? What if preparing for class became for us a kind of gardening that turned out to be profoundly connected to both play and justice? If the categories we habitually think in have worn thin, perhaps the most practical thing we can do is learn to imagine differently.

We believe that there is fresh depth to be gained by letting a biblical imagination and its play in the Christian tradition reanimate our ways of seeing and talking about learning. This is not a "how-to" manual or a collection of tips. This book offers lenses, not recipes, opening possibilities rather than laying out instructions. It is an opportunity to refresh your imagination, to step back and *see* differently. It invites you to explore how your faith and your imagination can dance together in ways that bring grace and truth into your daily service to your students and your school.

Talk of imagination does not mean escapism; we do want to address the reality of teaching and learning. But we are convinced that this reality cannot be grasped solely by means of the countable and measurable. The world opens itself up more fully to a larger, faith-filled vision. Our goal here is to recover theologically vibrant ways of seeing teaching and learning that have been mislaid, forgotten, or eroded into clichés. We suspect that these un-trod or well-trod paths might enrich and renew us if we wandered them a little. Perhaps refreshing our imaginations in conversation with Scripture and with Christian educators past and present might be exactly what we need in order to better come to grips with the real world. Perhaps if we could learn again to inhabit visions of classrooms as fruitful gardens, teaching as breaking bread, learning as a pilgrimage, or curriculum planning as cathedral building, new possibilities might come into view and familiar moves might appear in a new light. If so, then imagining teaching and learning in ways that resonate with faith is an urgent and practical task for the Christian educator as well as a path to refreshment and renewal.

Fact and Fancy We often associate imagination with creativity or fantasy. Our capacity to imagine lets us break free from what is immediately in front of us, allowing us the possibility of various excursions into the unreal. It lets us replace the chores list with unicorns, fairies, mid-morning mental vacations in the Bahamas, and events a long time ago in a galaxy far, far away. But that's only one side of what our ability to imagine allows us to do. Exercising imagination need not mean inventing things; it's also a way of putting things in context and knowing where we really are. We come to see what kind of world we actually inhabit and how we should act within it by glimpsing it from the right angle. This side of our imagination is active every day as we process the perspectives on the world that come at us from others and frame our own intentions and actions.

Imagine this. You're glancing a little more intently than you should be at a piece of chocolate cake (you are dieting). Or at a cigarette (you've quit smoking). Or at the smart phone that you had decided to leave turned off for a while (you've been way too connected). The familiar tensions between *I shouldn't*, and *I want to*, and *I don't want to want to*, and *I secretly do want to want to but know that I shouldn't* kick in. You remind yourself who you are, or bargain with yourself, or feel a little proud of your self-control, or pray for strength to guard your heart. Temptation has arrived, and some important things are going on in your brain.

Now listen in to two psychologists debating what is "really" going on when we feel the impulse to grab for available pleasures or resources. Psychologist one points to the role of glucose, suggesting that "The brain is always monitoring its resource levels. . . . If sugar is rising, we feel like we can defer indulging ourselves. In other studies, investigators control people's willpower as if with a joystick by putting them on a glucose infusion and regulating it up and down." Psychologist two disagrees, noting that the brain does not need a lot of sugar resources to operate willpower. He argues: "The glucose model is metabolically implausible . . . The brain isn't a hydraulic system that needs a constant pressure; it's an information processing system. If your browser's running slowly, you don't check your battery."

Listen to the language here. Although these scientists are describing physical facts, they reach into their imaginations to explain how we do or do not employ our willpower. In fact, they use quite different images — different metaphors — to make their points. If we pause to ponder their words, we are faced with some weighty questions. Are people computers that we can program, or machines that we can control with a joystick? Are our brains plumbing systems with pressure levels or information systems with data moving around? And what happens to how we see ourselves if we acquire the habit of talking about ourselves and others in terms of resource levels, joysticks, hydraulic systems, and browsers rather than discipline or holiness or the temptations of the wicked and deceitful heart?

We are not dealing with flights of fancy here. These images are competing attempts to interpret scientific findings and steer expensive research. They offer orienting images that might consciously or unconsciously influence the way we think about ourselves and our behavior, and so get woven into the lived tapestry of our choices. They are examples, plucked from current media, of the images *through* which we think and speak and act. Our imagery offers direction for our actions and inquiries, not only when we are reading fiction or studying art, but also when we are focused on real-world tasks. Imagination is one of our basic ways of getting at the world, and this recognition is at the heart of this book.

Classroom Imaginings So now imagine the classroom. Consider a child being taught about the roundness of the earth and its place in the solar system even though the land looks flat. Imagine the mental image of the world that needs to be formed for it to make sense to point at a spot on a foot-wide globe and say that we live "there." Or consider a first-year college student wrestling with visions of her future that awaken fear, ambition, or hope. Does she picture herself as a doctor, an engineer, a teacher? Does she imagine herself living close to her family or perhaps moving to another country? Does she foresee prosperity or poverty or sacrificial simplicity? Do these possibilities excite or worry her? Or consider a teacher preparing for tomorrow, wondering if an idea that crosses her mind really has a chance of connecting with her students. How does her professional knowledge begin to combine with an understanding about who students are and what it means to be a chemistry teacher?

Imagination opens up possibilities. For that reason, it can surely lead us astray, constraining us to live within a false picture of things. But our ability to imagine things that elude our immediate grasp — the shape of the earth, or our place in the world, or what comes next, or where the boundaries of wisdom lie — is often also essential to our ability to see things the way they really are and the way they could and should be. Teachers are not only shaped by their own ways of imagining, they are engaged in influencing the imaginations of those they teach. A teacher's imagination is a serious matter.

Patterns and Practice Some images are just passing illusions, moments of play, a brief sparkle on the rippling pond of language. Some delight us more deeply, but in a manner that remains conscious of their artifice. Some, however, take hold, and worm their way deeper into our ways of thinking and doing. They form consistent patterns that begin to guide and mold us.

A recent report from a medical forum discussing cancer treatment illustrates how an image can shape actions. One participant told of a six-year-old patient who would lash out against the nurses, kicking and hitting them while being treated. It turned out that the girl's mother had repeatedly told her that she must "keep on fighting" in order to "beat the cancer," and the girl had obeyed rather literally. When it was explained to her that the fighting was not fighting with fists, the behavior stopped.

Perhaps this story provokes an indulgent smile, but the focus of the discussion was on adult behaviors. Here again, growing up does not free us from the reach of our images. "We have inundated our language with bellicose metaphors," comments another oncologist, noting that in immunology "lymphocytes are 'deployed' or 'mobilized,' the protagonists are 'killer' cells and the images are all of 'battles' for supremacy and survival." What happens when fighting images become dominant? Thinking in battle images can help some patients retain a sense of dignity and control, but for others the same images arouse fear. For still others they can create a sense of guilt and defeat as the disease progresses and they are left feeling that they did not fight hard enough. Doctors note that battle imagery can influence treatment choices, through a "seduction that aggressive treatment is better."

There's some history to this, too. In the 19th century, the application of military metaphors to the profession of nursing helped create an ethos built on ranks and uniforms, nursing "stations," the giving of "shots," and an expectation that patients would obey orders, submit to hardship, and not ask questions. Today these images nest inside a larger cultural habit of thinking of prevention in terms of warfare: wars on terror, on poverty, and on drugs. Imagination connects our personal mental worlds, our institutional practices, and our orienting cultural frameworks by telling us what is plausible and how we should act. We work out our lives within patterns of imagery that offer direction for our dreams and our energies.

Cubes and Cathedrals   As Etienne Wenger points out, even when our outward behaviors appear similar, what is in our imagination may change our sense of what we are doing, and so our experience of doing it. He asks us to imagine encountering two stonecutters at work, and asking them what they are doing. One of them replies: "I am cutting this stone in a perfectly square shape." The other, apparently carrying out the same actions, says: "I am building a cathedral." In terms of chisel-holding skills, there may be little difference between the two of them. They are, however, experiencing what they are doing differently. As a result they may well be learning quite different things from the activity, even growing into different people. In teaching and learning, as in stonecutting, we need more than a set of techniques; we need a way of telling ourselves what it is we are doing and why. The visions we adopt will help shape the kinds of teachers and learners that we become.

Educators today work in environments that seem to work harder at keeping us cutting square shapes than at helping us to see ourselves building cathedrals. It's not that our talk about education is devoid of imagination. Our talk about education is full of implicit tales about journeys in which some get left behind, computing devices in which information gets processed, marching cohorts from which some drop out, heroic super-teachers who save the day, and so on. But most of these images do little to spark the sacred in our imagination, to help us to see the act of teaching and learning through the lens of faith, hope, and love.

Our educational imaginations inspire us, caution us, nurse our enthusiasm or our cynicism, nudge us in this direction rather than that. The images that we let take hold of our thinking influence the kinds of teachers we become. This matters especially for those teachers and institutions that aim to be Christian. While conversations about how to educate in Christian ways commonly focus on the relationships between beliefs and behaviors, the shaping role of imagination has not always been given its due. Our confessions of faith may commit us to seeking God-honoring practices even as our daily ways of speaking about teaching and learning draw mainly from an essentially secularized imagination. The renewing of our minds is about vision as well as beliefs.

Journeys, Gardens, and Buildings   This connection between faith, vision, and practice is the concern that gives rise to this book. Out of the many metaphors that have influenced visions of teaching and learning, we have selected three: journeys, gardens, and buildings. Each one easily lends itself to dreary, clichéd uses. Here we will explore them in ways that stretch beyond the familiar clichés, listening especially for the biblical echoes and Christian resonances that can be heard in them. We wish to recover a sense of their theological richness so as to bring alive connections between Christian ways of seeing and educational practice.

Take gardens, for instance. The natural focus on growth and patient nurture makes gardening an easy metaphor for teaching, one frequently appropriated throughout the ages. The ideal garden has ranged from the walled enclosure of medieval times to the mathematical patterns of French Classical gardens or the wilder, less tamed vistas of English landscape gardening — and so the implications of thinking of schools as gardens has varied. We might recall Romantic images of learning as natural growth spoiled by the mechanical invasions of adult discipline, and children as little flowers best left to blossom in the sunshine. But that is just one possible direction. The image can also be seen in terms of the need for careful planning, pruning, and cultivation in order to bring a more disciplined beauty out of nature's wild tangle. Talk of plants and gardens (and of journeys and buildings) gets bound up with wider networks of ideas, beliefs, stories, and frameworks that have taken root in our thinking, and so yields varying educational visions. What happens when the Garden of Eden, the tree planted by streams of water, or Isaiah's unfruitful vineyard are drawn into focus?

Each of our three metaphors has roots in the Bible, and each has been used throughout Christian history as a way of thinking about education in faith-informed ways. As a result, for ears that are attuned to biblical texts, some uses of these images can evoke a larger background narrative. Spending time reawakening the rich Christian tradition associated with each of these images offers fresh angles on the connection between faith and teaching. Each image can serve as a prism through which Christian theological sensibilities can refract into our conceptualizations, our classrooms, and our callings.

What if the generic notion of journeys, which risks descending into tourism, became a more specific meditation on learning as Christian pilgrimage, with its particular focus on formation, fellowship, and purpose? What if the

Bible's picture of gardens as places of beauty and virtue or of God planting a vineyard and looking for the fruits of justice rooted our imagining? What if talk of learning in terms of buildings began to evoke temples, cathedrals, and abbeys, forcing us to question just what kind of an educational edifice we are constructing? What if each of these images became a bridge connecting our imaginations to theological stories? These questions animate this book. We approach the nature of teaching and learning on this occasion not by diving into the detail of the classroom, but by stepping back and gathering the ingredients of a different vision. We offer these reflections convinced that there is fresh life to be found in wrapping our educational imaginations around Scripture, and that this fresh life is something we sorely need.

How to Read This Book

All that has been said so far implies a challenge that we have faced throughout the process of researching and writing. Our goal is to refresh minds, not just to inform them, with the ultimate goal of evoking new visions for teaching and learning. That has implications for the kind of book we offer and the kind of reader we hope for. That's why this book is a little different from most books on Christian education. A word on how best to approach it is in order.

The book emerges from four years of rich discussions among an interdisciplinary team of college faculty. The authors of this book all teach at Calvin College in Grand Rapids, Michigan. Barbara Carvill is an emeritus professor of German. Susan Felch is professor of English and the director of the Calvin Center for Christian Scholarship. Kurt Schaefer is professor of economics. Tim Steele is professor of music. David Smith is director of Graduate Studies in Education and of the Kuyers Institute for Christian Teaching and Learning, which sponsored this project. John Witvliet is professor of music and director of the Calvin Institute for Christian Worship.

As we worked together we found ourselves very clear about what we did *not* want to produce. A traditional collection of scholarly essays on the importance of metaphor seemed too pedantic. We wanted to avoid an exhausting enumeration of past Christian images — we were not trying to write a history, even though we were drawing deeply from historical sources. At the same time we did not want to end up with something vaguely inspirational in a greeting card kind of way — we felt that there should be some provocative details and spiky corners rather than everything tied neatly together. We especially wanted to avoid the impression that it is possible to move in simple, straightforward recipe fashion from a group of theological images to a set of pedagogical prescriptions. While an image can be profoundly direction-setting, it does not tell us exactly what to do.

The result is that if you approach this book expecting a tight logical argument, a masterly survey, a quick collection of practical tips, or a consistent set of answers you are likely to experience disappointment. We offer instead a more loosely linked collection of reflections, close readings, and examples of practice in the hope that as you ponder the harmonies and dissonances that emerge they might serve as a playground for your imagination. You will find that ideas take different directions, that a change of topic or of perspective jolts you towards a new train of thought. We may place things alongside one another without spelling out the connection or the application; we are trying to help you to make new connections as much as we are trying to tell you things. We linger over biblical texts and voices from the Christian tradition that have allowed these texts to mold its imagination, resisting the temptation to leap too quickly to strategies and solutions. What we are after here is a kind of engagement with biblical thought that might seep into the way we imagine; that calls for something more like an ongoing, meditative conversation than a ready-made set of conclusions.

You will at times detect different voices in the prose. The book has multiple authors, and while we have worked to make it readable, we have not aimed at a completely homogenized result. (We have steered away from single-author chapters, but where a section refers to "I" or is mainly the work of one author we indicate who that is in the notes. In order to keep the text itself free of apparatus, we have placed the notes at the end of the book). Our own discussions were marked by freewheeling fertility, perplexed wrestling, and happy surprises. We tried to leave some space for the reader to experience the same.

Our sustained conviction has been that a rich engagement with some of the deep veins of past and present Christian imagination could foster renewal — but only if these images are played with, lived with, and meditated upon rather than merely understood and filed away. Each image, and each facet of each image, reveals some things about teaching and learning and hides others. No single image provides a master metaphor. Each can resonate in different ways even within a Christian context. Sometimes it is through tensions and contrasts that our thinking might be nudged in fresh directions.

This book calls for a meditative kind of reading. We hope you will be willing to meander a little, to linger in some spots and make creative connections. We hope to provoke thought more than prescribe solutions. We suspect the best way to *think with* each image rather than just *know about* it is a process of gradual reflection. When you encounter an illustration, pause and ponder it before reading the accompanying text. When you find an exploration of a biblical passage, take the time to enter its world before worrying about what it might be telling you to do. When you come upon an example from the classroom, resist approaching it as a template to be approached in terms of whether it can be immediately applied in your setting. Dwell instead on the kind of educational imagination that has shaped it. When you experience a tension between different parts of the text, different directions in which an image might be taken, let it sit for a while and ponder what might be lost if the tension were too quickly removed.

While the book may be read from start to finish, we suggest it might be best digested at intervals during a semester, an academic year, or a summer or two, perhaps focusing on just one of the images for a season. Slow down, lay aside the impulse towards quick solutions or getting it all straight. Give each text and image a chance to settle, put out tendrils, roll around the mind, and strike up a conversation with daily tasks. This will increase the chance that the book might touch your imagination in generative ways. We invite you to take enough time for the journey, and revisit the places where you enjoyed the view. Linger in the garden and find a favorite corner. Explore the rooms of the house, and try out some of the furniture. Read with others and find out how they see. It might just transform the way you approach your craft and experience your calling.

PART ONE

Journeys and Pilgrimages

Setting Our Feet on the Road

THE FIRST OF OUR THREE chosen metaphors involves journeying, and more specifically pilgrimage. The notion that life is a journey is regular fodder for sentimental greeting cards; in classrooms we too *get stuck, press forward*, are *left behind*, and reach *finish lines*. Clichés these may be, but they offer tracks for our thoughts. Sometimes it is not the fresh and striking metaphors, but the images that have become our contact lenses — images habitually looked *through* rather than looked *at* — that guide our thinking and doing.

Journeys are all about movement, departures, and arrivals. Thinking of learning in terms of journeys encourages us to imagine learning as taking us away from our origins into new lands, requiring us to let go of some cherished attachments and embrace the new experiences and the new sense of self that arise along the way. Travel images conjure up questions about pace (forced march? mad dash? refreshing stroll?), and about how long to linger in a given spot. Plans for learning become maps and progress reports; we find ourselves looking forward to crossing thresholds and reaching milestones and destinations. Journey-talk raises questions of where we begin, what direction we choose, which maps we will trust, and what wonders, dangers, and distractions might lie along the way. It may also nudge us to think in terms of traveling companions and needed encouragement.

In this part of the book we will explore what happens when we start to think about our educational journeys in a less clichéd manner as pilgrimages. How might it change our approach to teaching if instead of planning learning as though each week were an identical container to be filled with content, we began to think about the rhythms of a journey together? We begin where every journey begins: with the challenge of taking the first step. Pilgrimage is not automatic. In fact, we begin with an image of learning as a prevention of travel, as an enterprise that pins the learner firmly to the ground and makes sure that things stay put.

PINNED TO THE GROUND

In your dream you are walking along a country path near the edge of a forest, the late afternoon sun warming one side of your face. All is quiet; no cars, no planes, no farm machinery in the distant fields. Just the unpaved path, the creak of trees, the stirring of grass, the low buzzing of insects.

Then something else reaches your ear, faint, just around a bend where the path turns behind a hillock. A muttering, then a strangled gurgling, retching sound, like an incompetent hangman's handiwork in full swing. It sounds like need and almost involuntarily you break into a run.

What first strikes your senses are the clothes of the three men standing huddled under a dead tree by the side of the way. They are clearly not of your day, not even of your century. Lacking the familiar reference points that speed recognition, all you can take in at first is a jumbled mix of pointed beards, waxed moustaches, felt boots and gauntlets, elaborate embroidered capes, feathered hats, ribbons, and pantaloons.

As the details resolve into the figures of three stern men, you realize that there is also a fourth, the source of the pained gurgles, lying at their feet, hands raised in what might be abject surrender or feeble efforts to ward off their attack. It seems that a fellow traveler has been waylaid, pinned to the ground. You call out in protest. One of the men standing looks over his shoulder and notes your presence, but the three show little intention of desisting.

Caught between the impulse to defend the victim and your awareness of being outnumbered, you take a hesitant step closer. It is only now that you realize that although they look sharp and dangerous, the objects being used to pin the unfortunate to the ground are not weapons. At the center of the huddle is a large funnel, its narrow end inserted into the throat of the recumbent wretch. It is this that causes his helpless immobility and his inarticulate noises. Aside from this funnel, no hand is being laid on him. The three standing over him are instead engaged in a comically laborious attempt to stuff a large tangle of awkwardly shaped objects down the broad end of the funnel and into his digestive system. You catch sight of the various paraphernalia of the learned:

The Nuremberg Funnel, engraving by David Mannasser, ca. 1650

musical scores, calipers and rulers and other tools of geometry, a globe and some related astronomical artifacts, books of grammar rules, philosophical tomes. Items crush against one another and catch on the edges. Apparently, these are teachers.

Most of these objects could not possibly fit through the narrow aperture at the bottom. The attempt to stuff them in seems hopeless. But the trio continue undeterred, exerting a steady downward pressure, ignoring the feeble cries from below. As they labor on, their student is motionless, going nowhere. His assigned role is to lie still and be filled up with things, not to venture forth for a destination beyond his teachers' designs.

Filled with pity, you reach to help, to say something, but you can't find the words. You find yourself frozen with the familiar immobility of the moments before waking. Soon you are back in the present, back in the more familiar world where you and your students engage in education together. *What thoughts do you carry with you?*

Is There a Destination?

The unsettling vision of teachers stuffing things into the head of the helpless learner haunted the European imagination for a long enough period to be given a name: the Nuremberg Funnel. Teaching here means forcing a mass of dense material through a narrow tube, all the while making sure that your students stay submissive and don't cause trouble. The student becomes a passive sufferer, an inanimate object at the teacher's feet, contributing nothing to the process, not even chewing and swallowing, yet expected to trust that the strangulation of his voice and subjugation of his body will be for his benefit someday. This student has been made into a receptacle, not a pilgrim.

The picture is, of course, satirical. Like all memorable satire it both offers a grotesque caricature of reality (but that's not how we teach!) and cuts close enough to give us pause (could that be how we teach?). Both the teachers and the learner are immobile; it is only the knowledge that travels from one place to another. The student has been interrupted on his journey through life, as if by a group of roadside bandits. Pinned to the ground beside the path, he is required to stop moving so that the funnel can be inserted accurately. The comically abject posture provokes imagination of other possibilities. What if the learner were standing too? Where was he going before he was knocked to the ground? What if he were walking down the path alongside his teachers, deep in conversation?

Education is traditionally associated with sitting still; an early modern satirist of education noted that one would not get far in school without "buttocks of lead". Yet we also have a long history of talking about learning in terms of journeys. Students follow a "curriculum," a Latin word that literally refers to the act of running or to a race track. More colloquially, we refer to a "course" of study, to "covering a lot of ground," and to learners "falling behind," "staying on track," or "making good headway." We might get "stuck in a rut," fail to "get to" some particular piece of knowledge by the end of class, or we may "not get very far" with mastering a new skill. We "go into" some things in more detail, explaining them "step by step," while we quickly "run through" (or even "skip past") other things. We may "go back" to something that we need to "revisit" or add some illustrations "along the way," and this might help us "get closer" to understanding or "reach a conclusion." We think that education can provide a "head start" in life, perhaps enabling some students to "go far"; some learners might even be on the "fast track." In a great deal of our talk as we teach and learn, it is apparent that we are thinking about the changes that happen during education as a form of journeying.

The journey metaphor offers us a different picture of the learner than the passive receptacle. And yet it still leaves the nature and purpose of the journey open for debate. As educational history has walked hand in hand with cultural history, imagery associated with educational journeys has shifted from travel on foot to riding in a coach and then to driving along a highway. In older Christian appropriations of the image, the path was given by God and led (at a more deliberate and deliberative pace) towards God as its destination. In the Enlightenment, the sense of destination remained, but the goal was reframed in terms of movement towards the virtuous life of the useful citizen. As travel became more widely available, the idea of education opening up new horizons took hold. The image of the 19th century explorer offered a version of travel as deliberately leaving the well-trodden path and collecting new experiences in exotic, uncharted territories. Later still, the rise of mass tourism tilted the image of travel towards comfort, efficiency, and consumption, evoking anxieties concerning educational tourists whose shallow gaze skims the main sights but does not linger for long enough to be changed. The educational path is now giving way to talk of an educational superhighway with a powerful emphasis on speed of information. Alongside these shifts came a gradual yet momentous reversal in which the experience of journeying itself overtook the pursuit of a hallowed destination as the central emphasis; simply being in motion at increasing speed and with increasing range became an end in itself. Eventually, with the fading of a shared destination, any self-chosen destination became equally valid.

The role of the teacher in all of this journeying also remains open to interpretation. Is the teacher a guide, walking the road with the students, or a signpost standing authoritatively at the crossroads, or the proprietor of a roadside strip mall hawking wares? Is the teacher to set or point towards the destination, or is the teacher's role simply to keep students in motion, to ease their journey, and perhaps provide guard rails to keep them from straying too far from the road? Is the teacher providing students with a route — a set of steps to be followed that will successfully lead to a destination — or a map — a bigger picture of a connected whole across which various journeys can be creatively plotted? How would a pilgrim answer these questions?

THE FIRST STEP

It was quite a few years ago, while reading aloud from a Bible story book written for young children that Abram's departure from Ur of the Chaldees suddenly became more human for me. I had grown used to thinking of Abram, the "father of all who believe," as a model of faith, a figure challenging us to step out and follow God wherever he leads us. The biblical account is sparse — God told Abram to "Go from your country, your people and your father's household to the land I will show you," and in response "Abram went, as the Lord had told him; and Lot went with him" (Genesis 12:1-4). There is more than enough space around this terse summary to launch heroic tales of the man of faith sallying boldly forth and providing a glowing model of courage to the rest of us who sit mired in our comfortable apathy. I have heard that sermon more than once. And there is something to those tales. God's plans for the world are at stake and when called away from his homeland, Abram indeed "obeyed and went, even though he did not know where he was going" (Hebrews 11:8).

But as I sat one evening reading the story of "Abraham's Big Family" from a small picture book to my small son, I was moved by a simple picture of a very worried-looking Abram sitting up in bed in the middle of the night, worry lines creasing his features, his knees hugged tensely to his chest, his wife asleep beside him. The picture brought his world-changing departure down to size. The text read:

Abram trusted in God.
But he was puzzled and afraid.
He lay awake all night,
worrying,
asking himself
all sorts of questions
— which way shall I go?
— what sort of place will it be?
— will I have a nice house?

At the time I was preparing for a precarious move to another country with my family, following our conviction that God was leading us to graduate study there. Learning commonly involves leaving home to some degree, and sometimes literally and radically. It felt like a risky journey to undertake, full of unknowns, and full of very concrete, anxious, human questions that stuck to me more closely than any incipient sense of heroics. How should we travel? When can we get the best deal on flights? What sort of place will it be? Will the visa come in time? Will the studying go well? Will I be good at this? Will I have a nice house? While the children's book account employed some poetic license, its description of Abram's sleepless night rang true.

Abram is not alone; the Bible is filled with accounts of fraught departures and fateful travels. Adam and Eve are sent east of Eden. Abraham continues his journeys, as do his descendants. Joseph travels to Egypt, eventually followed by his family. The people of Israel are led out of Egypt and journey to Canaan, and later into distant exile, and then back again. The people of Israel journey as pilgrims, year after year, to the Jerusalem temple for the major festivals. Elijah is one of many wandering prophets. Mary and Joseph journey to Bethlehem, as do magi from a distant country. Jesus and his disciples undertake three years of itinerancy, and ultimately Jesus sets his face toward Jerusalem. Encountering the risen Christ, the disciples are told that they will be witnesses to the ends of the earth; soon after, they are scattered far and wide. Paul, among others, embarks on great missionary journeys. To read Scripture is to encounter on a regular basis people leaving the security of home and setting out into the unknown.

Sometimes the journeys begin in hope, sometimes in shame, and sometimes amid suffering. There is always a first step to be dared. The travelers are opened up to the risks of the road — but also to the faithfulness of God. The learning that takes place along the way varies: the sudden, blinding transformation of the Damascus road, the patient, systematic dialogue of the Emmaus road, and the hard life lessons of the Jerusalem road, where one might learn not to travel alone after being beaten and stripped by robbers. But always, there is the vulnerability of the road.

The Bible not only narrates a panoply of journeys, but also frequently speaks of journeying in such a way that it becomes a pattern for faithful life before God's face, a life offered up to the risks of obedience. Psalms describing the journey to worship in Jerusalem have become patterns for prayer for believers who never literally travel more than a few blocks to attend church. 1 Peter 1:17-2:11 calls on Christians to live "as foreigners and exiles," while Hebrews 11 connects this sojourner status with journey to a heavenly city. The pilgrimage to Jerusalem thus becomes an enduring image for the Christian life. For medieval Christians it was a commonplace that life was lived as a pilgrim journey through an uncertain world — we face life as *homo viator*, "pilgrim humanity." John Bunyan's *Pilgrim's Progress* is nowadays perhaps the most famous and influential depiction of the Christian life as a pilgrimage, but it was far from the first. Gregory the Great, for instance, wrote in the 6th century:

> To the just man, temporal comfort is like a bed at an inn to a traveler: he stops and he endeavors to retire, he rests himself bodily, but his mind is inclined elsewhere. Truly, sometimes he even desires to endure difficulties, refusing the prosperity of transitory things lest he be delayed from reaching his homeland by the pleasures of the road, and lest he fix his heart on the way of the pilgrim and come to the heavenly homeland without reward when it eventually comes into view. The just man, therefore, does not accumulate wealth in this world, for he knows himself to be a pilgrim and a guest in it.

Little wonder that Abram's departure recurs in sermons. Throughout the history of the church, "journey" and "pilgrimage" have been recurring master metaphors for the life of faith before God's face.

But does biblical wayfaring have anything to do with educational journeys? We have so far dipped in a general way first into education and then into biblical talk of journeying. What would happen if we let these two strands mingle a little, if we let images crafted to articulate the Christian journey through life, images of paths and pilgrimages, walk for a while alongside the way that we think about teaching and learning? What kind of conversation might result? Would it redraw any of our mental maps? If teaching and learning could be about journeying together, then where are we headed? What resources are needed for the trip? What is the motivation for traveling? Do we travel alone or together? What are the rhythms of the road?

How would you begin to answer those questions?

Are We Tourists or Pilgrims?

THEY GO FROM STRENGTH TO STRENGTH

How lovely is your dwelling place,
    LORD Almighty!
My soul yearns, even faints,
    for the courts of the Lord;
my heart and my flesh cry out
    for the living God.
Even the sparrow has found a home,
    and the swallow a nest for herself,
    where she may have her young —
a place near your altar,
    LORD Almighty, my King and my God.
Blessed are those who dwell in your house;
    they are ever praising you.

Blessed are those whose strength is in you,
    whose hearts are set on pilgrimage.
As they pass through the Valley of Baka,
    they make it a place of springs;
    the autumn rains also cover it with pools.
They go from strength to strength,
    till each appears before God in Zion.

Hear my prayer, LORD God Almighty;
    listen to me, God of Jacob.

Look on our shield, O God;
    look with favor on your anointed one.

Better is one day in your courts
    than a thousand elsewhere;
I would rather be a doorkeeper in the house of my God
    than dwell in the tents of the wicked.
For the LORD God is a sun and shield;
    the LORD bestows favor and honor;
no good thing does he withhold
    from those whose walk is blameless.

LORD Almighty,
    blessed are those who trust in you.

                             (Psalm 84, TNIV)

In Whose Heart Are Highways

Pilgrimage is a significant theme in the psalms of Israel. Psalms 120-134 are commonly regarded as pilgrimage psalms or psalms of ascent, evoking the annual processions of worshipers from the towns and villages of Israel to Jerusalem for Passover, Pentecost, or Sukkot. These psalms place us on the road, ascending the hill of the Lord together to worship at God's dwelling place. Here we focus on a related psalm, Psalm 84, which chimes in with the psalms of ascent and offers a striking vision of the place of pilgrimage in the life of Israel.

We enter the psalm amid the glad strains of arrival — after the long, dusty journey, how lovely is Jerusalem! The psalmist has craved to be in Yahweh's courtyards, has longed to be at journey's end, and now, a glance down reveals feet standing within the gates of Jerusalem. Relief and joy burst forth. The road has given way to refuge and the pilgrim is like a bird in its nest after evading the hawk and the hunter. The destination is delightful because God's house is there. The expectation that God might "give ear" to pleas for favor and provision is now vivid. Worship is the proper home for heart and body, making both resonate with wholeness. "How lovely is your dwelling place!"

the psalm invites the congregation to exclaim, "Blessed are those who dwell in your house; they are ever praising you."

Arrival is joyful, yet it is only part of traveling. The heart of the psalm reflects on the relationship between dwelling and journeying. For the worshiper will not, in fact, be able to remain living in the temple, but must return to the road and to life in the villages until it again becomes time to set out for Jerusalem. There are children to be raised, fields to be tended, livestock to be fed, and neighbors to be consulted. This raises a natural question: if the temple is the refuge, the place of security and joy, then what of the times when the worshipper is not at the temple, or even near it? What about the journey back to the village, and the days in the fields?

In the middle section of the New Revised Standard Version translation of this psalm we find a curious transformation. After all of the emphasis on place, on dwelling, on nests, on houses, and on being near, we suddenly find a blessing pronounced on those with *highways* in their hearts:

> Happy are those whose strength is in you,
> in whose heart are highways. (NRSV)

These are the highways trodden by pilgrims in their annual journeys to the temple. The worshipers find their strength not ultimately in the place of worship, but in the one worshiped there, who is with them on the road as well as in the sanctuary. After all, the journey to Jerusalem is a journey across the Promised Land. It is not a journey from where God is not to where he is, but a celebration of God's rule over the entire land, a journey to the heart of a land, of a cosmos that belongs in its entirety to God.

This theme is peppered through the psalms of ascent (find them in your Bible, they are Psalms 120-134). Those who look fearfully to the surrounding hills, wondering whether enemies will strike, know that their help comes from the LORD, who surrounds his people as the mountains surround Jerusalem (Psalm 121:1; 125:2). Without the realization that God's rule extends out across the land, and even to the ends of the earth, the prayers for favor offered at the temple would have little reach. For those "whose walk is blameless" (v. 11), who traverse the land and travel through life in obedience, no good thing will be withheld, no matter what their location: "The LORD will watch over your coming and going, both now and evermore" (Psalm 121:8).

The highways are a place of blessing, but also a place of hardship. The journey passes through withered places, through the "valley of Baka," a name that evokes balsam trees and dry areas, and also weeping. We can imagine the personal and communal sufferings being carried along the road to Jerusalem with the hope of being heard by God, who is our "sun and shield" (Psalm 84:11). Once again we discover that blessing is not tied to arrival. As the pilgrims pass through the valley of Baka they make it a place of springs and the rain follows with provision of blessings. The pilgrims carry hope that the dry ground will soften, planting can begin, and eventually there will be a harvest. "Those who go out weeping, carrying seed to sow, will return with songs of joy, carrying sheaves with them" (Psalm 126:6). There is joy in arrival, yet the journey itself can be a place where fellowship and hope give life to the journey, where dryness is transformed into fruitfulness, where weeping becomes joy, and where tears become life-giving water. There is no passive waiting around for something better to happen. People journey and weep and make the valley a place of springs; God adds pools of blessing; the people plant; and God does not withhold the harvest. On this road, human toil and divine blessing kiss one another in greeting. Christian understandings of life as a pilgrimage find roots and resonance here. On their walk through life, Christian pilgrims are not just passing through, leaving the world untouched. Neither do they travel as tourists who merely take souvenirs and leave litter. They doggedly seek blessing, practice works of mercy, and erect signs of the kingdom.

Treading a pilgrim path involves placing oneself within a tradition. The pilgrim routes were not paved areas designated by planners and mapped out with aerial photography. They were ways trodden over the years, hardened and made sure by the passing of feet. They were created, at least in part, by previous travelers who had reached the same destination. The path was the visible trace of their wisdom concerning how to get there, inviting trust in the aggregate of their decisions over time. Here there is active responsibility — the paths were not already cut into the landscape, but had to be made and maintained by walking. There is also receptivity — the paths offer themselves as proven ways, inviting trust and a willingness to follow.

Ways that prove too dangerous do not become paths. Without well-trodden paths, the risk increases of wandering aimlessly, of finding "crooked paths" that can lead one astray, or of having one's foot slip on unnavigable terrain (Psalm 121:3; 125:5). The individual pilgrim learns the path both from elders, who passed this way in previous years, and by walking, by going along it for the first time and gaining a familiarity that might lead to becoming a future guide for others. Adding one's own feet to the process that wears the path into the landscape reinforces the way for future travelers. The imagery of springs and pools made as one journeys through the valley of Baka suggests both that there are known dry places along the road and that in journeying through them, one can leave behind blessings for others.

If learning is to be a pilgrimage, Psalm 84 offers images that reflect on the nature of the journey. It is a journey not towards spring break, towards a strong grade point average, or towards employment, but towards standing in the presence of God and seeing God give new life in the world. That does not mean that everyday tasks are made lesser, or that chapel services put class work in the shade. God's glory fills creation, and setting our faces towards God and our hearts on the highway is a celebration of God's sovereignty over every territory through which we pass. As we progress through the smaller journeys of our courses and semesters, are we able to see them in that light? How might the ways in which we journey together as teachers and learners turn dry places into springs and weeping into harvests, leaving blessing behind for those who follow? What kind of syllabus might result if learning is pilgrimage?

PERILS AND PITFALLS OF PILGRIMAGES

Between the writing of the Psalms and our own day stretches a long history of people making pilgrimage. Some pilgrimages are so well-known that they have become emblematic. For instance, alongside pilgrimages to the holy land, for over a thousand years pilgrims travelled the ancient Roman roads through France, across the Pyrenees, past the ancient frontier of Moorish Spain, to the tomb of St. James the Greater, Santiago de Compostela, a few short miles from the "end of the world" (Finisterre) on the Atlantic coast.

The route represents a journey of some 700 miles on foot, horse, or mule. Alone or among fellow travelers, men and women of every nation, tribe and tongue on the continent of Europe made this journey. Accosted by insects and robbers, taxed and swindled at many a crossing, risking illness and injury, braving wars and weather, perhaps possessing nothing but a robe, hat, scrip, staff, and a scallop shell token to mark one as a pilgrim, those who made the journey encountered both hardships and blessings, death and life. It was a heroic undertaking, a noble commitment inviting admiration — and yet one with which plenty of critics found fault. The pilgrimage of faith toward the heavenly Jerusalem translated imperfectly into flesh-and-blood journeying across Europe.

A key problem lay in the possibility that the pilgrims were pursuing a mirage. After all, the stories that nourished the pilgrim's sense of call, the tokens and signs that fed his or her imagination, were often largely the product of legend and superstition, and the interests at stake could be all too worldly. A newly militant church in the 11th and 12th centuries was intent upon recovering Spain for Christendom after Islamic incursions. The story of the 9th-century discovery in Santiago de Compostela of the tomb of James the apostle, the supposed cousin of Jesus Christ, offered convenient justification. The story also furthered the interests, both political and religious, of the supremely powerful abbey of Cluny, which supplied monks and bishops to Compostela. James was the patron saint of Spain, and his intercession was regarded as the key to victory over the Moors at Toledo and elsewhere. This intertwining of pilgrimage and conquest was also seen in the crusades to the Holy Land, which were initially framed as militant pilgrimages. Another powerful story was the secular and historically unfounded legend of Charlemagne's friend Roland, the paragon of knightly honor, celebrated in the *Song of Roland*. This song was sung in the inns along the pilgrim road and celebrated at the great abbey constructed at Roncesvalles where, it was believed, Roland had given his life to defend the rear guard of Charlemagne's defeated and retreating army.

Other fictions abounded. In medieval Europe, devotion to relics reflected the desire to have contact with something real, something full of potency because it had been in the presence of Christ or his mother. Given the difficulty of assessing their authenticity, these sacred objects could easily turn out to be frauds designed to attract visitors. Amid this fusion of secular and sacred stories, of economic and religious interests, of truth and swindle, the most earnest pilgrims risked pouring their devotion into a deception.

That might be enough to give us pause, but there was more. Further questions focused on the motives of the pilgrims themselves. Many pilgrims were doubtless motivated by fear. The judgment of God was displayed in stunning relief at the entrance to every church built along the pilgrim roads. One's hope of eternal life rested on the decree of Christ, the magnificent judge who dominated the scene. But the images of eternal punishment and the horrors that await the damned likely captivated many a pilgrim's attention. Pilgrims set out in response to serious illness (their own or that of a child or loved one) or after serious moral lapses that threatened their Christian standing. At the same time, amid these profound anxieties, there were those who traveled the pilgrim way lustily, punctuating their journey with drinking parties, ribald singing, and sexual adventures. Some traveled in pomp and treated the journey as a holiday.

There were also doubts about the spiritual value of pilgrimage. Critics argued that even devout pilgrims lapsed into old habits on their return, and that those freed by pilgrimage from the social restraints and obligations of their home church and community became more likely to sin and commit crimes. Many would have their money stolen by thieves posing as traveling companions. Many more would fall prey to the new temptations offered by the brothels and taverns that lined pilgrim routes. Some, the critics alleged, undertook pilgrimage largely in order to shirk responsibilities at home, to avoid taxation, or to wear the pilgrim's token as a badge of status and boast about where they had been. False pilgrims, it was said, took to the road without following the path of moral obedience or the spiritual journey towards God, thus betraying the very realities that might give genuine meaning to the outward journey. Concerns were raised that pilgrims might be deceiving themselves, coming to think that the act of pilgrimage itself was enough to cleanse from sins. Serious observers lamented that pilgrimage became for some a way of attaining a sense of forgiveness without repentance, converting the act of pilgrimage from devotion to superstition. Bernard of Clairvaux complained of churches along pilgrim routes investing resources in beautifying themselves to attract income from visits by passing pilgrims, while the poor went hungry within reach of the same churches. Such concerns helped to fuel a reaction against pilgrimage sites from the Reformation onward, and doubts concerning the Christian value of practicing bodily pilgrimage are expressed to this day.

Clearly pilgrimage has its dark side. If we want to explore honestly the idea of learning as a pilgrimage, it will not do to dwell only on its ancient aura of sanctity. There are real tensions between pilgrimage as a biblical idea and pilgrimage as a historical practice. But perhaps those tensions themselves can teach us.

Drawing together the perils of pilgrimage, we get a picture something like this: year after year a fresh group of people sets out on an expensive, difficult, and time-consuming journey that might, at least in part, rest on false stories about what matters. What is offered as true knowledge might in the end be largely deceit and self-promotion, or just not that relevant to the purpose for traveling. The maps offered may serve particular religious, economic, and political ideologies and interests as much as the will of God and the traveler's ultimate flourishing. Powerful hopes of future prosperity intertwine with powerful fear of failure. Some can afford to travel in style; others begin with inadequate resources and are further impoverished by the costs of the journey. The institutions that frame the journey invest disproportionately in upgrading their facilities to attract more visitors and therefore more income. Those offering assistance by the roadside may help, or they may abuse and exploit. New temptations abound as home is left behind. Serious travelers seek to glorify God and hope for a more faithful future walk; they walk alongside others more focused on drinking, laughter, and getting the credential without the arduous process of personal transformation.

Now tilt the picture so that the light catches it at a different angle; which parts of this could describe our schools?

To think of education as a pilgrimage can invite misty-eyed nostalgia or easy judgment of past pilgrims. But perhaps it should lead instead to serious soul-searching regarding our motives, methods, and shared sense of purpose more than it invites either. Medieval Christians distinguished between several varieties of pilgrimages. There was the outward pilgrimage of physical journeys to holy sites, the ongoing pilgrimage that each person was called to make through life by means of daily obedience without necessarily leaving home, and the interior pilgrimage of the soul's journey toward God. For the outward pilgrimage to be authentic, it had to align with the other pilgrimages as an outward enactment of an inner walk of obedience and fellowship with God. The journey was to be one of personal transformation, rooted in prayer. Through this process of inward change, one became fitted for the eventual destination, arriving as a different person from the one who set out. As she traveled, the serious pilgrim rehearsed the stories of redemption presented in stone and glass along the way and saw grace in the gifts of protection and hospitality offered to her. Hope that sin and its effects could be overcome, grace received in the sacrament, and forgiveness attained in the acts of contrition and penance were intertwined in the pilgrim experience. Arriving whole testified to the power of Christ and his victory over the devil. The daily labor of the journey forged the pilgrims into a fellowship of faith, walking in biblical footsteps. The earthly pilgrimage stood as a hopeful sign of the ultimate journey still to come.

What of us? Do our noble educational visions match our outward practices? Which of our practices actually sustain faith and move us Godward, and which justify movement without growth, experience without discipline, achievement without transformation? What stories do we weave for students to justify the journey, and how do students come to understand their calling? Do we beautify educational sites without satisfying the thirst for wisdom? What is preached by our buildings, our art, and our brochures? Could serious reflection on ourselves as educational pilgrims, subject to the risks and temptations that have always been part of pilgrim journeys, help us focus more clearly on our goals, expectations, and practices?

A JOURNEY INTO LEARNING

Late last summer I drove one of my daughters back to college in Georgia, near Chattanooga, Tennessee, for her senior year. The direct route would have taken about 14 hours, principally on interstates 65 and 24. But with a few days to spare we decided to take the long way, travelling west to Independence, Kansas, spending a weekend with my parents, enjoying our time on the road. Such an opportunity to share several days and many miles with a daughter poised on the threshold of adulthood turns a necessary trip into a crafted journey, giving us time to cement and extend our relationship.

During the autumn of that same year, my wife began another, much less pleasant journey. Her left hip alternated between cramps and numbness. At times it would, as she tried to explain it, "lock up" so that the joint was unable to straighten out or support her. Unable to stand, sit, or lie down for longer than five minutes without experiencing excruciating pain, it became clear that hip-replacement surgery would be needed were she to have any hope of "getting around" on her own. Throughout the months of her ordeal, I was constantly reminded of the delights of mobility and the terrors one confronts in the face of a potentially serious injury. To stand; to walk; to run; we hardly notice how much space these verbs occupy in our mental picture until they suddenly withdraw.

Recently I agreed to teach my department's World Music course, and these images of journeys tumbled around in my mind. Among other things, this course is an introduction to music from societies across the globe, from sub-Saharan Africa, to Japan, Bolivia, and so on. Traversing the bewildering complexity of the world's music leaves me breathless, particularly because it takes me far from my own specialization. How can one teach what one does not know? And what does it mean to know the Carnatic musical traditions of southern India, let alone the music of the Kabuki theatre or the fusion of Andalusian and North African practices in the music of Algeria? Is this another road trip? How do I avoid sinking into pedagogical immobility or reinforcing the tendency of American students to be merely tourists and consumers of world culture?

Participating in a road trip that encompasses a rite of passage, witnessing descent into pain and ascent into recovery, and searching for a route through the unfamiliar terrain of a new course; the images that emerge in these stories map onto one another in intriguing ways. The unfamiliar and potentially fearful encounters; the moments when weakness gives way to insight and renewed determination to continue; the poignancy of unrecoverable loss that remains part of the alloy of hope and faithful perseverance. As aspects of journey, these elements seem to make sense. So imagine a course syllabus that begins with these words:

I want to invite you to consider your work in this class as a kind of journey. In some ways this journey will seem like a pilgrimage, abandoning the safety of home and country to follow a call to seek transcendence and meaning in a place of spiritual encounter. As with any pilgrimage, this is something we do together. I will be your guide, and as your guide, I will be journeying too. As we journey, I fully expect to see things I have never seen before, especially because of you and the questions that you ask.

As a detailed map of the terrain I've chosen a recent textbook, but in selecting the best routes to take I've relied on my own experience and judgment. As your guide I intend to offer some insights into less travelled paths that may enrich your journey. Once in a while I may invite you to settle with me in a place where we'll want to form some attachments and gain some deeper empathy with the local population through more direct and sustained interactions and conversations. The point of this pilgrimage is not efficiency, but attentive awareness. To see a city, you can fly through it on a crowded expressway or wander through the neighborhoods. The first gets the job done, but it is the second that leads to deeper knowledge.

In addition to a good map, we also need a clear goal. In this course, the obvious goal is for you to demonstrate that you know the essential facts of the history of music by completing various assignments and taking the final exam. But I would raise one caution here. Although you should certainly do your best to get a good grade in this course, the success of our journey is not dependent upon reaching this goal. The best journeys are rarely the ones in which we merely check off the sites we visit as from a list, collect a few souvenirs, and return mostly unaffected by where we've been or what we've seen. Merely accumulating facts is not the same as knowing history, and remaining unchanged by one's study is not learning. I hope that you will go beyond the memorization of facts to grasp the gift that history offers us in the great abundance and diversity of music making, and that you intentionally and faithfully undertake the stewardship of this art for your own generation. And I hope that you will become experienced travelers for whom the journey is about honoring and respecting those we encounter, rather than colonizing and appropriating their work. Perhaps in time you will be able to serve as a guide for others.

This is a tall order for a music history class. But context is important; not only the context of history in which we learn to see and hear the presence of music in the past and the past of music in our present, but the context of our own journey of discipleship. It is not our attempt to master the details of music history that should be foremost in our minds as we set out. Rather we seek wisdom in our learning, in our performing, in our teaching, and in all our ways of being musical. The details (all the facts, interpretations, documents, scores, opinions, criticisms, and recordings) will be more meaningful — and we'll remember them better — if we see them in light of our own journey of faith. We will remember them like we remember the places that have special significance for us. They will be as meaningful as places where we felt close to God, or as the place where we saw for the first time a perfectly executed architectural program, or a view of the Tuscan hills that will forever define our idea of the sylvan wood of the ancient world. At the same time, pilgrimages often involve dangers, many of them unforeseen. In this course we will read texts and encounter worldviews that could prove to be alluring, but deceptive. We'll need to keep our wits about us.

And I hope you will find that the end of the journey is not a place but a person, and that we will be successful if we hold to the promise of Jesus Christ: "And surely I am with you always, even to the very end of the age" (Matt. 28:20). What we seek, in the end, is to know him and all his ways, to gain more intimate fellowship with our Lord who accompanies us and who has set up his tent among us, and to be with him where he is, in the presence of God who reigns over all.

Now pause and ponder these questions: What expectations are evoked in the minds of the students if I begin class in this way? Are any of them different from average course expectations? In what ways have students been invited to imagine their learning differently? How will this course now need to be taught in order to make this introduction an honest description rather than a pious flight of fancy?

The Rhythms of the Road

A different time, a different course, and a different discipline; this story comes from a language class. A student came to visit me during the first week of the semester. It wasn't his choice; I had asked all of my students to drop by during the first week so that they could connect with me individually and I could find out a little about who they were. Joe was polite and personable, but also quite clear that he did not want to be on this particular road. The course, beginning German class, was one way of fulfilling a foreign language requirement. Joe explained that he saw little purpose for language learning in relation to his future plans, found little aptitude for the task in himself, and felt that his time was not being used well by insisting on this requirement. He would do the work, he assured me, but he wanted me to know how he felt. I thanked him for his candor, found out a little more about his hopes and interests, and he left. I did not try to change his views in that one conversation; we would journey together through at least a semester, probably more, which allowed time for matters to unfold.

One of my goals for the semester was to help my students rethink their relationship to other languages and cultures in the light of Scripture. I wanted them to see that learning the languages of others was part of a bigger story than getting verb endings right or gaining marketable skills. Yet I wanted to avoid an approach that would lay out a Christian perspective in the first week, perhaps in a reading or a lecture, and trust that it would frame everything that followed. Themes announced in week one may not be very vivid in week ten, however clearly they might have been stated.

I decided to pursue the matter in a way more akin to the rhythms of journeying together, in which threads of conversation are picked up, dropped, rejoined, and gradually elaborated in a way that draws us into relationship. Each week I spent a few minutes in class offering reflections on biblical passages that addressed our attitude to language, to culture, and to those foreign to us. We read of words that bring light out of chaos, making delightful spaces for others to live, and of words wielded like swords. We traced the recurring call to love our neighbor — and to love the foreigner. We considered what it might mean, linguistically and culturally, to do to others as we would have them do to us. We considered hospitality to strangers as a Christian practice. We mused over Babel and Pentecost, and the final multitude from every nation, tribe, language, and people. Each episode was brief — approaching the matter in terms of the rhythms of a longer shared journey removed the burden of needing to lay out everything at once or fret too much about what had been "covered" on a given day.

After six or seven weeks, Joe came to my office, this time of his own volition. He had been pondering the biblical themes discussed in class. They were new to him — he had never before considered how language classes could connect with love of neighbor, or with hope and reconciliation. He asked if there was more he could read on the topic. I gave him an article and some other pointers, and he left.

Two weeks later he was back. He had followed up on the reading and had sent a copy to his high school teacher. Was there more? I provided him with some more reading, and he left again, with thanks for the help.

Towards the end of the semester he came with a different request, one that took me aback a little. He had to write an argumentative paper for a composition class on a topic of his choice. His chosen topic was why every freshman at a Christian college should be made to learn a foreign language and he wondered if he could interview me as part of writing the paper.

Not every student goes through such a dramatic shift during any given semester, though the transformations (for good and ill) that take place during the years of our education are far-reaching. I still think of Joe not as a template for what should happen with every student, but as a reminder to take time for the journey and its unfolding conversation rather than relying on maps and outlines posted at the point of departure. God may experience all times and places simultaneously, but we can't, even though the internet may tempt us into thinking otherwise. Our learning unfolds over time and in particular relationships. As it does so, the patient rhythm of connecting each day's walk to the bigger purposes of traveling through God's world can change everything, however mundane the steps might seem.

MEEKLY GALLOPING FULL-TILT

Medieval pilgrim pictures often show travelers dressed in simple clothes, with sturdy staffs, a small satchel or backpack, and perhaps bare feet. There is something right, we think, about such simplicity and something quite wrong about Chaucer's noisy Canterbury pilgrims, jostling along on their well-fed horses, telling bawdy stories to pass the time, eager to reach the next tavern and next meal. It is no accident, then, that one of the virtues associated with the true pilgrim is that of meekness. And if we want to shape our classrooms as a pilgrimage and our students as pilgrims, we will want to cultivate that virtue. But meek is a tricky word to understand.

In the classroom, it is often misunderstood as self-deprecation. Good students in particular may think of meekness as the antidote to pride. Make an "A" on a paper? Score an "excellent" in a piano competition? Win an award for writing or a scholarship to college? A little voice squeaks in the background, "Now don't be proud." But how to respond to that not-so-subtle command? Write more sloppily on the next paper? Miss a few more notes? Hide the award? Give back the scholarship? Or just mumble — "ah, it really wasn't anything; I'm not really that good" — whenever a compliment appears?

Such remedies for pride are totally ineffective. False humility of the "Oh, shucks, I really didn't do very well" variety is bogus and counterfeit. Hiding good work seems a strange way to obey God's commands to "rule over the earth" and to love him with all our heart, soul, strength, and mind (Deuteronomy 6:5; Matthew 22:37). Parrying every compliment with a joke or a putdown is tiresome and uncharitable to those who offer it. Yet if we as students and teachers can see ourselves as meek pilgrims, it may free us up not only to do our best work but also to delight in it. And we may be able to glimpse meekness via the third beatitude and a poem by Mary Karr.

We know the beatitude: "Blessed are the meek," Jesus says, "for they shall inherit the earth" (Matthew 5:5), but the poem by Karr, "Who the Meek are Not," poses a challenge: do we actually know what meekness looks like? Karr begins by discounting some familiar images of "the meek." The meek are not Russian peasants bending under heavy loads, or tenant farmers eking out a living, or the poor who labor to fill the pockets of the rich. Meekness does not require a beaten down, beaten out life.

Yet when we hear the beatitude, we often either discount its grand promise — the meek shall inherit the earth — or we retreat, perplexed, from its apparent paradox: how can wimpy, nerdy, quiet, mousy, and meek people possibly inherit anything, let alone the whole world? Perhaps this verse is just a way to keep downtrodden, oppressed, marginalized people quiet in the here and now with a vague promise of a better life in the far-off future.

But the promise, "for they shall inherit the earth," is not a throw-away line, or a distraction, or a pretty greeting-card sentiment. It is not even a paradox. Rather, it is the key to understanding the first part of this beatitude, to understanding just exactly who the meek are. The structure of Matthew's Gospel text encourages us to think in this direction. Certainly there is a close and logical connection in many of the other beatitudes between the second and the first clauses: Those who obtain mercy are those who are merciful (v. 7). That makes sense; there is a logical connection between the first and second clauses. Those who will be satisfied by God are those who hunger and thirst for righteousness (v. 6). That makes sense, too. So perhaps those who are fit to inherit the earth are the stout-hearted, sturdy, talented, all-around meek. Because inheriting the earth is certainly not for the faint of heart. When God wants to impress Job with his own power and glory, he doesn't begin talking directly about the incommunicable attributes of the Trinity — God's omniscience, omnipresence, or omnipotence. Oh no. He awes Job into silence merely by asking him to look around at the world:

> Have you entered the storehouses of the snow, or have you seen the storehouses of the hail, which I have reserved for the time of trouble? (Job 38:22-23)

Can you bind the chains of the Pleiades or loose the cords of Orion? . . . Can you guide the Bear with its children? (Job 38:31-32)

Can you hunt the prey for the lion, or satisfy the appetite of the young lions? . . . Is the wild ox willing to serve you? (Job 38:39; 39:9)

Do you give the horse his might? Do you clothe his neck with strength? (Job 39:19)

Can you draw out Leviathan with a fishhook? Can you put a rope in his nose, or pierce his jaw with a hook? . . . Will you play with him as with a bird? (Job 41:1-2, 5)

Snow, stars, lions, horses, and the Leviathan himself — to inherit this earth is to inherit a creation that is bursting at the seams. And yet, incredibly, it is this wild, grand, untamable, and expansive world that God has given to us as our inheritance: "I have given you dominion over the works of my hands," God says to us in Psalm 8. "I have put all things under your feet — all sheep and oxen, and also the beasts of the field, the birds of the air, and the fish of the sea, whatever passes along the paths of the sea." To inherit the earth is no casual task to be undertaken while sitting on the deck, ball cap pulled down over eyes, feet up, coke in hand. It is not a job for slackers. It is a call for ready pilgrims who will muster all their energy, creativity, and intellectual moxie to walk through the land God has given them and make it a better place.

On the pilgrim journey, the best antidote to pride is not something negative — false humility, hiding our talents, or side-stepping compliments — but something positive: cultivating the meekness that will inherit the earth. Here the second part of Mary Karr's poem, her exegesis of Jesus's words, "Blessed are the meek," is helpful. In place of Russian peasants, tenant farmers, and poor laborers, she sets before our eyes the image of a great horse, a stallion — full of natural gifts and abilities. An honors horse, we might call him.

Certainly he is an honorable horse. A horse who doesn't merely canter across the meadow, but runs at a full gallop. A horse whose immense natural gifts have been fine-tuned by discipline and hard work. The stallion knows his power, and so do we who look at him. There is no hiding the honor that attends his magnificence; it is a cause for celebration.

Yet in the picture that Karr paints, all this natural ability, all the discipline and training, all the craft of horsemanship is tuned in one direction — toward the master's voice. As the stallion gallops across the field, he suddenly, instantly stops. He has heard his master call. One foot raised, nose pointed forward, body aquiver but still, he strains toward that sound. Strength, courage, grace, elegance, accomplishment—all stand rippling and eddying along his great neck. But the stallion holds himself in check; only the ears move, pricking forward to catch the master's command. The joy of galloping is dissolved into the joy of service. The stallion lives to obey his master's orders. The stallion is every inch a stallion — not a pack horse, not a broken-down drab. He is full of honor and accomplishment and pleasure in his strength. But his deepest pleasure, his deepest delight, comes when he is able to put all that honor, accomplishment, strength, and energy into purposeful motion, to obey and please his master. If the horse could speak, surely he would echo David's closing words of Psalm 8: "O LORD, my Lord, how majestic is your name in all the earth!" But perhaps the stallion does speak those words; he speaks them through his meekness, by offering his strength to his master's voice.

When we and our students recognize gifts and abilities, when we discipline and shape them, and when we accomplish hard tasks and are honored for them, we lay the foundation for meekness. We may, and should, take pleasure in our strength and speed as we gallop full-tilt across the meadow. But we are fit to inherit the earth only when, at the sound of our master's voice, we draw up, in Mary Karr's words, "to a stunned but instant halt," quivering with eagerness to obey his next command.

Longing for a Better Country

The New Testament picks up and runs with images of pilgrimage that we have seen in the Psalms. It also asks us to rethink the notion of pilgrimage, its route and its destination. For the Hebrew pilgrim on the road to Jerusalem, sacred space mapped clearly onto geographical space. Yahweh rules over all of creation; the land of Israel and Judah is the focus of Yahweh's covenant with his people; and the temple in Jerusalem stands at its heart. One's feet are quite literally directed toward Jerusalem for the recurring worship festivals. Jesus transforms this scenario. The temple falls, Jesus himself and the church that is to be his body become the hands and feet of God's presence on earth. We are reminded that God does not live in temples built by human hands (Acts 17:24; 1 Corinthians 5:1). "Don't you know," asks Paul, "that you yourselves are God's temple and that God's Spirit dwells in your midst?" (1 Corinthians 3:16, TNIV). In Jesus, God dwells with us, and in coming to Jesus we have already come into the presence of God, with no need to first load a donkey or pack a suitcase.

Rather than a renewed regular pilgrimage to the holy city, we find a call to go with the good news to the ends of the earth. Rather than a focus on the geographical Jerusalem as the place where God is especially present, we find a new focus on a heavenly Jerusalem, in which there is no temple but the Lamb who dwells there (Revelation 21:22). Rather than a prescribed journey to a particular mountain to pray, we hear a call to worship in spirit and truth. The journeys have shifted, yet a central truth remains: the whole earth is a place where life can be lived before the face of God.

The epistle to the Hebrews pictures the lives of believers who went before, from Abram onwards, as an ongoing pilgrimage:

> All these people were still living by faith when they died. They did not receive the things promised; they only saw them and welcomed them from a distance, admitting that they were foreigners and strangers on earth. People who say such things show that they are looking for a country of their own. If they had been thinking of the country they had left, they would have had opportunity to return. Instead, they were longing for a better country — a heavenly one. (Hebrews 11:13-16, TNIV)

Those who have encountered Jesus find themselves at a different point in the story; like the Psalmist in the opening verses of Psalm 84 they can rejoice in safe arrival and the chance to dwell in God's presence:

> You have not come to a mountain that can be touched and that is burning with fire; to darkness, gloom and storm . . . But you have come to Mount Zion, to the city of the living God, the heavenly Jerusalem. You have come to thousands upon thousands of angels in joyful assembly, to the church of the firstborn, whose names are written in heaven. (Hebrews 12:18-23, TNIV)

At first sight it might seem that the journeying is over, that continued Christian attachment to the idea of pilgrimage is a throwback now best left behind.

And yet, alongside the joyous sense of arrival, "you have come to Mount Zion," there remains a sense of "not yet" and a reminder that we still have roads to travel. Sandwiched directly between the evocation of pre-Christian pilgrimages towards the "better country" and the celebration of having caught sight of the "heavenly Jerusalem" are reminders that the call to have highways in our hearts is still needed. "Let us throw off everything that hinders and the sin that so easily entangles," we are urged. "And let us run with perseverance the race marked out for us." We are to set our eyes on Jesus, so that we will "not grow weary and lose heart." We are not to sit back and stop moving — "strengthen your feeble arms and weak knees" is the cry, "make level paths for your feet" (Hebrews 12:1-13, TNIV). Present discipline will produce a harvest of peace and righteousness. As we set our eyes on the heavenly Jerusalem, there is transformation that needs to happen in us so that as we journey, we become fit to dwell there when we fully arrive. Emmanuel, God with us, has come. But the kingdom is not yet complete, and there is still a narrow path of discipleship to be walked and a vale of tears to traverse. "Guide Me, O Thou Great Redeemer, pilgrim through this barren land" remains the song of Christians.

The idea of a heavenly Jerusalem does not shift our journey away from creation, away from mundane realities, and therefore away from most of the things that daily make up the content of our education. Our central prayer asks for things to be done on earth as they are in heaven, and as we meet the heavenly Jerusalem we find it descending earthward:

> And he carried me away in the Spirit to a mountain great and high, and showed me the Holy City, Jerusalem, coming down out of heaven from God. It shone with the glory of God, and its brilliance was like that of a very precious jewel, like a jasper, clear as crystal. (Revelation 21:10-11, TNIV)

The hope of our journey is not that all we learn here will be abandoned, but that as the heavenly Jerusalem descends, "the glory and honor of the nations will be brought into it" (Revelation 21:26). The kingdom of the world will become the kingdom of our Lord and of his Christ (Revelation 11:15). Christ is the one in whom "all things, whether things on earth or things in heaven" are reconciled (Colossians 1:20). Like the Hebrew pilgrim turning hopeful eyes toward Jerusalem and finding there a vantage point from which to see that God reigns over the whole land, the Christian pilgrim sets out for the heavenly Jerusalem and finds in it a vantage point from which to see all things reconciled and made new.

If we imagine the educational journey as pilgrimage, it may remind us that the destinations on which we set our heart — a high school diploma, the right college, exam success, mastery of a field, graduation, or career — are penultimate. Success in such matters will not mean arrival, and failure in them need not be the end of hope. They are dethroned as ultimate destinations, and therefore freed from the impossible task of bearing such weight. Both teachers and students need that reminder at times. We will also find that our march through the stages of education will, at times, indeed be passage through a barren land, one in which feeble arms and weak knees will stand in much need of strengthening. We are not just would-be achievers, but fellow pilgrims in need of hope and fellowship.

At the same time, seeing education as pilgrimage does not render the educational journey trivial. It calls us to examine whether our movement towards our educational goals could be described as the walk of a pilgrim. Is it rooted in worship, consecration, gratitude, and hope? Is it characterized by mutual encouragement and help? Do our educational practices step us toward humility or pride, patience or apathy, meekness or self-promotion? Can we remember the bigger story, the larger journey-arc, as we plod through particular moments along the way? As we study the world, do we remain aware of God's presence in the whole land through which we travel, and seek the reconciliation of all things in Christ? If the educational journey turns out to be part of a pilgrimage, then we will be required to consider the manner of our travel and the vision that sustains it.

Walking the Path

HAVE YOU CHOSEN A PATH?

This picture might not at first glance look as if it is about journeying, but it portrays a parting of the ways and the necessary choice of which road to take. Spend a little time with it, see how many of its details you can piece together.

The picture, a German print from the early 15th century, evokes those moments when life is poignantly Y-shaped. Paths fork before us (or, in this case, beneath our very feet) and each choice precludes the other; for each way there is a way not taken. The everyday process of choosing one thing over another leaps into dramatic focus as the picture reminds us that there are some choices that will alter our whole trajectory. The decision to go left, or right — or even to stop and do nothing — will give the story of our life a different shape, different characters, perhaps a different ending.

Classical antiquity offered an iconic image of the two ways, depicting the hero Hercules standing in front of a path that divided into two directions. He had to choose between the path of virtue and the path of vice, and his choice for virtue became an emblem of moral education for the youth of Athens and Rome. The letter Y, visible beneath the feet of the young man in this picture, came to symbolize the moment of moral choice, especially for adolescents entering adulthood.

Scripture also admonishes us to choose the right path, and some early Christians embraced the tale of Hercules and the Y-shaped symbol of the forking paths because it seemed to resonate with Jesus' Sermon on the Mount. "Enter through the narrow gate," Jesus urged. "For wide is the gate and broad is the road that leads to destruction, and many enter through it. But small is the gate and narrow the road that leads to life, and only a few find it" (Matthew 7:13-14). The pagan Hercules had to choose between vice and virtue; the Christian also had to choose between two paths, with an eschatological destination at stake. When the Christian stood at the crossroads, the choice was eternal life with God or eternal torment in hell. Guidance was promised for finding the right path: "I will instruct you and teach you the way you should go" (Psalm 23:3 NRSV).

Unlike many figures in such pictures, the young man here does not stand in front of a forked path pondering which way to continue his journey. We see instead a well-dressed young aristocrat in the center of the picture, straddling two tree branches shaped in the form of a Y. This tells us that we should ponder the two paths, but also suggests that this young man is failing at the task of deciding. He wants to have it both ways, to travel the one path without leaving the other. Look at his stance. He has put his left foot on the branch where the devil is standing, and his right foot on the branch where a divine messenger also has a foothold. It is not just his feet that display his indecision.

43

His posture is S-shaped, showing the pull from both directions. He has an ear for the contradictory lessons of both sides. His face, his right hand, and his lower body are turned toward the godly way; his upper body and his left ear are inclined toward the way of darkness. His left hand goes for the gold, and his heart is where his treasure is. The ample, long sleeve of his garment is shown in full, suggesting its use as a deep pocket into which he can drop the gold that he grabs, so that his right hand will not know what his greedy left hand is doing.

The young man does not stand alone, making up his mind in peace and quiet which path to take — from each direction there is a pull, there are voices calling to him to journey in their direction. Look at the margins of the picture. He is surrounded by three teachers (a devil, an angel, and God) who, judging by their hand gestures, each have a substantial lesson for him. Banners, or text scrolls, fill most of the empty spaces of the woodcut. Today they would be speech bubbles.

The great tempter, Satan, is on the young man's left (our right as we view the picture), promising: "You shall satisfy all the desires of your flesh and live with pleasure in the world," and urging: "If you live according to my will, I will give you this money to own." On his right the young man hears an angel admonishing him: "You shall follow my teachings; you should always turn to God." And God, who looks down from a cloud, pronounces: "[Young] man, turn to me; I will give you the kingdom of heaven."

What is going on in the young man's mind? Despite the lack of urgency in his features, he seems dimly aware of his precarious perch. A prayer scroll hangs down limply from his right hand: "I have [chosen] two paths [at odds with each other]; may God help me so that I'll be able to stand." It is dawning on him that he cannot serve God and mammon, that a house divided cannot stand. The rest of the picture, however, suggests that he might be praying the wrong prayer. A better prayer might have been: "Teach me your way, LORD, that I may rely on your faithfulness" (Psalm 86:11).

Why is the prayer wrong? Take another look at the tree beneath his feet. The viewer sees what he does not — that his need at this point is not to stand but to walk, to start journeying in a definite direction. At the bottom of the tree, death and a devil covered with the flames of hell are already busy sawing at the tree trunk. They are saying: "Day and night we are sneaking up to you; you cannot escape us." According to Matthew 3:10 (and Luke 3:9; 13:7-9), a fruitless tree will be cut down and thrown into the fire. The branch on which the young aristocrat's left foot stands is already almost fully cut off — the idea that he can stand there indefinitely is illusory. The other branch is still whole — God's gift of grace is still available, there is still time for repentance, for rejecting a life of greed and self-indulgence and embarking on a life of charity, of doing justice and loving one's neighbor. Soon he will have to choose one journey or the other, or the failure to choose will make the choice for him as his perch collapses.

This woodcut was made to invite 15th century German Christians to meditate on the choices they had made in their pilgrimage through life. It also functioned as a visual sermon preached to secular leaders who were in power. The picture invites the wealthy noblemen to think about their use of money and to ask themselves: "Where do I stand? Do I walk through life with grabbing hands or with giving hands? Do I live a dishonest life before the Lord?" It reminds them that there is still time to repent and change.

How might the picture speak to us as we help students frame the formative life decisions that face them during their student years? We can probably all think of students whose figurative posture resembles that of the young man in the picture, swaying between duty and desire. Perhaps we can think of students who are waiting for life to push them into some perfect calling, when perhaps they simply need to begin walking, to begin using their gifts to honor God and meet the needs of others, so that in the very walking they become pilgrims whose path God can guide. Perhaps we can think of students who want to keep the big questions indefinitely in suspension instead of genuinely seeking a path as they commit themselves to action. Our picture offers a reminder that while the work of education often involves opening up alternatives, expanding the palette of possibilities, it should also lead to points of decision, and the decisions matter profoundly.

At the same time we should beware of loading students' decisions about how to invest their energies with the weight of eternal significance. While the picture does indeed tell us that there are times when we cannot walk in two directions at once, it also locates the full seriousness of such decision-making at a level deeper than decisions about which major to pursue or whether to do extra work on the term paper to avoid a low grade in biology. There might even be times when choosing the kingdom of God means neglecting study for a season to invest time in some more pressing human need. The fundamental decision in view here is to journey towards life or towards death, to seek first personal affluence and self-indulgence or to seek first the kingdom of God. That decision may be worked out in a host of smaller decisions, but it also relieves many of those smaller decisions of their apparent magnitude. The image can warn against mistaking twists in the path for ultimate decision points. The deepest question is neither "should I study English or Engineering?" nor "which of these majors will best help me get ahead and give me the most comfortable life?" but rather "how can I realistically commit to serving God along either of these paths?" Once the student becomes a pilgrim, then the teaching and learning task comes to include seeking those virtues that both embody the kingdom of God and enable godly learning: learning humility and patience in weighing the words of others, seeking justice and loving mercy as new learning is applied, loving one's neighbor inside and outside the classroom.

Another caution: we should not walk away from this picture without questioning the direction of our own gaze. It is easy to look at the young man, nod sagely and gossip inwardly about the weaknesses he shares with our students. If only they would commit whole-heartedly, cast off their entanglements, and set their heart on Christian learning. But the picture is not inviting us to judge, but to examine ourselves. At times the ideals that we project onto our students allow us to conveniently overlook our own vacillations and shortcuts in our eagerness that the young should step up and show their commitment. Where are the tensions in our own posture and our perch as we stand before students, offering ourselves as pilgrim-guides? At what points do our own desires for ease, for status, for control, for being listened to, for winning arguments, for being thought of as someone of consequence who knows things, or for career building, come into tension with the kingdom of God, love of neighbor, and service to our students?

HARBORS AND HAZARDS

For either God or nature or necessity or our own will or some or all of these in combination have cast us forth into this world as though upon a stormy sea, apparently without purpose or plan . . . And so, how many would know the direction in which they should struggle or the way they should return if a storm, which the foolish regard as unfavorable, did not at times force them unwilling and struggling against it into that land of their great desire while they were wandering in ignorance?

Everyone journeys, says Augustine, as he embarks on a treatise about the happy life and how to find it. But not everyone journeys in the same manner, and not everyone makes it home. We are "cast . . . forth into this world as though upon a stormy sea, apparently without purpose or plan." We find ourselves in the world, already on the ship with no clear memory of boarding. We are in motion, the days passing and carrying us further into the future whether we like it or not. We hurtle headlong and then are becalmed, apparently going nowhere. We are regularly perplexed as to the direction we should take. Should we drift with the tides, fly before the wind, or doggedly tack into the face of the gale? Is there some particular shore towards which we should be struggling? Storms come, waves crash. Are they disasters sent to overwhelm us or gracious interventions designed to force us into what will eventually turn out to have been a better course? In the midst of the ocean it's easy to lose one's bearings.

We are lost at sea, says Augustine, but we need to regain a fair land that we have lost, the land of "the happy life." In this land, faith, hope, and love join us to God, and the possession of true wisdom blesses us with perfect peace. God is our origin and ought to be our destination; in the time stretched between the two we find ourselves journeying, seeking, cast upon the sea.

Augustine glimpses three sorts of travelers among the spray. The first type only journeys a short distance from shore, and it requires only a little labor with the oars for these travelers to flee back into the harbor when the waves get rough. Not everyone has to reach the truth through momentous crisis — it's possible to be more teachable from the start, to stay at least within sight of the lighthouse. These first sailors, once they have reached the harbor, put their efforts into raising beacons "for whomever of their fellow citizens they can," in the hope that they will be able to help others to find their way. Learners become teachers, pilgrims become guides. Here Augustine evokes a string of biblical texts that speak of Israel as a light to the gentiles, of the wise as shining like stars, and of the church as the light of the world that is to be placed in full view (Isaiah 42:6-7; Daniel 12:3; Matthew 5:14-15). These travelers demonstrate an authentic journey to the truth as they reach out to teach others.

A second group of sailors is not so easily drawn home. They voyage forth, perhaps boldly, perhaps thoughtlessly, striking their own course. They believe that they can navigate the waters by their own lights. They forget that they have a homeland and a destination, thinking that their journey justifies itself. Some travel so far that they forget the shore from which they departed.

Perhaps they lounge lazily below decks, heedless of where the tides carry them. Or perhaps they rejoice in the thrill of the flapping sails that carry them further into the trackless distance. If a wind speeds their progress and appears to blow in an appealing direction, they welcome its push, and "enter the depths of misery elated and rejoicing." If the wind dies, and life is serene and stable, then "the deceitful calm of pleasure and honors seduces them." What should we wish for such sailors? Interruption, says Augustine. Perhaps the mild kind, some moderate stress or failure or weariness that pushes them beyond empty ambitions. Turning from their vanities, they may find themselves taking up the books of the wise, not necessarily with determined purpose, but perhaps simply "as if they had nothing else to do." Even so, they find themselves directed back on course toward truth. For many, this might prove enough. Should more drastic change be needed, however, then we should hope that they might meet "a violent storm and hostile wind which might lead them amid tears and groans to certain and solid joy." Either way, it is God's rule over the wind and the waves (and the books and the words), not their own sense of direction or skill at navigating, that pushes them home. Lost at sea, they "wake up" through trials and providential redirections and find themselves in the harbor.

Members of the third group fall between these extremes. They too might have ventured out to sea, tossed by the waves and blown too far to have a clear sight of home. Conscience, however, speaks more insistently; they are more aware that there is a harbor that they must seek, and when signs appear showing the direction in which it lies they set sail. Their journey might be swift and straight, though more often they wander along a circuitous route. Cloudy skies give them few chances to take their bearings. They are distracted by "signs" that turn out to be nothing more than shooting stars. These sailors too might need a storm along the way to push them home. Nevertheless, they are seeking, looking out for the harbor lights.

As Augustine surveys his fellow sailors, ships and books get mixed together. The journey that he has in mind is towards the wisdom that leads to the happy life, and so study and inquiry are pertinent ways of moving the oars. The three kinds of travelers are three kinds of learners — can we discern ourselves and our students in their company? Perhaps we know learners like the first sailors who have never ventured far from faith, who need only a few oar strokes to correct their course, who have a comfortable sense of the truth that grasps them. Has this left them complacent, or have they realized that their safety is not to be squandered on themselves? Have they heard the call to teach others?

Learners of the second kind sail aimlessly on through their studies with little apparent sense of why they are learning or where they are headed, focused on pleasure and satisfied with a passing grade and the next experience. Do they need interruption more than they need continued progress? We should be cautious here: Augustine says that these sailors might need God to provide a storm that shatters their complacency, not that we should set out to engineer one. Augustine's personal storm involved pain in his lungs that forced him to give up teaching. Perhaps a better question, then, concerns how we view setbacks and struggles, and how we share with students the realization that they can be markers of hope.

Perhaps many of us are in the third group, knowing that we want wisdom, but finding ourselves easily distracted, easily discouraged, easily disoriented. We know about the *telos*; we can name the kingdom of God as our goal. But the path leading there does not seem straight, we are not always sure which signs to rely on, and we are too prone to follow detours. How do we help one another to grow in discernment and sustain perseverance?

> For all these who are brought in any fashion to the land of the happy life there is one huge mountain set in front of the harbor itself. This mountain also creates difficulties for those entering and should be much feared and carefully avoided . . .

There's another complication, Augustine notes. Even with the harbor in sight, it turns out that planted in the ocean before it is a "huge mountain," a navigational hazard greatly to be feared. It shines out like a beacon, "wrapped in deceitful light." Those arriving from sea and even those already in the harbor are tempted to mistake it for the destination and land on its flank in hope of fulfilment there. For those who succumb to the temptation, it "delights them with its height, from which they can look down on the rest." Like those who raised beacons on the shore, these mountaineers begin to teach others from their mountain perch, pointing to the harbor (which is after all close by), offering detailed advice on how to avoid dangerous submerged rocks. They want everyone to know how much work and skill it took to gain their lofty spot, and make sure that newcomers don't think they can easily climb up too and join them on the mountain. Convinced of their own superiority, "puffed up with pride," they are happy to point those they regard as simpler than themselves toward the truth. The image of teaching from the mountainside hints at usurpation of divine authority, offering our advice as if it carried divine weight. The mountain represents "the proud pursuit of empty glory that has nothing full and solid within." It gives the illusion of having arrived somewhere, but "once it has wrapped them in darkness it snatches away from them the shining home which they had scarcely glimpsed."

There are, then, at least two kinds of teachers in Augustine's allegory. Some seek wisdom for themselves, aware of their continuing need. They set up beacons for others when they have given themselves to the truth and are living thankfully in it. They can beckon towards the happy life because they can say with honesty that they are living at least on its shores; they are guides who themselves walk the pilgrim trail, not bystanders dispensing tips. They have arrived not just at expertise, but at wisdom.

Others seek the status and superiority that comes with being known by others as one who knows things. They enjoy letting others see how hard it is to achieve what they have achieved, and teach with an implied condescension. They chuckle at their students' stupidity as they gossip with colleagues. Teaching brings status, the chance to stride onto the podium and tell others what to do, to expose others' weaknesses while concealing one's own. These teachers like to give directions, to map hazards and warn the world, but have themselves ceased to journey before reaching the destination. They talk about the truth, but have not yet humbled themselves in living it.

Do we find ourselves in either of these pictures? Might they call us back to our oars?

Augustine's tale of the ocean is filled with the uncertainties of the journey. We glimpse the light, and sometimes the light is a beacon. But sometimes it is just a shooting star, or a reflection from a dangerous rock to be avoided. For stretches of time we labor under cloudy skies, pressing on without clear direction. We meet fair winds and violent storms that threaten to capsize us. Sometimes, from a later vantage point, we realize that the fair winds were our enemies and the storms our friends. We teach and learn. Sometimes those who point to the destination are not themselves headed there, but teaching only words. Some of those sailing aimlessly will find that by grace they have arrived. There is a mystery at the heart of learning.

Each must journey, but we need not journey in isolation. Augustine's picture is not of lone journeys and arrivals, but of a variety of travelers helping and needing help, giving and receiving light, pursuing by whatever means we can find ways of teaching and learning that might lead all of us to the happy life.

SETTING OUT AND LOOKING OUT

In the last two sections we have pondered a young man perched at the parting of the ways and Augustine's account of a sea voyage toward happiness. Pause a moment to see them side by side. In both cases, the metaphor of journeying engages the whole person. All significant learning has the potential to alter our life's trajectory and destinations; it changes who we are. Journeying requires engagement and exertion, it involves moral decisions, bodily actions as well as cognitive judgment. It places weight both on God's actions and our own. This immersive quality of journeying means that it is never merely a cognitive act. Reading a map can be a mostly cognitive affair, but making a journey requires both knowledge and know-how, both cognition and commitment.

Journeying also requires the willingness to walk down some roads rather than others, accepting that not all possibilities can be left open, that there is a harbor that calls. For both the precarious youth and the Augustinian sailor journeying is not an end in itself, as if the mere fact of being in motion were inherently virtuous. As for Bunyan's pilgrim, the destination matters, and the dangers along the way are dangerous precisely because they threaten the attainment of the destination. In terms of how we get there, however, the two images tell different sides of the story.

The woodcut focuses on the drama of decision. Procrastination leads to destruction, and choices have consequences. The forking path reminds us that there comes a time when we must commit. It can, however, also be a destructive and incomplete image, leaving us with a fearful awareness of our own finitude and fickleness, but with less sense of divine grace. Augustine broadens the picture, showing a variety of ways, some more circuitous than others, of reaching the harbor. Rather than admonishing at the crossroads, God is abroad upon the seas before we begin our journey. God, the running-out-to-meet-him Father, travels alongside disciples on the road to Emmaus and sends Philip to walk alongside the Ethiopian's chariot. Awareness of divine agency and involvement in our journeying is why Christians pray "Guide Me, O Thou Great Redeemer" and "Lead Us Not Into Temptation," joyfully resisting a deist worldview with every word they sing. As another author puts it, our challenge is not just "choosing the correct fork, but learning to walk with the Savior who can use any road to bring us home," trusting that "our lives will end up in the right place not because of our good choices, but because of the choice God made to love us. . . God owns all the roads." And all the tides, winds, and weather systems, and even the books of the wise. Unlike roads, oceans carry ships along, sometimes even against the best efforts of the sailors. Alongside the drama of choosing, where our own efforts and decisions are in view, Augustine offers the image of being buoyed up by the waters and assisted by the winds, where God's grace sustains and directs the journey.

Augustine imagines the journey not from the perspective of our own determined sallying forth, but in terms of being pulled toward a destination, drawn towards the luminous glory of God. Rather than seeing the forks in the road as a strictly present-tense exercise in weighing costs and benefits, we can begin to see them as exercises in eschatological yearning. Will we allow ourselves to be pulled by a vision of God's glory? Are we open to being drawn along by a vision of our gifts being purified for kingdom service? Can "I have decided to be a lawyer" become not just "I think God is calling me to be a lawyer," but "I feel compelled by a vision of God's justice to study law"? Can "Becoming a teacher seems a sensible plan" become "I sense God's passion for the beauty of truth and the thriving of children, and it gives me a sense that I need to teach"?

Perhaps both teachers and students need reminders of both perspectives. Decision time challenges our sloth and apathy; the call to trust and hope counters over-anxiety. While we journey, learning along the way, we do so as responsible agents and as grateful recipients of divine grace. Journeying calls us to act, to decide, to commit, to risk, to persevere. Yet even the steps we take, the decisions we make, are themselves made possible by, shaped by God's agency. To take a journey, we must "set out," whether by foot or car or plane. But we must also "look out," to discern God at work. A faithful journey asks what God may be accomplishing today and seeks signs of God already traveling the road. We journey not in despair, but in hope; not in drudgery, but in wonder.

DRIVER EDUCATION

Sometimes teaching and learning are quite literally concerned with how we move through the world. Here too our normative images of what it is to journey faithfully challenge us to focus on the kind of imagination fostered among our students.

Matt Phelps and Scott Waalkes, two professors at Malone University, designed a capstone course to help students reflect on how they move through the world, both literally and morally. Their course addressed the desires and choices that inform car culture, manifested in North America's love of cars, road trips, and road movies, and looked for ways to imagine hopeful alternatives.

Rather than beginning with critique, the course fostered exploration. It began with an appreciative look at the things we love about cars, and an invitation to students to share their own car stories. The class went on to examine car artifacts, listen to car-themed songs, and watch advertisements and movies alongside reading about the role of the automobile in modern society. Students were led to gradually acknowledge how car culture had shaped their imaginations, habits, and practices, as they confessed on mid-term papers. One student wrote:

> We live in a culture that mandates that no second be wasted even while we are driving. . . . I myself totaled my first vehicle because of the cell-phone I was looking at instead of the road.

Another student wrote:

> The realization that we are on the roadways with other living, breathing creations of God's own image instead of simply riding besides lifeless metal machines should be a central way of thinking for Christian drivers. It is very possible to be too focused on productivity and efficiency.

The link between cars and the pace of life was explicit in another student's reflection:

> The car has . . . provided a means by which haste and hyper-efficiency have driven many people into extremes of task accomplishment that have left them void of the slower-paced relational life that I still see in the Scriptures and my Amish neighbors today.

As the course unfolded, it explored the various ramifications of the role played by cars in our culture for an array of topics that included suburbanization, church membership, road rage, and environmental sustainability. The group reflected on the impact of car ownership on our sense of self, our relationship to material possessions, our relationships with those around us, and our commitment to the wellbeing of others, including those with whom we share the roads. In what ways does our decision to travel fast, efficiently, and often alone erode our relationships with our neighbors? How far does the status of our ride infiltrate our sense of our own worth and the worth of others? To what degree are we willing to put others at risk for the sake of our own convenience, whether in terms of getting there quicker or multitasking while driving?

As the class journeyed together through the course, the focus on how we journey through the world led to discoveries. A student discovered that staying within the speed limit fostered a greater sense of calm and a more peaceable attitude towards other drivers. Others considered ways of achieving lifestyles that minimized car use. Some time after the course, a student sent the following report.

> I just want you to know that it has now been two full months since I gave up my
> car and decided to bike instead. . . . I use family vehicles every once in a while
> but I have been biking pretty religiously and it is liberating. One of my favorite
> things about it is that on my trips, mostly to and from work, I am many times
> more likely to stop and talk to my neighbors than if I am driving. I passed an
> old friend one day, who was also biking, and she invited me to have breakfast
> with her family. I'll see my neighbor . . . sitting in his lawn playing his banjo and
> I'll just swing in for a bit. There are more instances but there's something about
> the open air and reduced speed that promotes friendliness and makes it harder
> to seclude yourself. I seem to always have a little time to stop in. (I stopped to
> say hello to one of my elderly neighbors as I saw her watering her flowers and
> then she in turn invited me to a dinner locals were having with a group of Swiss
> travelers who were in the area. I learned a bunch about my heritage and now I
> have people in Switzerland who want me to come see them!)

Perhaps unsurprisingly, a focus on literal movement through physical and social space became intertwined with meditation on the journey of learning and living. As one student put it, reflecting on the possibility of reducing car use, "I see the need for change and would consider doing this if I feel God calling me to follow this path."

At another level, the journey together towards insight offered by Phelps and Waalkes invites reflection on the rhythms of the educational journey. When are our courses like quick trips to the mall, just far enough above the speed limit to cover maximum terrain at speed while sustaining the hope of averting arrest or disaster, each participant focused on his or her own bubble, those around us mostly felt as potential obstacles to getting everything done? When are they like slower journeys through a neighborhood, with time taken to pause for conversation, listen to stories, make new connections? At what point does the exhilaration of forward progress turn into the blur of landmarks barely noticed? Or does the patience of slow pedaling turn into dawdling and losing sight of the destination? Is our course conducted on foot, on a bicycle, or in a car, and what concerns might each bring into focus in terms of how we journey together?

WALKING IN CIRCLES

Each spring when I teach Senior Seminar, I find that students are horrified to discover that they have become increasingly more ignorant each semester they have spent in college. We draw this diagram together. As first-year students, they knew this much:

As sophomores this much:

As juniors this much:

As seniors this much:

They nod their heads in agreement. Then realization dawns. Alas, as their knowledge has increased, so also has the circumference of their ignorance. Every article they have read comes with a list of references to other articles not yet read, and so draws a larger map of what they don't yet know. Each trip to the bookstore uncovers more novels from authors to whom they've just been introduced. Every new field they tackle opens up new vistas beyond, all of which demand to be known. And what they are learning this last semester in college makes them feel less certain of the things they thought they once knew. Some of them feel as if they are moving in circles: coming back to matters once mastered and now forgotten and in need of re-learning, being puzzled again by the same questions, confronting again ideas that now seem both pressing and tedious. As they quickly acknowledge, the remedies for such ignorance can be lethal: bluffing, defending a few positions more loudly, seeking to master an increasingly small body of knowledge, despair, lethargy . . . the list goes on.

Learning to be a pilgrim student can bring some ease to their bodies and minds. Because a pilgrim is always in progress; a pilgrim is never alone. When an insect emerges from its chrysalis, it is called an *imago* — a perfect insect, fully formed, having completed all its metamorphoses. But a pilgrim is not an insect: a pilgrim never completes her metamorphoses. Her *imago* is to be continually formed into the image of Christ. To be a pilgrim is to be still on the way, in the middle of things. As a wise teacher once said, "We don't move toward heaven in one gigantic, decisive step after another. We move in small, repetitive, cumulative patterns — learning to make a habit of what we do well, and repenting, again and again, what we do badly." Pilgrimage, in other words, is a life lesson in revision. And to their great comfort, pilgrims make these small, repetitive patterns in the company of others. My circumference of ignorance bumps up against your circle of knowledge, and in this way we both grow and change and move forward.

To be a pilgrim is not just to move forward in a straight line, but also to enter into a circular motion of journeying forth and returning home, perhaps multiple times. This circularity may sometimes feel tedious, as if we were failing to make progress, yet the deeper movement is a spiral, an old reality caught up and transformed into a new reality. In a culture deeply permeated with ideals of linear progress yet paradoxically enchanted with its ability to multi-task and randomly surf in multiple directions, it is well to remember the contrasting circular rhythm of pilgrim journeying. The pilgrim leaves for Jerusalem each year, worships again at the festival, and returns to the village, enacting a cycle that bodily recalls God's continued faithfulness. The prodigal son sets off for a distant country, but in the very failure of his trip and his ignominious return home he finds that neither he nor his home are the same as when he left, that new possibilities for reconciliation are waiting in the village he abandoned with such disdain. Flight becomes pilgrimage; self-confidence is turned into self-knowledge. The disciples travel with Jesus for three years, assured that they are moving up the ladder of their ambitions, only to be scattered at his death. Yet when Jesus calls them back together after his resurrection, they start again, they resume their pilgrimage with the Comforter that Jesus sends.

Pilgrimages are not just about a distant destination; they are also about the hope of returning, of finding one's relationship to home transformed, of finding one's self renewed by the journey, of seeing the familiar with a fresh perspective. We set out for a dimly glimpsed site and in the end, as T. S. Eliot put it, "arrive where we started / And know the place for the first time." My students find this comforting as they recognize, with new urgency, that graduation will inevitably push them a bit more quickly along their pilgrim paths. Their ignorance seems a little less lethal, the fellowship of companions a bit more real, the resolve to persevere a task they are ready to undertake, the promise of home a sure and steady light.

WHAT STATIONS STRUCTURE YOUR JOURNEY?

Heinrich Böll, in a remarkable short story titled *Traveler, if you should come to Spa,* . . . describes a journey that lasts less than an hour, traverses perhaps a hundred meters, and yet maps a looping path all the way from childhood to death.

The story opens in the closing years of the Second World War. A vehicle pulls up outside a secondary school in a burning German city. A soldier is lifted from the van on a stretcher and carried into the school. We follow his progress from his semi-delirious, pain-fogged perspective. As he moves along the corridors, his surroundings begin to look familiar. He passes a portrait of Medea, who killed her children in revenge against Jason, and a replica of a Greek frieze displaying military exploits. A portrait of Nietzsche is glimpsed through an open door. Busts of Roman emperors stand alongside portraits of Frederick the Great and Adolf Hitler, and charts depicting the varieties of Aryan facial features to aid in identifying those fully human.

The soldier suspects that many of these pictures hang in plenty of schools, but gradually suspects that he knows this school. A picture of German colonies in Togo glides by, as does a First World War memorial with its laurel wreath and iron cross. A statue of Hermes offers a vision of lithe physique, and a bust of Zeus provides a manly and martial vision of deity. Small details gradually confirm that this is indeed the school that the young soldier recently left for the front; even in his reduced state of awareness, the sequence of images seems vivid in his mind, engraved there by long daily repetition.

After two flights of stairs and three corridors lined with images, the stretcher is carried into the art room, where a discolored patch on the wall renders visible a spot where a crucifix has been removed. The soldier is given water and a cigarette, and we glimpse the pathway worn in his internal world by romanticized images of military conquest as he briefly admires the glorious sound of the artillery outside even as flames from the burning city light the sky red through a window.

Eventually he is carried behind a blackboard, on which a fragment of a literary text citing the famous epigram about the 300 Spartans who died to save Greece still stands in his own handwriting. He is placed on a table for examination. The last image that he sees is his reflection in the lightbulb overhead, wrapped up like a small, dirt-colored package. He is unwrapped, and as he tries to sit up he finally becomes aware that he has lost both arms and a leg. A figure in a white coat prepares an injection, and the story ends.

The succession of images and allusions that Böll weaves into his story articulates a sharp critique of Nazi propaganda and the unholy cross-breeding of humanistic education and classical motifs with the militaristic, racist worldview of the Third Reich. A still more profound layer is added when one begins to count the images; counting the vision in the lightbulb and the absent cross, there are fourteen images or clusters of imagery. As a Roman Catholic author, Böll was familiar with repeated symbolic journeys past a sequence of carefully chosen images; the practice of praying one's way round the Stations of the Cross is a form of Christian piety that has endured for centuries. As the believer moves from one picture to the next, a series of moments from Christ's journey to the cross, beginning with his condemnation and progressing through to his being laid in the tomb, invite reflection and identification. We are to walk with Jesus on the way of the cross. The repeated journey through the stations is intended to be formative, to invite the one praying to map the way of the cross onto their own ways, to walk the path that Jesus walked. In some versions of the tradition, the cathedral building in which the stations are displayed counts as a fifteenth station, the environment of post-resurrection faith within which those praying reiterate their miniature pilgrimage.

As we overlay the meditative journey through the Stations of the Cross onto the soldier's journey through the stations of his schooling, some striking parallels and contrasts appear. The charts identifying Aryan faces correspond in the sequence with Veronica wiping the Jewish face of Jesus. The representations of powerful military leaders parallel the repeated occasions on which Jesus falls under the weight of the cross. The bust of Zeus stands over against Christ on the cross, offering starkly contrasting visions of deity. The taking down of Christ from the cross echoes the taking down of the crucifix, removed because of its unacceptable focus on suffering, from the art room wall. The nightmare vision in the lightbulb identifies the soldier with Jesus in the tomb, offering one of several hints (including the truncated epigram that gives the story its title) that he does not survive the story's end.

Böll is suggesting something profound about schooling in these clashing layers of imagery. The school, like the cathedral, is a place where liturgy is enacted, a place of iterative, deeply formative journeys that shape us and mold our imagination. The liturgies of the school that he describes are, he suggests, profoundly deforming, twisted parodies of life's true pilgrimage as seen in the path of Christ.

Böll's story provokes reflection about our own iterative journeys, and brings questions into focus that sometimes remain in the margins of discussions of Christian education. He asks us to think about ideas, worldviews, and narratives, but also about buildings, pictures, memorials, motions, and daily routines. He calls us to reflect on the repeated patterns of schooling, not only in terms of the syllabus and lecture outline but in a way that might include the vending machine, the TV screens, the paintings, the trophies on display. We are invited to see schooling in terms of the movements and symbols and daily ways of being together that add up to a particular circuit around which we travel together daily, until its rhythms and contours and peculiar sights become inscribed in our gait. What if, he forces us to ask, we thought about Christian education not just in terms of ideas, perspectives, and standards, but also as a set of motions that we make together, a way of journeying together that forms us in ways that might go deeper than our knowing? And what might it then mean for us to be walking as teachers and learners in the way of Christ?

What Sustains the Journey?

AT SOME POINT IN ANY significant journey, travel means weariness. It means impatience, wanting to be there already, discomfort, frustration. Journeying saps our resources, our patience, and our courage. We are tempted to take dubious shortcuts, to attempt a mad dash or sink into a grim march.

The pilgrim, unlike the Olympic athlete, is not out to demonstrate that her own strength is sufficient to triumphantly reach the finish line. Pilgrims should not travel proudly alone, chalking up the achievements of each day to their personal prowess. The pilgrim counts on the sustenance provided by inns and hostels along the way, the hope born of shared eating and singing, the fellowship of traveling companions, and the rhythm of motion and rest that allows God to carry the burden of the world. In this final group of reflections on journeying we focus on these sustaining practices that open up the possibility of joy in the journey.

PILGRIMAGE IN THE DESERT

It is tempting to think of pilgrimage in romantic terms. I am a brilliant visionary setting off on my personal pilgrimage, marching to a different drummer, embracing life's rich journey. I will be admired by people who can only dream of breaking free from convention and complacency. I will look back with nostalgia on my pilgrimage as a personal victory.

The Bible undercuts an image of pilgrimage as an enticing, self-directed avocation. Biblical imagery of paths and journeys is replete with talk of slipping feet, of deceptive, crooked paths, of the danger of one's foot striking against a stone, of the need for level paths, of robbers and wild animals, and the weariness that besets the traveler.

The Bible frequently uses the Hebrews' exodus from Egypt and wanderings in the wilderness toward their promised land as a touchstone for thinking about life's pilgrimage. The great Hebrew migration begins with a sprint for their lives from a superior army in pursuit. The Hebrews narrowly escape by water, and in the morning the rising sun brightens a shoreline covered in enemy corpses. Then come days in the stifling desert without adequate water or food, civil wars of rebellion, attacks by hostile clans, plagues by snakes and scorpions and earthquakes . . . in the end, over forty years of parched pilgrimage, and still no promised land. Virtually no one who set out so hopefully from Egypt actually arrives in the land that was promised. They all die in the desert, no more successful than the army that initially pursued them.

Why are there such difficulties during pilgrimage? What breaks the pilgrim's stride and keeps her from making good on all of her first and best dreams?

It's worth considering the diversity of reasons that are given for the Hebrews' waywardness. It was not just the heat of the afternoon, the steepness of the mountains, or the remoteness of the destination. The Hebrews' most notable desecrations happen on the plains, in the cool of the evening, and right on the property line of the Promised Land. Demoralization and infidelity are never deprived of opportunity by our comforts, never obligated to strike at the obvious time. That would be too predictable. And predictability would steal their great advantage: the element of surprise.

Yet the heat of the afternoon and the simplest of needs — food, water, warmth, shade, clear orientation toward a goal — also proved to be the allies of temptation. The desert is, after all, a place where things usually die. If the forces of demoralization ignored such willing allies, they would hardly be the worthy opponents they have proven to be.

So we might not be surprised that the teaching pilgrimage encounters the familiar cast of distractions, demoralizers, and demons that the Hebrews engaged on their trek — some coming predictably in the heat of the day, some sneaking up when all seems well.

Some teachers lose their passion and experience burnout, the depletion of their source of energy. Thinking in terms of our source of energy turns the focus on things that are going on *within* the teacher; this emphasis has the good sense of anticipating that burn-out is not entirely attributable to external, harsh surroundings. Pilgrimages are supposed to get the pilgrim all the way to the pilgrimage destination; trekkers who expend all their energy too early in the process and fail to take heed of the length of the journey aren't successful as pilgrims.

Teachers tend to lose their inner energy when they do not take good care of themselves. And they fail to take care of themselves when they fail to live intentionally — with forethought, deliberation and follow-through. There needs to be planned self-care — clear priorities, and integrity in pursuing them.

This sort of intentionality requires that a teacher is in touch with herself — knows what she actually needs, knows what exacerbates the needs, knows how those needs can be met. Like the Hebrews craving water and food, each teacher has some common non-negotiable needs; fail to meet them, and an internal rebellion breaks out. Some needs are fairly pedestrian and immediate — ample sleep each night, enough exercise, enough healthy relationships and not too many unhealthy ones, enough intensity of friendship without too much, spiritual feeding in devotions and communal worship. Other needs develop on a slow simmer of unresolved internal conflicts — from family, or work, or the past — and silently drain energy.

Beyond these internal needs there are challenges on the border between the internal and the external. The marathon teacher — the one who will make it to the pilgrimage destination — needs to keep her teaching in the right perspective, in the right relative relationship with the rest of life — not growing lax in remaining professionally current and updating knowledge, skills, and insight, while not obsessing about performance and perfection. Either leaning — perfectionism or self-indulgence — can end a pilgrimage. The aim should be growth with contentment, giving, while yet receiving from life.

And then there are the purely external factors. Institutional and communal failings can create forms of chaos that overstretch the individual teacher's resources. The aging process affects energy levels and abilities, and rapid cultural and educational change dates us. A lack of opportunities for retooling or even getting credible feedback leads to isolation, and separates daily life from the vision of faithful pilgrimage that originally motivated it. The press of duties encourages teachers to mass produce — rather than seeing each student as a unique person in God's image, for whom one can do something that is both special and limited. The treadmill of uncompleted tasks from an overabundance of roles turns at a non-human pace. "Treadmill" can feel like the right metaphor, because most teachers lack clear external finish lines, clear moments of completion and accomplishment, clear ways of celebrating staging posts with others. Treadmills are antithetical to the daily, measurable progress of a pilgrimage; one goes through lots of motion, but gets nowhere. The common pull (perhaps especially among men) is to not include other people when one's stride falters. Life on the treadmill leads to unmaintained friendships, so that there is no one to connect with when times become tough.

The Hebrews sometimes failed to appreciate that they had left the pilgrimage route. Even Golden Calf worship was framed as a celebration of the god who had brought them out of Egypt and into pilgrimage. A set of "wrong way" signs can help warn when your stride is being broken.

Lack of hope for an extended period of time, inability to be excited about the future, pain or stomach ache when the future is discussed, or ongoing frequent cycles of hopelessness, should get our attention. (Unfortunately, perfectionists seem especially prone to breaking stride, but also have habits that can blind them to this symptom.) Changes in dependability — missed deadlines, forgotten appointments, unanswered mail — are markers of a treadmill existence. Sleeping disorders, chronic fatigue without a clear cause, irritability and short-temperedness indicate that you're unhappy and needy. Compulsive behaviors, frequent desires to change jobs, restlessness, loss of self-confidence, loss of the ability (or even desire) to play, and fear of new things all show that you're burying things rather than facing them and strategically making an effective plan.

And what's to be done when your pace has been broken? First, regain some perspective. Periodic retreats, both "away" and "embedded within" our regular world, can break patterns and adrenaline cycles in a helpful way. They are the equivalent of a respite at a roadside inn along a well-traveled pilgrimage highway, or a pause at one of the ubiquitous European roadside chapels that punctuate pilgrimage routes. Both restore perspective — inns by nurturing the physical needs of the pilgrim, chapels by restoring the vision that animated the pilgrim's departure. Both distant and embedded retreats come in a lot of flavors: accountability partners and confidants, times for reading beyond what is required, regular lunches with a coach or two, creative hobbies, time at a monastery or on the porch. All of them help break up patterns so that we can breathe some fresh air and perspective. You might take some of your restorative time to explore what is happening in your life, and why it is happening. For example, try identifying one symptom of your negative situation, and then ask why it is happening. Then ask why that "why" is happening. Continue asking until you think you're getting close to the core issue.

Second, take note of the challenges your new perspective reveals. Journal, and keep a log of how you actually spend your hours. Become aware of whom you spend time with, and what you're taking on from their lives. Log the number of things in a week that inspire you; if there aren't any, log that. Make a log of things that energize you and things that deplete you in a given week; the first list needs to be longer and weightier than the second (and may need to remain longer for some years in order to restore your depleted reserves). Think about the processes you're a part of that have led to the situation you face — they need to be addressed, or you will eventually end up back in trouble, no matter how you accommodate the immediate problems. Many pilgrims throughout history have kept such a record of their pilgrimage; perhaps the keeping of the record is central to maintaining the action of the pilgrimage.

Third, make a plan. Pilgrims have a planned destination, and the process of life-pilgrimage for teachers deserves a similar strategy. If your log indicates imbalance among work, play, worship, family, body care, rest and creative recreation, take charge of rebalancing. (Plan to respect others who are wired for a different balance among these things!) Deliberately say "no" to something; it will give you confidence that you are not out of control. If you say "no" enough it will eventually clear space for saying "yes" to some small, more important thing . . . a thing that will bring vitality and fresh focus to the pilgrimage process. If you've discovered unresolved issues in your family or work or other relationships, decide how you're going to face and resolve them. Don't fear to get the help of a professional, and don't fail to maintain an appropriate, "current" support system — sometimes trouble has festered because your support system is massively outdated and needs an upgrade. Think about ways to draw strength from others not only in relationship terms, but in terms of your call to teach — find another teacher who loves teaching and loves students and arrange to meet periodically with a few ground rules (such as no grumbling or gossiping about students). Brainstorm constructive ideas for your classrooms and pray for your pedagogy.

This focus on strategy must happen within a larger framework; the failures of the Hebrews' journey were not just a matter of keeping up morale. At the outset of Torah, humanity is exiled from God's presence because of sin, and this sin is motivated by the desire to escape the limits of creatureliness. Not content to be human persons, Adam and Eve over-reached. They wished to be gods, not creatures. This was of course impossible, but they insisted on constructing their lives around things that could not possibly be true. Their rebellion and disobedience centered on setting goals that they could not possibly achieve.

This is a core sin of us stride-breakers. And the core message of Torah is that this sin is too strong to be overcome by a mere self-help program. Reflection and planning only find their power after the pilgrim has addressed the motives, failures and guilt that have broken the pilgrim's stride.

This finally points us to another need: thankfulness. Instead of giving thanks to God in humble acknowledgment of our need and God's generosity, we easily become focused only on what has not been received, on our own strivings and dissatisfactions and unfinished tasks stretching to the horizon. A regular focus on thanksgiving, individually and with others, can put things back in their proper order and allow us to celebrate milestones reached and draw strength from grace received. It also fosters a healthy sense of limits, allowing us to turn from seeking to carry the world and acknowledge that God knows what our portion should be.

> We thank you for setting us at tasks which demand our best efforts, and for leading us to accomplishments which satisfy and delight us.
>
> We thank you also for those disappointments and failures that lead us to acknowledge our dependence on you alone.

HURRYING TO THE TENT ENTRANCE

Pilgrims need places to stay. "Pilgrimage" conjures up images of winding roads, weary feet, and days spent traveling, but the journey is punctuated each night by a place that, ideally, provides rest, refreshment, and directions to the next stopping place. To be a pilgrim means movement, but also the recurring need for food and shelter. Throughout Scripture, the vulnerability of the journey is coupled with the call to extend hospitality. In fact, welcoming the stranger becomes a way of welcoming God.

Early in the story of Abraham we encounter him sitting by the entrance to his tent. Three visitors show up, and his response offers a vivid picture of eager hospitality:

> When he saw them, he hurried from the entrance of his tent to meet them and bowed low to the ground.

He said, "If I have found favor in your eyes, my lord, do not pass your servant by. Let a little water be brought, and then you may all wash your feet and rest under this tree. Let me get you something to eat, so you can be refreshed and then go on your way — now that you have come to your servant."

"Very well," they answered, "do as you say."

So Abraham hurried into the tent to Sarah. "Quick," he said, "get three seahs of the finest flour and knead it and bake some bread."

Then he ran to the herd and selected a choice, tender calf and gave it to a servant, who hurried to prepare it. He then brought some curds and milk and the calf that had been prepared, and set these before them. While they ate, he stood near them under a tree. (Genesis 18:2-8, TNIV)

Strangers arrive, and everyone begins to scurry. Elderly Abraham races around making hurried preparations. All of his energies are focused on providing hospitality to his visitors. Then, instead of holding court, he stands to one side, ready to serve as his guests sit and eat. Only later does Abraham discover that it was God he had welcomed.

In the New Testament Jesus declares that "Anyone who welcomes you welcomes me, and anyone who welcomes me welcomes the one who sent me" (Matthew 10:40-41, TNIV). His parable of the sheep and the goats underlines that "whatever you did for one of the least of these brothers and sisters of mine, you did for me." The list of actions that separate sheep from goats includes: "I was a stranger and you welcomed me" (Matthew 25:35, 40, TNIV). Peter's acceptance of the inclusion of the gentiles in the church of Christ, with its momentous consequences for the church as a whole, happens amid mutual acts of hospitality (Acts 10-11). Hebrews 13:2 offers a direct exhortation: "Do not forget to show hospitality to strangers, for by so doing some people have shown hospitality to angels without knowing it."

This call to recognize Christ in the face of the stranger at the door undermines any vision of the host as someone who condescends to make space for the poor guest. Genuine hospitality is not an act in which the host sees him or herself as the heroic rescuer and noble provider to the needy. In biblical terms, hospitality is an act of decentering in which the guest is honored and the host brings his or her resources to bear in willing service. We see this in Abraham's eager bustle, and in that story's presentation of Abraham as the one begging for favor as he serves his guests. Amy Oden puts it this way:

Hospitality requires that the host recognize both the need and the full humanity of the stranger. There is a respectful balance in successful hospitality that neither denigrates the guest's neediness nor denies it. The other is fully honored as a child of God, while at the same time needs are addressed.

The stranger on the road has real needs, and these are met, but they are met without condescension. Hospitality begins at the level of basic physical needs, involving provision of food and shelter to those who find themselves vulnerable. However, it goes beyond this to encompass social and spiritual needs. It includes a focus on welcome into table fellowship. It requires openness of heart and genuine attentiveness to the guest.

What would it mean for our classrooms to be hospitable spaces for students on their educational journey? How might the biblical picture of hospitality shape the way we see ourselves as teachers?

Of course, travelers do not always meet with hospitality. The Bible affirms hospitality as the normative response to strangers, and also starkly acknowledges that part of the likely suffering of the traveler is complete failure of hospitality. Abraham's own fear that as a stranger he will face violence rather than hospitality later twists his behavior in disastrous ways as he passes his wife off to Abimelek as his sister (Genesis 20). One of the more distressingly sordid tales in the dark corners of Judges centers on sexual violence directed towards journeying strangers (Judges 19). Jesus himself, the Word of God come to dwell among us, did not receive a hospitable welcome (John 1).

To exercise hospitality is to enact an alternative to indifference, exploitation, or violence. A hospitable stance rejects an understanding of others as threats to be feared, as too much trouble, or as resources to be used. The people of God are themselves strangers who know what it is to be mistreated in a foreign land. They are not to repay evil with evil, but rather with kindness. "Love your neighbor as yourself," says Leviticus 19:18. Jesus points to this text as part of his summation of the Law and the Prophets, and explains it with a story in which a traveler is attacked by robbers before being brought to an inn by a wayfaring stranger, who turns out to be the "neighbor" in the story (Luke 10:25-37). The choice of illustration is not accidental. A few verses after the "love your neighbor" command in Leviticus 19 the phrase "love . . . as yourself" recurs: "When a foreigner resides among you in your land, do not mistreat them. The foreigner residing among you must be treated as your native-born.

Love them as yourself, for you were foreigners in Egypt" (Leviticus 19:33-34, TNIV). We are aliens, sojourners who have been welcomed by God; in turn we are to welcome those who have become vulnerable by traveling from home.

What kinds of violence do learners come to fear from teachers and fellow students? How do we learn to repay students imperfections with hospitable kindness?

Both the traveler's need for hospitality and the ever-present threat of violence can be seen throughout history. Early church writers pointed to the provision of hospitality to vulnerable travelers as a characteristic form of Christian service to the world. Jerome wrote:

> Our duties in our monastery are those of hospitality. We welcome all who come to us with the smile of human friendliness. We must take care lest it should happen again that Mary and Joseph do not find room at the inn, and that Jesus should be shut out and say to us, "I was a stranger and you did not take me in."

Chrysostom similarly urged his flock in a sermon on the Acts of the Apostles:

> Have a room, to which Christ may come. Say, "This is Christ's space. This building is set apart for Him." Even if it is just a basement and tiny. He won't refuse it. Christ goes about "naked and a stranger." It is only a shelter he wants. Abraham received the strangers in the place where he himself lived. His wife stood in the place of a servant, the guests in the place of masters. He didn't know that he was receiving Christ, didn't know that he was receiving Angels. Had he known it, he would have lavished his whole substance. But we, who know that we receive Christ, don't show even so much enthusiasm as he did who thought he was receiving humans.

Medieval monasteries developed rules for hospitality in part because they were inundated with pilgrims who threatened to disrupt the daily pattern of work and prayer and yet who needed to be fed and sheltered. Along the routes of major pilgrimages a network of hostels developed to serve the needs of travelers. Along the same route the unwary pilgrim might encounter groups of bandits offering apparent hospitality and companionship on the road as a preface to robbing their targets in lonely places. Classic journey stories — and here we might think of the *Odyssey* or *Pilgrim's Progress* or even *Huckleberry Finn* — are likewise full of tales of seemingly hospitable places that trap pilgrims or distract them from their journey. Odysseus's men are turned into pigs by Circe, Christian and Faithful linger in Vanity Fair, and Huck and Jim barely escape from Mississippi river towns.

Think of our own classrooms and educational institutions. Are they places that offer genuine hospitality and sanctuary? Do they provide rest for the weary and safety for the vulnerable? Are they free of patronizing or hostile gestures? Do they aid pilgrim students on their path toward God, or do they provide distractions and road blocks?

What would it mean for our schools to be hospitable spaces for students on their educational journey?

How Do You Host Your Students?

What makes a classroom an inviting and hospitable hostel for pilgrim students? And conversely what turns a hostel into a hotel of horrors? The negative examples — the men of Gibeah, medieval bandits, Circe's island, Vanity Fair, and Mississippi river towns — have this in common: the hosts all want to possess and control their guests. Rather than offering a respite and encouragement to pursue the journey, these hosts write the guests into their own scenarios. It isn't hard to see parallel temptations for teachers, particularly because we often think of our classrooms, at least implicitly, as *an* end point if not *the* end point, of a student's journey. We expect students to have taken enough preparatory courses, to have learned critical thinking, to be able to write an argumentative paper, so that when they arrive in our classes they are ready to master the material we've put on the syllabus. We can be tempted to approach the learning space as a struggle for control, bouncing between the poles of "teacher-centered" and "learner-centered." The metaphor of the classroom as a pilgrim way-station offers a different model.

The Rule of St. Benedict, which guided many medieval monasteries, is clear that the life of the monastery — work and prayer — exists apart from the presence or absence of pilgrims. In this respect, the pilgrim way-station is very unlike a hotel, or some classrooms, whose entire business is to cater to guests.

Pilgrims are welcomed at a monastery, and they are invited to participate in the community as appropriate. But their contact is limited to the abbot and to an assigned guestmaster, whose chief virtue is that of prudence. The community is not entirely focused on pleasing customers, but has its own rules. At the same time the wellbeing of the guest is not sacrificed to those rules. The abbot and the guestmaster, who are allowed to "break" rules of the community such as injunctions to fast or to keep silent, mediate between monastery and pilgrim.

In a classroom that functions as a pilgrim way-station, the teacher/guestmaster must have a clear sense of the student pilgrim's destination and the needs that the way-station can appropriately meet. The entire journey is not to be completed here and now — it stretches out before the beginning of this class and long after its final week. The goal of such hospitality is to enable the student to continue his or her journey, not to encourage a dependent lingering in the classroom. It might be useful to ask near the beginning of a semester, "If you thought of your life as a pilgrimage, what is its destination? How do you see this class helping you along that journey?" Having raised this question, we can formulate or reformulate with students more appropriate or more nuanced responses as we proceed, and then re-ask the question at the end of the semester.

The guestmaster must also prudently mediate between the stable community and the passing pilgrim, with an eye toward both protecting the community and helping students on their way. For instance, whether the community is an academic guild, a tradition, or an ecclesiastical institution, the guestmaster respects the work of the "experts" and works to protect the community's integrity while selectively choosing those activities that will refresh and nourish the pilgrim. That means, among other tasks, selecting not just what is fun to teach or what comes easiest to hand or what is currently recognized as "excellent," but rather what students need to know or receive from a community in order to continue their own pilgrimages.

The guestmaster will also be concerned with whether visiting pilgrims feel safe during their stay. Classrooms can be places of substantial risk for some students, exposing them to possible ridicule, denigration, and failure. The risk comes not only from fellow pilgrims, but even from the teacher, whose conscious or unconscious desire to control, to display prowess and mastery, or to maintain a sense of superiority to the hapless youth being instructed can lead to overbearing behavior or outright abuse of power. Henri Nouwen sees the role of host as calling on the teacher to provide a fearless space in which personal as well as intellectual growth can happen. Parker Palmer similarly claims that three major characteristics of a learning space are "openness, boundaries, and an air of hospitality," noting that participants' sense of security is bound up with how ideas are treated. Learners who are treated with hospitality may themselves learn to be hospitable to the ideas of others:

> To be inhospitable to strangers or strange ideas, however unsettling they may be, is to be hostile to the possibility of truth; hospitality is not only an ethical virtue but an epistemological one as well. So the classroom where truth is central will be a place where every stranger and every strange utterance is met with welcome.

When we reconfigure our classrooms as hostels along the pilgrim way, we may glimpse a more robust image of what it means to be hospitable, beyond simply being "nice." We will recognize the necessary limits of such a classroom — it is simply one way-station among many. We will also recognize its potential — it is a place where pilgrim students are welcomed, provisioned, and sent out again, equipped both to walk more sturdily on their own and to deal more charitably with others they meet along the way. And we will learn perhaps to ask questions like these: Have the students in this class thought about how what we are studying relates to their larger life-questions? Have I created tasks or experiences that encourage them to do so? Do students feel an appropriate sense of safety? Have they also learned to ask and listen to questions? Will students walk away from this way-station with a greater understanding of the tradition of which it is a part? And will they have been nourished by that tradition?

TEACHING IS BREAKING BREAD

> The instructions that I address to you, my brothers, will differ from those I should deliver to people in the world, at least the manner will be different. The preacher who desires to follow St Paul's method of teaching will give them milk to drink rather than solid food, and will serve a more nourishing diet to those who are spiritually enlightened: "We teach," he said, "not in the way philosophy is taught, but in the way that the Spirit teaches us: we teach spiritual things spiritually."

Hospitality involves food, and also how we share it. As various teachers have discovered, the literal preparation and sharing of food in learning settings can make a tangible difference to the sense of welcome, community, and security experienced by students. But there does not have to be literal food in the classroom for reflection on how we eat together to be relevant.

Teaching itself is breaking bread, so says Bernard of Clairvaux.

The setting is a 12th century sermon, the first of a long and famous series of sermons that Bernard composed on the Song of Songs. He addresses the reader as one of his monastic brethren, inviting us into the intimacy of the chapter house. He announces a course of instruction that will stretch long into the future (the series was interrupted by his death in 1153, with the first 86 sermons completed). He opens with reflections on how his teaching will proceed, in a voice that yearns to harness his hearers' imagination and shape their idea of the kind of learning demanded of them. He invites his learners to share an image of teaching and learning as breaking bread and practicing hospitality.

His teaching will, he assures them in his opening sentence, be different from that which he would address to "people in the world." Desiring to follow "St. Paul's method of teaching," he will teach in a way appropriate to the spiritually mature (compare 1 Corinthians 3:2). "Be ready then," he urges, "to feed on bread rather than milk . . . bread that is splendid and delicious, the bread of that book called *The Song of Songs*."

Bread versus milk. How does invoking this pair of images from Paul offer ways of thinking about teaching? What might teaching have to do with spiritual maturity? What if the contrast had been bread versus cake?

Bernard quotes the Bible here not to prove points, but to begin to build a shared imagination around the question of what is at stake in learning. The brief biblical allusion not only points to the need to fit teaching to the capacities of the learner, but also implies that the learner's capacities are not merely cognitive but spiritual. The progress made in learning will have as much to do with maturity as with memory or quickness of wit. Learning important things is more than processing information; it puts to the test our capacity to grapple with wisdom, our ability to bring our very selves to our learning. A book may be bread and nourish the bones — but for it to have savor, the learner too must be prepared, must bring an unspoiled appetite and a readiness not merely to nibble but to feed, not to swallow whole but to meditate through patient chewing. With milk all we need to do is suck and swallow; enjoying bread takes more investment.

Be ready then to feed on bread rather than milk. Solomon has bread to give that is splendid and delicious, the bread of that book called "The Song of Songs." Let us bring it forth then if you please, and break it . . .

The bread offered to learners is not just a contrasting foil for the milk of basic instruction — it is "splendid and delicious." The teaching must appeal to learners, must be capable of being experienced as something fragrant. However, this is not the sugary, gratifying appeal of cakes and candy, but rather the hearty, wholesome savor of bread to the hungry. Bread may be fragrant, but it is primarily designed not to titillate but to satisfy daily need. There is a world of difference between teaching and learning that delight and nourish, and teaching and learning that are only amusing.

A book may be a loaf, but a loaf is not yet a meal. "Let us bring it forth then if you please, and break it," continues Bernard. Loaves are not to be swallowed whole or gnawed in solitude, but broken and shared. This requires not only baking bread in preparation for the encounter, but also breaking bread so that portions match appetites and all can share. Offering plates of grain or throwing whole loaves at learners would be a poor act of welcome, as would casting educational content at learners without breaking it down pedagogically so that it becomes fitted to those who are to learn it. As the host stands between oven and guest, the teacher stands between those who assemble knowledge and those who would digest it.

This mediating task does not, however, put the teacher on a pedestal. Someone must break the bread for there to be a meal, but the prospect causes Bernard to strike a note of caution: is this service or an arrogant attempt to own a shared blessing? "Who is going to divide this loaf?" Bernard asks. The teacher is herself dependent on receiving knowledge as a gift, knowing that it is not ultimately hers to own and control. There is another who is to be recognized in the breaking of bread.

But who is going to divide this loaf? The Master of the house is present; it is the Lord you must see in the breaking of the bread. For who else could more fittingly do it? It is a task that I would not dare to arrogate to myself. So look upon me as one from whom you look for nothing. For I myself am one of the seekers, one who begs along with you for the food of my soul, the nourishment of my spirit.

To teach is not to claim status, but to model a hunger for learning. Our daily need for bread speaks of our human fragility and calls for our gratitude, and in this teacher and learners are one.

Presenting gourmet delicacies at a banquet can turn into an act of self-aggrandizement and personal display; sharing bread at the daily table places the focus on the simplicity of the day's shared need. The focus is nourishment, not culinary prowess. Bernard emphasizes not his superior learning, but his lack.

> Poor and needy, I knock at that door of his which, "when he opens, nobody can close," that I may find light on the profound mystery to which this discourse leads. Patiently all creatures look to you, O Lord. "Little children go begging for bread; no one spares a scrap for them"; they await it from your merciful love.

What kind of picture does this offer of the teacher's calling? What kind of authority does this teacher wield?

The teacher comes not as a master ("the Master of the house is present," but his name is not Bernard and he is not standing behind the lectern), but as a child, aware of his own need and yet daring to desire that he might be a means of meeting the need of others. The teacher comes to his task in an attitude of supplication. Does it make a difference that God is present in the classroom?

> O God most kind, break your bread for this hungering flock, through my hands indeed if it should please you, but with an efficacy that is all your own.

Hunger, hands, humility — how do these three dance together? How do we, teachers and learners, approach our tasks with the meekness, expectancy, gusto, and gratitude that go with sharing bread when hungry?

Like Abraham bustling about his tent, the host hopes that the guest will welcome the food that is offered, just as the teacher hopes that her teaching will be welcomed by learners. Try it, she urges. It will taste good. And I have your good at heart. I'm not here to lord it over you. You can trust that it's good to eat.

> Now, unless I am mistaken, by the grace of God you have understood quite well from the book of Ecclesiastes how to recognize and have done with the false promise of this world. And then the book of Proverbs — has not your life

and your conduct been sufficiently amended and enlightened by the doctrine it inculcates? These are two loaves of which it has been your pleasure to taste, loaves you have welcomed as coming from the cupboard of a friend. Now approach for this third loaf . . .

Before arriving at the Song of Songs, Bernard reminds his hearers, they have had the "pleasure to taste" the books that came before, and test whether the one who taught them was really their friend, committed to their wellbeing and not merely to his own ego-satisfaction.

How do students learn this from us? Trust matters for deep learning. It is a poor host who offers the meal mechanically, without care and goodwill. Any meal, however well cooked, can be spoiled if accompanied by an underlying tone of thinly concealed resentment or condescension.

Like all hospitality, this provision of learning is not to be closed in upon a small circle of favorites. The aim is not for a few to show how much they can eat while the rest go hungry. Here the traveler enters the picture. Bread (like learning) is not there to be possessed and displayed, but to be shared, and that sharing must be open to the wayfaring stranger who appears at the door.

I am sure that the friend who comes to us on his travels will have no reason to murmur against us after he has shared in this third loaf.

The one who is not from here, who arrives dusty from the road and seeks a place at the table, is to be met with hospitality. If some gorge themselves without taking account of the fact that others are hungry and vulnerable, then the joy of the meal cannot be complete. Who goes hungry in my classroom as the learning time draws to a close each day?

Turning at last to the content to be taught, the Song of Songs, Bernard wonders aloud whether to skip the book's title and begin commenting on the first chapter. No, he decides, let's not do that.

So now what shall we do? Shall we by-pass the title? No, not even one iota may be omitted, since we are commanded to gather up the tiniest fragments lest they be lost. The title runs: "The beginning of Solomon's Song of Songs."

Now we are talking about crumbs, about gathering them up. What stories does that bring to mind? What does that invites us to think about teaching and learning?

In a single image, Bernard here conjures up both frugality and extravagance. Of course, his various references to breaking bread and seeking spiritual sustenance evoke the Eucharist, and now his words bring to mind the liturgical image of the priest gathering the smallest crumbs of the consecrated loaf and adding them to the remnant of the wine, letting none fall to the ground. These crumbs are not consumer waste to be brushed aside as we look towards the next snack; they are fragments of something precious, deserving of care, calling for grateful reception of even the smallest part of the gift. If what is to be taught is indeed well selected (and not mere busy-work), something able to bring growth to those who learn, then the one who presides over the learning must model the most careful attentiveness. Her message will not be "you can skip this part," or "we need to get through this quickly," but rather "watch carefully, let's not miss this crumb here — what we have before us is precious."

At the same time the gathering up of fragments calls to mind another meal, other loaves, in a remote place as evening was drawing on. More than five thousand had left home and were hungry, and Jesus' disciples were sure that the few loaves available would not go far. "Taking the five loaves and the two fish and looking up to heaven, [Jesus] gave thanks and broke the loaves. Then he gave them to the disciples, and the disciples gave them to the people" (Matthew 14:19). Afterward there was a gathering of fragments: "They all ate and were satisfied, and the disciples picked up twelve basketfuls of broken pieces that were left over." The gift given is not lost or diminished — it multiplies, and the gathering of fragments becomes a celebration of plenty. What seemed like a competition for scarce resources turns into the gift of abundance. Once again, the fragments are not headed for a landfill; instead of careless waste there is a wondering gladness for plenitude — see how much more there is than we expected when we set out? Are there not generous riches here? Learning too is a gift that is not diminished through being shared. However much we treat it as a resource to be grasped competitively to secure our own success, it finds true fulfilment in grateful wonder.

This kind of fragment-gathering is the reward for attentiveness and obedience, the glad discovery that after the hard work of attending to the detail, we have come further than we thought, discovered more riches than we can take in right now, found that this meal will feed us and the traveler at the door and leave something to enjoy later too. We are fed (and taught) not so that we can hoard and gloat and gain status from our pile of crumbs, but so that we can feed and fellowship with others, seek their wellbeing, and give thanks together for shared needs met along our journey.

INTO THE LABYRINTH

Bunyan's *Pilgrim's Progress* is, of course, the most familiar and widely influential literary account of life as a pilgrimage, but it was not the first. In 1623 John Comenius, a theologian and educational reformer, published his own pilgrim tale, *The Labyrinth of the World and the Paradise of the Heart*. His Pilgrim is guided on a labyrinthine journey through encounters with a wide range of human professions and vocations, finding an abundance of vanity, violence, and deception. Finally he despairs and desires to flee the world, but instead receives Christ into his heart as his guest and finds a transformation that sends him back into the world with new eyes and new hope, traveling now toward an ultimate vision of the glory of God.

During his initial journey, the pilgrim visits the gate that leads to learning and follows some students on their educational path. Arriving at a library, he reports seeing scholars walking around a collection of containers containing "medicines against ailments of the mind." Each is engaged in selecting things to ingest. Some choose the finest, tear off a piece, and chew it thoughtfully, digesting it carefully. Others are not so patient:

> I saw some people who behaved very greedily, stuffing themselves with what-
> ever came into their hands . . . I noticed that they neither improved their com-
> plexion nor gained flesh or fat, but their stomachs were swollen and never
> satisfied. I also saw that what they crammed into themselves came out of them
> again undigested, either from above or from below.

For these people, eating only served to make them faint or ill.

As the pilgrim moves on he sees the contents of the boxes/books being prepared for consumption. Some exert care and patience, vying with one another to "shape more carefully and artistically the boxes," and to combine and distil "fragrant spices and herbs." Again, not all are so virtuous:

I saw some who merely took from the vessels of others and transferred the contents to their own. Of these there were hundreds. . . . Indeed, some seized others' vessels in order to fill several of their own, then diluted the contents as much as possible, even with dirty dishwater. Still others thickened it with various odds and ends, even dust or refuse, so that it would appear as if something new had been made. Meanwhile, they added inscriptions more glorious than the original ones and, like other quacks, they shamelessly extolled their own work.

Since all this dilution causes a vast multiplication of the boxes available, most of them go unused, "relegated to dusty shelves and back corners." As a result, their authors are forced to cast about for an audience, seeking patrons and prefaces and adding floral designs to make their work more attractive. Not content to make the product prettier, "they personally brought such potions to people, and crammed them down their throats against their will." Moreover, they engage in constant fights with one another. Shooting at each other with paper,

> they spared neither the wounded nor the dead, but mercilessly hacked and lashed at them all the more, each more gladly proving his valor against one who did not defend himself.

This Pilgrim's satire of the academy stands in sharp contrast to Bernard's evocation of teaching and learning as breaking bread together. As with all satire, the imagery is exaggerated, yet far from unfamiliar if we take a moment for honest reflection. Do we cram content into students in such a manner that they are forced to stuff themselves indiscriminately? Does our writing serve and nourish or dilute and jockey for position? Has due care gone into what is served or are we just filling up the hours? Is fighting with words a central activity, or are the conversations that we model and conduct seasoned with grace?

Traveling Companions

Reflecting on teaching as journeying, I think of classroom moments when the question of traveling companions insinuated itself into the journey through the semester. In my first year of teaching in higher education I found myself one day drinking tea at a campus café, talking to a college senior who had asked me to mentor him. I was fairly new to the college, and he asked me what my impressions had been. I began to talk about my realization in the closing weeks of the first semester that there were still students in my class who did not know the names of others sitting near them. I had asked a student to help me hand out some returned assignments, and heard her having to call out names to identify each paper's owner. I also noticed that if I moved the chairs around and then asked students to return the room to "normal," they would create straight rows of individual seats facing forward. I began to wonder how many at some level believed their presence in class to be for the sole purpose of their own learning, as if an invisible thread connected each to the front of the room but to no one else. Did they see the success or failure of those at their side as in any sense their responsibility or concern, or was everyone else just the professor's responsibility? It's a Christian college, I said, as I sat in the café, so what about "love your neighbor," or "am I my brother's keeper," or "the body is not made up of one part but of many" or "encourage one another as long as it is called today?" Does the way that we learn together from day to day really echo those texts? Are we taking the admonition to "run the race" a little too literally, focused on the educational equivalent of an Olympic sprint, each straining for maximum speed and success (or perhaps feigning injury in eighth place), but also keeping carefully to his or her own lane?

I suspect my tone was more than a little self-righteous, especially given the likelihood that some of my own teaching strategies helped support the reality that I was lamenting. But what stayed with me from this conversation was the reaction of my conversation partner. He had been through Christian elementary school, Christian secondary school, and had spent time at two different Christian colleges. Yet the idea that actively and intentionally caring for the learning of his neighbor while in class might be a way of connecting his faith to his studies seemed to strike him as new and exciting. Could it really be a new idea that the degree to which one helps fellow learners to flourish could be part of what success might mean for a Christian learner? That fellow learners are not threats who might drag down my grade if we have to collaborate, or bystanders as far as my learning is concerned, but fellow pilgrims pursuing a calling that is *ours*, not just mine? If this was a new thought, what did it say about my own teaching, about the layout of my classroom and the design of the assignments and the grades and the learning conversations that I fostered or suppressed? How was my own teaching furthering the individualistic culture that was also shaping my students?

Another year, a few weeks into another semester, I graded the first major test in a beginner-level language class and was alarmed. Almost all of the students fell into one of two categories, roughly equal in size: those with a solid grasp of the material and impressively high scores, and those who were floundering badly and scoring catastrophically. There was no steady curve; almost no one had grades in the mid-range. In other words, the test told me that I needed to move faster to challenge students more and that I needed to slow down or even backtrack to keep from leaving some lying abandoned at the roadside — and that aiming for the middle of the range might not be optimal for anyone. It was one of those moments that make teaching at once fascinating and infuriating.

After some pacing, gnashing of teeth, and staring at a blank sheet of paper, I resolved on the following. At the start of the next class I handed back the tests and explained the situation, deliberately stating not that "I" had a problem, but that "we" did. We would have to learn together for many more weeks, and we had differing needs and speeds. One of the learning challenges before us was now how to resolve that without those at either end of the spectrum failing to make progress. On this occasion I did not engage in a lengthy class discussion about what we should do; instead I offered a proposal. I handed out two different sets of response cards. On one was written: "On the evidence of the first test, it seems as if I am good at this, and have gifts to offer. I would be willing to be available to another member of the class who needs some help." The other read: "On the evidence of the first test, it seems as if I am struggling, and could use some additional help." Both cards had space for a signature and an email address, and I told students that it was entirely optional to hand in one of the cards, but that if they did so it would be a modest commitment to the wellbeing of the whole group. Many chose to hand in a card, and I was able to match needs with offers of help. As the semester continued I began to offer alternatives in the homework assignments — extension tasks and review tasks, so that some could press on and others could loop back. I also began to regularly include choices between a solo homework task and one to be conducted with a learning partner, in an effort to help sustain the connections through the structure of the class.

I am not recounting this as the perfect solution. What if many more students had asked for help than offered it? What if few had responded? What if the class had had better ideas? I am also unable to end the tale with an inspirational outcome in which every student became a professional linguist, though many made progress. What seemed important in the incident was the question it forced me to ask about how I could help construct a learning environment in which we rooted for each other rather than just for ourselves, in which we took notice of whom we were leaving behind or holding back and what kind of travelers we were becoming, and in which we set out to bear one another's burdens. The difference between a pilgrim class and an Olympic sprint is that in the pilgrim class it is not a happy outcome if one student turns in a record-setting performance and hits the headlines but others are left in the dust and quickly forgotten; the journey of each learner matters profoundly. Perhaps through such faltering steps as those described above we can become more like fellow pilgrims, with eyes still fixed on the destination, yet also glad for fellowship along the way.

SINGING OUR JOURNEY

Pilgrimages are not just traveled, but sung. There are basic bodily reasons why this is important on a long and arduous journey. Singing together along the pilgrim road is a means of mutual encouragement, keeping up the spirits of the weary traveler, and creating camaraderie and shared memories among the group; modern parents with kids in the car on the way to the cottage are hardly the first to discover this. The road is easier when threaded with melodies, the legs more limber when marching to a beat.

There is, however, more to pilgrim singing than therapy for the wayfarer's energy levels and short temper. Pilgrim songs are also an evocation of the true arc of the journey. They take footsteps and movement through the landscape and draw them up into a larger story that makes the walking much more than a way of changing location. *What* is sung together — bawdy ditties, romantic ballads, or psalms of ascent that turn progress up a mountain path into ascending the hill of the Lord — reveals much about the true spirit of the pilgrimage that is underway. True pilgrim songs help tie together inner and outer pilgrimage as the rhythms of the soul and the movements of faith are aligned with the rhythms of sound and motion. *How* songs are sung — with hope and determination, alone to God in the night, or in time with others along the road — draws us into fellowship with God and one another, reminding us as we sing *to* and *with* that we are not isolated worlds unto ourselves.

Liturgical scholar Don Saliers writes of the power of song to embody a theology, to unify a people, and to spark a collective conscience:

> The act of singing together is deeply and indelibly human . . . When we sing, words are given greater range and power than when we speak. Something is shared in singing that goes beyond the words alone. Among Christians, this something has taken shape over many centuries in a practice that expresses our deepest yearning and dearest joy: the practice of singing our lives.

It is no accident that most Christian schools and colleges create opportunities for students and teachers to sing together in worship during chapel services and devotions; Christian teachers and learners, like Christians in general, engage in the Christian practice of singing their lives into the kingdom of God. Could this connect further with learning beyond the bounds of chapel services?

Jeff Bouman meets regularly with a group of student leaders in the service-learning program that he directs. Pursuing his interest in how the learning that takes place outside the classroom contributes to the formation of college students, he decided to shape a set of shared practices for the group that included singing together. He wondered whether the students might be drawn into a clearer communal identity by committing consistent time to singing together.

The group's work was placing students in service-learning settings with partner agencies both locally and further afield. This involved careful communication, record-keeping, publicity, evaluation, and peer training. All of this helped generate a shared rhythm parallel to the rhythm of the academic year, with weekly commitments including staff meetings, one-on-one meetings with a supervisor, or site visits to community locations. Like all such communities of practice, the group also shared a lexicon, talking to one another about reciprocity, reflection, justice, and mercy, terms rooted in the field of service-learning. They also took part in three retreats together, designed to foster Christian community, faith development, and an appreciation for the particularities of place, especially in urban settings.

As the school year got underway, Jeff introduced some shared practices to the group. Each team meeting was to include communal reading of poetry and prose, prayer, and singing together. Various songs were chosen from the canon of traditional hymns, as well as from a variety of contemporary sources, each designed to accompany a variety of themes related to the larger mission of the community. Over the course of nine months the group framed its discussions by reading aloud and singing together in a focused, strategic attempt to tie together strands of life that are often left unconnected: the academic, the spiritual, the communal, the theological.

As they read and sang and discussed, the daily work of placing students in service-learning sites throughout the city went on. StreetFest, an annual day-long service-learning project for incoming students, came and went. Residence hall partnership activity began. Academically-based service-learning placements were made. Blood drives enabled life-giving transactions to occur. A few thousand food items were purchased, collected and disbursed to local food pantries. Spring break trips were planned and implemented. Data was collected and entered. Community partners were consulted and visited. A website was updated, and a weekly list of service opportunities was sent out. A blog conversation connected alumni staff members with current staff members. Reflection exercises were facilitated. Students wrote papers and journals for related classes. And along the way, the cadences of communal reading and the rhythms of shared song were woven together with the rhythms of the school year.

At the year's end the students reflected on the journey that they had sung together. Their comments resonate with pilgrim reasons for singing, the sustenance of hope, community, and an embedding of daily work into the larger story. Some found the process a little awkward at first, but still expressed appreciation. One wrote, "I consider songs and devotions as a way to remind myself of, and sometimes reconnect with, the reasons to serve," while another reported: "for me it helped create a mindset," and a third liked "how unified speaking can be a way to embody the idea of being a collective body of Christ." The sense of rhythm provided by reading and singing together was noticed: "I found that the consistent integration of songs and liturgy provided a rhythm and pattern that both gave substance to and set the tone for our meetings." Questions of meaning and significance came to the fore: "It was very significant to begin each meeting with a participatory reminder that what held our office together and what motivated our work was our worship" wrote one. Another echoed: "It was meaningful to regularly root the work of our office in something larger than logistical expectations or even shallow social justice philosophy. The effects of this, I think, were unspoken and rarely conscious, although ultimately a force of unity and motivation."

Through something as simple and ancient as singing together along the way, these students and their instructor found that their work had been dignified, that their sense of its connection to the kingdom of God had been enhanced, and that their awareness of working as part of a community of believers had been strengthened. Singing together helped to weave what philosopher Alfred North Whitehead called a "seamless coat of learning," making of that coat a pilgrim's robe.

A RHYTHM OF WORK AND REST

Pilgrimage is about journeying, but also about rest. There is a patience to pilgrimage, a necessary willingness to set the journey in God's hands each evening as well as each morning and give oneself over to the nourishment and rest needed to sustain the next stage of the journey. "In vain you rise early and stay up late" admonishes one of the Psalms of ascent, "toiling for food to eat — for he grants sleep to those he loves" (Psalm 127:2). Learning to rest well — not just to do nothing, but to balance forward progress with fellowship and meekness and trust — is as much a part of pilgrimage as learning to walk well.

Such rest seems elusive in our modern societies. Imagine a teacher who becomes passionate about the degree to which her students are caught up in the frantic pace of modern life. It seems they are always rushing from one activity to the next, never taking time to reflect, to rest. They need to take greater heed of the importance of Sabbath to the Christian life, the importance of having a time when we lay down our frenetic efforts to secure our own existence and allow God to be the one holding the world together. What is she to do?

Well, she could plan a series of classroom devotions about Sabbath in Scripture, or perhaps (lest it seem like merely a pious add-on) she could develop a unit exploring the theology of Sabbath in relation to modern culture. We can picture her choosing biblical texts to display, collecting examples to reinforce her argument, designing handouts that lay out the theological arguments for the role of Sabbath in a Christian view of the world, composing questions for class discussion about how we use our discretionary time. Perhaps we can hear her carefully explaining, then passionately exhorting her students to live more intentionally, more Christianly.

Or perhaps she takes a different approach. Instead of preparing talks and handouts, she decides to restructure her course so that is it not feasible for her students to work for her on Sundays. She plans her homework assignments so that they are always due to be turned in on Friday, or electronically by Saturday evening. She makes sure that no new assignment is known to the students before Monday morning. She insists on strict deadlines, with penalties for letting the task run past Saturday evening. As the semester progresses, her students discover that for this class at least there is no way to work for class credit on Sundays. Notice that we have shifted the emphasis here from information and exhortation to patterns of action. Rather than just telling the students that they should each live more faithfully, this teacher has created a shared practice within which there is a built-in bent towards obedience for the whole group.

Yet a practice, as opposed to a behavior, is at some level intentional — it involves a shared story, a shared imagination that helps make it a coherent, meaningful practice rather than just a collection of movements that happen to take place one after the other. Our imaginary teacher's second plan might count as a practice at some level — *she* has a narrative about Sabbath that makes sense of it, and the learners are being caught up in a communal set of moves that will help shape their sensibilities. But it risks falling short of being truly shared practice as long as the students are not invited into the narrative. Sabbath-keeping is about more than avoiding math homework.

Suppose, then, that our teacher decides to combine her first and second approaches. She decides to invite the students with all the winsomeness and creativity she can muster into an account of life in which pilgrims need to periodically lay down their efforts, and God calls us to Sabbath — and she implements a homework policy that supports this way of living through shared work patterns, refusing to claim a right to students' time on a Sunday. She is careful, moreover, not to settle for an inspiring talk in the first week and rely on memory for the rest of the semester. She takes frequent opportunities to graciously remind her students that the semester is a pilgrimage, and that that is why the homework is once again due Saturday. Sometimes on Fridays she mentions big questions about life before God that she plans to spend some time thinking about on Sunday, and suggests that others join her. Sometimes on Mondays she shares something that came from spending time meditating on a text or praying over a situation the day before, and invites students to do the same. Sometimes during the week she draws students' attention briefly to how the practice of Sabbath might make us view some other aspect of our culture differently. While doing her best to avoid becoming drearily moralistic, and certainly seeking to avoid a tone of I-know-how-to-do-this-and-you-youth-of-today-need-to-shape-up, she works to weave a consistent story through the semester — and she polices the deadlines to support it. She weaves a patient rhythm of work and rest, accompanied by an ongoing conversation along the way, and her class becomes a shared pilgrimage.

"Sabbaths 1979: X"

Whatever is foreseen in joy
Must be lived out from day to day.
Vision held open in the dark
By our ten thousand days of work.
Harvest will fill the barn; for that
The hand must ache, the face must sweat.

And yet no leaf or grain is filled
By work of ours; the field is tilled
And left to grace. That we may reap,
Great work is done while we're asleep.

When we work well, a Sabbath mood
Rests on our day, and finds it good.

— Wendell Berry

PART TWO

Gardens and Wilderness

Clearing the Ground

WE HAVE BEEN REFLECTING TOGETHER about pilgrimage — about journeying and rest and weariness and hospitality and beginnings and destinations. We turn now to a rather different cluster of images for learning: images nestled around the practice of gardening. Learners are like little plants, and teachers are like gardeners, says the cliché. Learning starts in a garden, in a kindergarten, says a tendril of cultural memory whose theological roots we have by and large forgotten. We want our students to grow, we want to cultivate their abilities, we want ideas to germinate — our vocabulary of learning often carries the scent of gardening.

We talk about *kindergarten* or about children *blossoming* without a second thought, perhaps not even consciously aware that we are using gardening language. When learning is pictured in terms of *gardens*, the focus is typically on growth and its relationship to deliberate cultivation. Just how much pruning and weeding is needed? Do we have the right soil? What will serve as fertilizer? How long should we leave things to compost? Do we want roses or potatoes, beauty or utility? Thinking of learning as growth can draw our minds to the need for patience and the limitations of invasive interventions, to the ease with which young shoots are crushed, to the need to work with what is given and respect its rhythms. It points to the recurring possibility of fresh growth after times of apparent dormancy, or to the hope of seeing hidden beauty unfurl. Places of learning have sometimes literally resembled gardens, as with the philosophers' groves of classical times and the green quadrangles of medieval universities. More widely, talk of schools as gardens, learners as plants, and teachers as gardeners with their watering cans and pruning shears recurs perennially.

The connection between schools and gardens seems intuitively plausible.

In both we have young, tender things that are supposed to grow and mature. People are charged with helping, but find that there is a limit to what they can make happen. We have a plan in our mind's eye of a well-ordered outcome, with hopes that it will bring us pleasure and pride. We have protective spaces set aside to try to improve the odds of healthy growth occurring, yet environmental factors, only partially under our control, can have a significant impact. If conditions are right, then a mysterious process unfolds at a pace not of our choosing. Sometimes growth seems agonizingly slow, sometimes startlingly swift, surprising us with shoots where we had become used to staring impatiently at bare ground. Teaching as gardening seems to make sense.

Pause for a moment, though, to let the picture get a little more complicated. Think about where your mental lawn chair is located, your place in cultural space and time. Many of us live in places heavily paved with asphalt and adorned with glass and steel. For us, the garden becomes associated with relaxation and refreshment. It offers a modest oasis of greenery to reassure us that we are still rooted, or to supplement the supermarket with fresh zucchini. Many of us live lives of constant motion, filled with scurrying and focused on the glimmer of small screens. For us, the garden becomes a place to rest the eyes, to exhale, to heed the clichéd call to stop and smell the roses. Many of us live at the limit of our available time and energy. For us the garden offers a romanticized idyll, or maybe just one more chore, a failing battle with dandelions in which chemical warfare becomes the shortcut around tiresome labor. What mental landscape conditions how you resonate with garden images? If the gardens of our minds tend to twinkle at us decoratively in the gentle dusk or if they remind us mostly of lawnmower-related procrastination, then thinking of classrooms as gardens may just evoke the protest that our classrooms are far from pretty and perfect, or remind us that teaching is often drudgery.

Mingled with our own garden experiences is the afterglow of other times and places, the ideas and stories passed down to us by others. "God makes all things good," wrote Jean-Jacques Rousseau famously two and a half centuries ago. However,

> man meddles with them and they become evil. He forces one soil to yield the products of another, one tree to bear another's fruit. [...] He destroys and defaces all things; he loves all that is deformed and monstrous; he will have

nothing as nature made it, not even man himself, who must learn his paces like a saddle-horse, and be shaped to his master's taste like the trees in his garden.

So much for the first Adam's calling to serve the creation by tending it. The romantic tension here between a pure natural state and the regimented disciplines of intervention splits our image of gardening into two. Growth is natural and innocent; cultivation is intrusive and to be viewed with caution. Our picture of learning splits similarly: learners are to blossom in the sunshine, and structure and discipline are viewed with caution. "A garden is not, except in so far as it contains plants, a 'natural environment,'" writes a more recent educationist,

> Rather, it is a contest, man's taming of nature, in which plants are placed, shaped, bred and cross-bred in accordance with human notions of form and order. . . . There is more than a hint here . . . of authoritarianism.

Opposing views of education, learner-centered and teacher-centered, are evoked; watering cans pitted against pruning shears. If these are the cultural conversations that have shaped our imagination, talk of schools as gardens might just evoke well-trodden arguments about traditional and progressive visions of education. Chances are we have already dug in on one side or the other of these debates, and talk of gardens might just prompt us to restate our existing convictions. We know the view from the kitchen window all too well.

Yet other vantage points might provide different views and allow us to see into some less explored corners. What happens to the idea of schools as gardens when the garden is Eden or Isaiah's vineyard, when the trees include the tree of life, when the fruits are love, joy, and peace, when the leaves heal the nations? Can biblical ways of imagining gardens speak to teaching and learning in fresh accents?

Of course, the biblical writers and those who have meditated on them share some of our experiences of gardens. They know that flowers are beautiful, water is refreshing, and trees give shade. They know that growth happens slowly and weeds all too easily stunt crops. They know all about stones and thorns and pests. They know that gardening is a rhythm of work and enjoyment — that the beauty must be tended and those tending it must rest and enjoy what has grown. They live in the same creation that sustains us, and so biblical garden imagery overlaps with garden imagery elsewhere.

What we find in the biblical writers, however, is something more than a collection of homely meditations on growing things. Their talk of plants and gardens is contoured into a larger redemptive story. Gardens, it turns out, are about generosity, virtue, and justice as much as growth, pruning and patience. Our shared familiarity with gardens becomes a point of contact, a bridge connecting our experiences to larger God-breathed horizons. The imagery of gardens is one way in which a biblical imagination can come to inform our own.

Generous Beauty: Is Your Classroom a Royal Garden?

A River Watering the Garden

This is the account of the heavens and the earth when they were created, when the Lord God made the earth and the heavens.

Now no shrub had yet appeared on the earth and no plant had yet sprung up, for the Lord God had not sent rain on the earth and there was no one to work the ground, but streams came up from the earth and watered the whole surface of the ground. Then the Lord God formed a man from the dust of the ground and breathed into his nostrils the breath of life, and the man became a living being.

Now the Lord God had planted a garden in the east, in Eden; and there he put the man he had formed. The Lord God made all kinds of trees grow out of the ground — trees that were pleasing to the eye and good for food. In the middle of the garden were the tree of life and the tree of the knowledge of good and evil.

A river watering the garden flowed from Eden; from there it was separated into four headwaters. The name of the first is the Pishon; it winds through the entire land of Havilah, where there is gold. (The gold of that land is good; aromatic resin and onyx are also there.) The name of the second river is the Gihon; it winds through the entire land of Cush. The name of the third river is the Tigris; it runs along the east side of Ashur. And the fourth river is the Euphrates.

The Lord God took the man and put him in the Garden of Eden to work it and take care of it. And the Lord God commanded the man, "You are free to eat from any tree in the garden; but you must not eat from the tree of the knowledge of good and evil, for when you eat from it you will certainly die." (Genesis 2:4-17, TNIV)

PLANTED BY STREAMS OF WATER

Imagine this. You find yourself at a convention for Ancient Near Eastern Kings, and over lunch you get stuck at a table with several leading potentates. As lunch progresses, an argument develops about who is the greatest ruler in the region. As boasts and banter are exchanged, what would you expect the main topics to be?

Sure enough, you'll hear plenty about wealth, wars, and wives. The gold and silver, the royal treasures, the building and palaces, the tracts of land and the livestock that graze them will certainly put in an appearance. Kings are rich; they own and build things. The size of the army and the extent of the conquests made will be added to the list. Kings are powerful; people far and near obey or fear them. The matches made with other kings' daughters and the size of the harem will come up for mention. Kings are important; they collect wives and concubines.

There are few surprises so far. But how would you react if the conversation dwelt on who was best at gardening?

In the second chapter of Ecclesiastes, we find Solomon boasting in precisely this vein:

> I undertook great projects: I built houses for myself and planted vineyards. I made gardens and parks and planted all kinds of fruit trees in them. I made reservoirs to water groves of flourishing trees. I bought male and female slaves and had other slaves who were born in my house. I also owned more herds and flocks than anyone in Jerusalem before me. I amassed silver and gold for myself, and the treasure of kings and provinces. I acquired male and female singers, and a harem as well — the delights of a man's heart. I became greater by far than anyone in Jerusalem before me. (Ecclesiastes 2:4-9, TNIV)

Solomon includes the more familiar points — the gold, the harem, the flocks, the slaves, the tribute received. But he starts with the gardening. He was not alone in this. Nebuchadnezzar, for instance, had some nifty gardens too, hanging ones no less. The story goes that he had the Hanging Gardens of Babylon built to please his wife, who was homesick for the plants of her home country and missed the mountains, and so a king's project of building a queen-sized garden became one of the Seven Wonders of the Ancient World.

Why would kings boast about gardens? No doubt they were as partial to a well-wrought arboretum as the next person, but the context in which they lived raised the stakes. Notice Solomon's focus on reservoirs. The environment was one where water was often scarce and streams were fickle. Natural water sources could be used as a poetic image for the frailty of human life; people live for a little while and then disappear, "as the water of a lake dries up or a riverbed becomes parched and dry" (Job 14:11, TNIV). Cisterns were important sources of life and health. A cracked cistern meant hardship (Jeremiah 2:13), and visions of joyous abundance promised a day when "each of you will eat fruit from your own vine and fig tree and drink water from your own cistern" (2 Kings 18:31).

Water was not only scarce, but also tied to certain locations. Moving water from one place to another often meant hard manual labor. Water is deeply in cahoots with gravity; if you want to make it go anywhere but downhill and lack modern plumbing, you'll need control over a work force. If you can provide a continuous water supply at an arbitrary location just for pleasure, you must be wealthy and powerful. Building gardens in the wilderness and making them flourish is an achievement to be celebrated, the provision of generous beauty.

God, the King of Kings, naturally turns out to be masterful at watering plants and building gardens. Psalm 104 boasts:

> He makes springs pour water into the ravines;
> it flows between the mountains . . .
> The trees of the LORD are well watered,
> the cedars of Lebanon that he planted. (v. 10, 16, TNIV)

God is so great he can water all the trees in the region. Psalm 1 applies the thought to people:

> Blessed is the one
> who does not walk in step with the wicked
> or stand in the way that sinners take
> or sit in the company of mockers,
> but whose delight is in the law of the Lord,
> and who meditates on his law day and night.

> That person is like a tree planted by streams of water,
> which yields its fruit in season
> and whose leaf does not wither —
> whatever they do prospers. (v. 1-3, TNIV)

The image of the righteous one planted as a tree by never-failing channels of water may echo the ancient ruler's boast that he could transplant trees from conquered lands and make them flourish in his own palace garden. Rulers plant gardens out of their abundance and generosity, and as trees in God's garden we are the recipients of his generosity. To sustain a garden is to lavish resources so that beauty can flourish in the desert.

In the Psalms, the healthy tree is planted firmly in the temple, and the healthy tree is the vibrant person of faith. Carefully planted, well-watered, the tree in the temple will flourish over the long haul, even into old age. As Psalm 92 puts it:

> The righteous will flourish like a palm tree,
> they will grow like a cedar of Lebanon;
> planted in the house of the LORD,
> they will flourish in the courts of our God.
> They will still bear fruit in old age,
> they will stay fresh and green,
> proclaiming, "The LORD is upright;
> he is my Rock, and there is no wickedness in him."
>
> (v. 12-15, TNIV)

How to be fresh and green and fruitful? Stay planted in the temple, rooted in the life of God. Talk of the temple evokes devotional practices, the rhythms of prayer and worship. Yet the temple in Scripture is also a more cosmic image. Genesis 1 depicts the creation as God's temple, and at the completion of the kingdom in Revelation 21 we see God once again all in all, the whole of creation drawn into his presence. Being planted in the temple implies cultivating a genuine sense of doing all of our work before the face of God.

In Genesis the human story begins in a garden within God's cosmic temple. The word "Eden" in Hebrew is related to a root meaning "fruitful" or "well-watered" and may be translated as "delight." This is a pleasant place, a place of abundance and beauty, a pleasure garden:

Now the LORD God had planted a garden in the east, in Eden; and there he put the man he had formed. The LORD God made all kinds of trees grow out of the ground — trees that were pleasing to the eye and good for food. In the middle of the garden were the tree of life and the tree of the knowledge of good and evil. A river watering the garden flowed from Eden . . . (v. 8-10, TNIV)

The garden is nourishing, beautiful, and generously watered, an environment fit for a king and queen, worthy of being in God's temple.

It is into this garden that God places humanity, made in the "image of God." This is language reserved for royalty in Babylonian culture but now extended to all humans, male and female; gardens are no longer just for the king to boast about. We are placed as co-regents "in the Garden of Eden to work it and take care of it." The bounty is ours to enjoy, and our hands are to work to bring it to full flower. We are not only trees; we are also called to be gardeners, to work at making things flourish in dry places.

Later on gardens become places of learning, and as they do so the thread connecting back to Eden stays intact. What might it mean to see classrooms as gardens and have these particular gardens in mind, places of plenitude in a dry landscape? These are places where work and delight are to be joined together rather than set in opposition. They are places where what once were royal privileges become the calling of all who are made in God's image. They are places where God's co-laborers take up their calling to tend the creation alongside and before the face of God, while also delighting in its beauty and generosity. If the place of learning is a garden and these are the biblical echoes, how might that inform the way we see the work of teaching and learning?

DOES IT SNOW IN YOUR CLASSROOM?

There is no straight line from Genesis, Ecclesiastes, and the Psalms to teaching mathematics or science, as if those texts told us how to run a class. But what might start to happen if at regular intervals we asked ourselves: could my classroom become a garden of delight? If gardens of delight are about generous beauty, about finding living water in dry places, about caring for God's creation and seeking its flourishing, then what about classrooms? Could they become gardens of delight? Is "generous beauty" a phrase we could ever bring ourselves to use about our teaching or about how students experience the world through our classes? Does the rich life of creation become visible? Does our teaching foster wonder?

Doug is a scientist. He teaches chemistry to undergraduates, and he thinks not only about understanding, but about wonder. Sometimes his students arrive at his classroom to find a sign on the door inviting them to enter in silence. That's already odd, outside the usual repertoire of science classes. It hints at reverence and respect more than test tubes and equations. As they enter they find gentle music playing, dimmed lighting, and pictures on the screen. They perhaps begin to wonder if there was some kind of last minute change today, and they have come to the wrong classroom. As they settle into their seats the quiet subdues the usual small-talk, and they find themselves watching the slide show, a series of high resolution photographs, one after another, each showing a different single snowflake. Each snowflake lingers in the screen for 15 seconds or so, long enough to notice details. The slow parade of beauty continues for several minutes. Perhaps some students fail to slow their minds enough to really tune in; others have become fascinated and have a new kind of anticipation for what follows.

Eventually Doug begins to speak. He talks about the mystery of six-arm crystal growth leading to highly symmetric crystals. He points out the numerous imperfections in each snowflake and yet their exquisite beauty in spite of that. He reflects that the vast majority of them go unseen by human eyes. Abundant, profligate, gratuitous beauty, poured out whether or not people are watching. What does that say to us about the nature of the world we are studying? What might it say about the generosity and delight in creation of the creator God?

Josh teaches science in a secondary school. His students are younger, but he has some of the same concerns. Do students see the information they are learning as simply items to be mastered for the test? Do they ever let themselves be amazed by what they are learning? Do the intricate pieces of creation paraded before them become just a series of chores, or things to be manipulated for grades or gain? He wants students to see beauty in the ordinary as well as the extraordinary. Salt is certainly ordinary. Plain, white, never the focus of a meal, scattered carelessly, left strewn across tabletops and wiped away without a thought. Salt and science class — could that combination evoke wonder?

Josh thinks carefully about how he combines words and images to provoke thought. Like Doug, he uses striking images to focus attention. Salt lakes, salt mounds, salt flats, close-up shots of individual salt crystals. Each picture is displayed with the same caption: 'Just Salt.' The more pictures go by, the harder it is not to catch the irony in the caption: just salt? He talks about some of salt's more remarkable properties and then hands out worksheets that probe students' understanding of these properties. At the top of each sheet is the heading: "Just Salt?" As he interacts with students, writes comments on their work, and talks about examples in class he looks for small opportunities to further nudge his students towards wonder at something daily taken for granted.

Sue teaches mathematics, and knows full well that not all of her students think it a wondrous thing. She decides to include some work on fractal equations. These involve repeating simple patterns a large number of times in order to produce patterns of increasing complexity. It turns out that this apparently gratuitous process can model certain aspects of the natural world. It can also produce images of startling beauty. Sue has her students work with fractal equations to produce two fractal images. Take a triangle, one with equal sides. Rest a smaller triangle on each side, in its center, so that the triangle becomes a six-pointed star. Repeat the process with each point of the star, and then do it again, and watch as the triangle gradually becomes a snowflake.

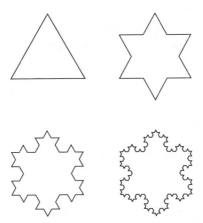

Or work in the other direction, inwards. Start with the same simple triangle. Draw another one upside down inside it, so that each of its three points touches the inside edges. The original triangle now contains four smaller ones. Now draw an inverted triangle inside each of those. And so on.

Students draw the Koch Snowflake and the Sierpinski Triangle, noticing how they have to stop because of the limitations of their pencils rather than because the mathematical process could not continue. They also collect photographs of fractal patterns in nature — the edges of cumulus clouds, fir trees, ferns, the rocky ridges of mountains, aerial views of river systems. They create a striking visual display of their work, connecting mathematics, beauty, and the natural world.

Does our teaching and learning reinforce a jaded view of the world as filled primarily with things to be used, things to be memorized, things to be bought and sold, things to be written down in exchange for grades? Do our pedagogical choices reinforce a sense of the generosity and abundance of creation, of the beauty and intricacy of the world, and of the possibility of delight as a response to learning?

PAINTING YOUR CLASSROOM

Imagine painting your classroom as a garden.

Biblical imagery of flourishing gardens as sites of God's presence, God's generosity, and God's call echoes down the years. Around 1410 an unknown artist from the Rhine Valley painted this *Paradiesgärtlein,* or "little garden of paradise." It was most likely created for a convent as a devotional piece. The

Frankfurter Paradiesgärtlein

hortus conclusus, the enclosed garden, with Mary as heavenly queen was a popular theme in art and literature during the 15th and 16th centuries. These images drew from the richly metaphorical love poetry of the Song of Songs, where the lover compares his beloved to an enclosed garden full of delicious fruit, a sealed fountain, and a well with fresh, cool water (4:12-15). Medieval exegesis of the Song of Songs was highly allegorical, and the beloved bride was understood as the human soul in love with and being loved by God, or as the Church, or as the Virgin Mary, the new Eve, placed in a garden of love. The garden recalls the Garden of Eden and looks forward to paradise regained at the end of times.

The carefully tended garden in our painting is enclosed, but not closed off from the viewer. Because the painter shows only part of the protecting wall, we are invited to enter. The table invites us to commune. The painter beckons us to explore the sacred place with a meditative, reverent mind, to step into the presence of holy figures and find out what such a visit can teach us about the life of faith.

As we enter the garden, a spirit of joy and playfulness infuses the atmosphere. It's late spring or early summer. The air is filled with sweet music played on a psaltery by the Christ Child, seated at the center. This child is the focal point of a series of triangles formed by the three trees, the three people in blue robes, the three people in red robes. He is the center around which the riches are arranged, the one for whom and in whom creation unfolds its beauty. He is helped along by the humming of Saint Cecilia, his music teacher. Deep male voices come from two warrior saints who, with the Archangel Michael, form a group on the right. Twelve varieties of birds chirp praises into the heavenly blue sky from the treetops and the crenellated wall. These are the biblical birds that do not worry about tomorrow, because they trust in God's faithful provision of food each day. We approach softly because the Virgin Mary, sitting on a large red cushion, is prayerfully reading her devotional Book of Hours. The garden is a place of God's presence.

Blooming flowers fill the garden with fragrance: the strong aroma of the lily of the valley, the delicate scent of violets, the rich perfume of roses and carnations. On the big table, which is draped with a delicate table runner, stands a green glass half filled with red wine and a bowl full of apples and apple peels. Mary has given the Christ Child, the New Adam, an apple to eat. The apple (which tradition came to associate with Genesis 3) is no longer a forbidden fruit in paradise regained. To the left, St. Dorothy picks a basketful of cherries, a fruit associated with healing, from the tree of the knowledge of good and evil. Another virgin saint sits at the well. Look at the color of her dress, her face, and the tilt of her head, and see how they imitate the Virgin Mary. This saint is ladling a cupful of cold fresh water, the living water of the Holy Spirit that will refresh our spirit. Here we "can taste and see that the Lord is good" (Psalm 34:8) and "be like a well-watered garden" (Isaiah 58:11).

While the female saints are diligently working, the male saints seem to be busy watching, listening and talking. Saint Sebastian, a warrior saint, leans against the tree of life. He is a martyr, once brutally pierced by arrows, but now miraculously restored to health. Sitting under the same tree in the pose of a serious thinker is the Archangel Michael. Michael has brought a trophy along, Satan, the slain archenemy of God. The prince of darkness and the father of all lies is almost invisible; in a ridiculously diminished, harmless form he sits chained to a tree stump at Michael's feet. One horn peeks out from his shrunken head. God has broken the power of Satan; small, fresh branches sprout from the stump to which he is tethered.

Nearby, a small animal lies helplessly on its back. It is the shrunken evil dragon killed by St. George, the other warrior martyr. Evil, lust, heresy, pride, all the ungodly vices represented by Satan and the dragon have been defeated in this new garden of delight. The message to visitors: fight the demons in your own souls with confident hope of victory, and celebrate the garden as a sign of suffering's end.

The Archangel Michael lifts his gaze in our direction. Maybe he wants to tell us: "Don't just look with your botanical eyes at the plants, the flowers, and the fruit. Learn how to hear, smell, taste, touch and see with your spiritual senses. Learn the symbolic language of this garden." We follow his counsel and discover that the color of the seven blooming blue irises at the wall points to Mary, and that they symbolize the Seven Sorrows of the Virgin and the seven gifts of the Holy Spirit. The blade-like shape of the iris leaf recalls the sword piercing the heart of the *Mater Dolorosa* (Lady of Sorrows). We find that the colors, shapes, and fragrances of the flowers speak of the virtues of humility and chastity, about the love, suffering, healing, and compassion modeled by Christ and Mary. This garden invites us to plant a garden of healing and virtue in our own soul, a garden where we can be what we were meant to be. The painting is sensually rich, with full colors, implied fragrances, beautiful flowers, dresses, birds, each in plenty. This garden is a pleasant place, a place of fruit and beauty, where we can learn, praise, harvest, study, and delight in the presence of God and the saints.

Imagine painting your classroom, not a literal, realist painting but a painting displaying your vision for the learning and growth that are to happen there for you and your students. Imagine painting it as a garden. Would it resonate with this garden? What would you change or keep? What would be at the center and the periphery, what things would be joined together through their colors and shapes? What fruits and flowers and living creatures would you want to highlight? What would the picture say about the way you see learning?

YOU ARE A GARDEN FOUNTAIN

How delightful is your love, my sister, my bride!
    How much more pleasing is your love than wine,
    and the fragrance of your perfume
    more than any spice!

Your lips drop sweetness as the honeycomb, my bride;
    milk and honey are under your tongue.
The fragrance of your garments
    is like the fragrance of Lebanon.
You are a garden locked up, my sister, my bride;
    you are a spring enclosed, a sealed fountain.
Your plants are an orchard of pomegranates
    with choice fruits,
    with henna and nard,
    nard and saffron,
    calamus and cinnamon,
    with every kind of incense tree,
    with myrrh and aloes
    and all the finest spices.
You are a garden fountain,
    a well of flowing water
    streaming down from Lebanon.
                (Song of Solomon 4:10-15)

DO STUDENTS KNOW THEY ARE GARDENERS?

The formal part of the workshop was over (thump) and a freewheeling conversation was underway. The setting (thump) was a vibrant urban elementary school on the east coast (thump). As it happens, the teachers and I were discussing the notion of schools (thump) as gardens of delight. Our words were punctuated and our thoughts harried by the persistent rhythmic (thump) of a pile driver from the construction site immediately adjacent to the school, where a hospital was being renovated (thump). The room was hot and sticky; the afternoon was winding towards its (thump) end. The world around us was no garden. We pressed on anyway. Thump.

Then Elisabeth spoke up about an incident earlier in the day, and captured our attention. The school used a nearby park for physical education classes, generating careful rows of children being shepherded across pedestrian crossings and counted out and in again. Today the walk to the park had a pounding accompaniment, in a rhythm far from jazz. As the students walked and the teacher hovered, one nine-year-old began clapping in time with the hammer. Then she began improvising around its beat, building a more complex clapping rhythm around it. Other students began to join in, and by the time they arrived at the park the mechanical pounding had been transformed from an invitation to migraines into a shared source of pleasure. A fresh tone was set for the lesson that followed; teacher and students continued with their day. Now that fleeting interlude came up in our conversation.

We wondered together whether the student realized how much she had contributed. What if the teacher had mentioned to the students how the clapping game had just taken a little piece of the wilderness of the world and made it delightful? What if she had thanked the student for her contribution to the learning of her fellow students and the quality of their day? Would the student have seen it that way? Learning, after all, is about writing in books and following instructions, not clapping on the way to class . . . isn't it? And creating beauty out of ugly things is just fun and games . . . isn't it?

It was our conversation about wildernesses and gardens of delight that drew the story into our midst, turning it from a piece of passing fun between classes into a provocation to see learning afresh. Thinking about gardens of delight helped us to see the good that had sprung up, and connect it with school. It got us thinking about the images of learning that we communicate to learners, and about other ways in which learners might catch themselves making beauty in the world, and about what is celebrated and offered back to God, and what simply gets missed.

Shaping the Soul

BIBLICAL GARDENS DRAW OUR THOUGHTS to the provision of water in dry places, to generous beauty and fruitfulness, and to care for creation. As the biblical images of well-watered gardens, and the Garden of Eden in particular, echoed in the minds of Christian thinkers, they twined together with their views of learning. This garden is the place where the drama of obedience or disobedience towards God unfolds. It is the place where we grow spiritually and bear fruit. The early church began to picture the soul as a garden, the place where God cultivates *us* and makes us fruitful, the place where wisdom and virtue grow through careful tending. Tending the garden became an image for shaping the soul.

SHE IS A TREE OF LIFE

Blessed are those who find wisdom,
   those who gain understanding,

for she is more profitable than silver
   and yields better returns than gold.

She is more precious than rubies;
   nothing you desire can compare with her.

Long life is in her right hand;
   in her left hand are riches and honor.

Her ways are pleasant ways,
    and all her paths are peace.

She is a tree of life to those who take hold of her;
    those who hold her fast will be blessed.

By wisdom the Lord laid the earth's foundations,
    by understanding he set the heavens in place;

by his knowledge the watery depths were divided,
    and the clouds let drop the dew.

(Proverbs 3:13-20, TNIV)

Do You Tend the Garden of the Soul?

In the Christian tradition, gardens are connected not only with delight and beauty, but also with virtue and spiritual formation. The garden of delight became an image for the believer's soul, where the fruits of the Spirit should grow. Gardening and growth in faith and virtue became interleaved. There are many examples in early and medieval Christian writings; instead of cataloging them we will linger over one early account, found in a manuscript unearthed in colorful circumstances.

Picture yourself as a young Italian student in the early 15th century. Your name is Thomas d'Arezzo, and, having the means to travel, you have decided to spend time abroad to expand your learning. Wanting in particular to improve your Greek, you are currently staying in Constantinople. One day, perhaps finding your mind meditating more on the possible shape of supper than on the intricacies of Greek verbs, you wander down to the fish market. As you meander among the stalls watching buyers making their choices and fish being wrapped in paper, something catches your eye. In a pile of old paper awaiting its final fate as travelling clothes for dead herrings, you notice an old, worn out book. You're a sucker for old books, and your curiosity is aroused. It takes very little haggling to purchase the volume from a surprised fishmonger who had entertained little thought of profiting from fish-free wrapping paper.

You turn for home with a renewed thirst for learning, little realizing that you have just secured for yourself a small footnote in the history of the church. The book contains, among other things, an anonymous epistle from the second or third century, today known as the *Epistle to Diognetus*. It has been lost for so long that its very existence had been forgotten, but over the ensuing centuries (and further adventures involving lost copies and library fires) it secures a place among the writings of the church fathers. Its chief burden is an explanation of Christianity written for a pagan audience, and it closes with a chapter on "The importance of knowledge to true spiritual life." Much of this last chapter turns out to be about gardens, and so that is where we will linger.

The final chapter begins like this:

> Once these truths have been brought before you, and you have listened heedfully to them, you will know what God bestows on those who rightly love Him.

Learning starts with listening and loving. *Listen heedfully* to sound instruction about God, and *rightly love Him,* and you will learn something, you will *know.* This is more than having one ear open or letting words register on your ear drum. We are asked to *heed* what is said, not just to hear it. That involves the kind of close attentiveness that is willing not only to work at capturing what is said, but to change in response. This kind of listening is rooted in love. As a more recent Christian thinker puts it, "Lovelessness, indifference, will never be able to generate sufficient attention to slow down and linger intently over an object, to hold and sculpt every detail and particular in it, however minute." Love, not objective detachment, is what moves us to linger and give of ourselves. If we let ourselves become this kind of learner — listening, heeding, loving — then a reward is promised — we will come to know what God bestows on his attentive lovers.

No mention of gardens so far — but wait, it's just around the corner. These heedful listeners to truth are changed:

> Once these truths have been brought before you, and you have listened heedfully to them, you will know what God bestows on those who rightly love Him. They become a very paradise of delight, cultivating in themselves a flourishing tree, which yields all manner of nourishment and adorns them with fruits of every kind.

Paradise of delight — that's Eden language, and the familiar biblical resonances continue to pile up as we meet a tree in the garden, a call to cultivate,
and the promise of fruits. But when was the last time you encouraged someone
at church, or in school, to *be* a garden of Eden?

That is what our epistle does, and it is not alone. Irenaeus, an early church
leader, also wrote that "the Church has been planted as a garden (*paradisus*)
in this world." A while later Saint Ambrose, bishop of Milan, insisted that "by
Paradise is meant the soul," and expounded the story of the garden in Genesis
2 as an allegory of how God cultivates our souls. Saint Augustine, while pre-
ferring a more literal reading of Genesis, translated Genesis 2:15 like this: "The
LORD God took the man whom he had made and placed him in Paradise to
cultivate him (that is, to work in him) and to guard him" — we become the
ones cultivated. And so it went on, the Garden of Eden becoming the garden of
the soul, a place of spiritual growth. The image of gardens of delight cultivated
by God became a recurring Christian image for talking about our learning and
formation, and carried over onto the tools of learning. When Herrad of Landsberg, a twelfth century abbess, decided to write a book gathering together all
the knowledge that her nuns might need to learn, a kind of illustrated encyclopedia, she titled it *Hortus Deliciarum,* or *Garden of Delights.*

And so, our epistle says, we *become a very paradise of delight.* Through loving
attentiveness to the truth, we become a well-watered place of abundance and
flourishing. There are no magic wands, though. The transformation involves
Christian learners *cultivating in themselves a flourishing tree* — we are called
to have a hand in our formation. It will be a patient and careful task; trees,
of all things, are not cultivated overnight. Particular disciplines will aid our
flourishing even as God showers us with what we need — God *bestows* and we
cultivate. God teaches and we work to become the kinds of learners in whom
the truth can be truly fruitful.

In this picture, learning includes a commitment to gradually grow into the
person in whom heedful learning is connected with fruitful living. As we grow,
we start to find an inner nourishment, we start to bear fruits — *gathering its
fruits, you will at all times enjoy a harvest.* It is not hard to hear an echo of Paul's
talk of the "fruits of the Spirit," and of Jesus' talk of his Father the gardener and
the true, fruit-bearing vine of which we are part. This harvest of fruit has the
potential to benefit others, not just ourselves.

Character, spiritual hunger, and genuine learning are inseparably connected, rather than belonging to separate domains. Learning serves virtue rather than ambition, and aims at nourishment more than achievement. There are fundamental choices at stake here in terms of what kinds of learners we are to become.

THE SOUL OF STATISTICS

Paradise: beautiful but distant. Talk of gardens and souls and virtues may be uplifting, but given our cultural tendency to split the world into hard and soft, the "real world" of brute facts and the fuzzy world of personal values, we might wonder whether soul growth has much to do with real classrooms, especially those classrooms where we are not reading poetry or discussing theology.

Imagine this classroom. (You weren't there, but it really happened.) A college statistics class, the first class of the fall semester, winds to a close. As the students head for lunch, one stays behind to talk to Jim, the professor. Instead of the expected question about some detail of the day's work, he launches into a more fundamental problem. He has a strong dislike for mathematics, he explains. He is only here because the class is required for his program. He has already tried through other channels to get the requirement changed or waived, without success. His doom is now upon him, and he wants to know how much mathematics he needs to understand in order to get through the course.

The professor responds with reassurance — even for the mathematically average student, the course should not be an impossible hurdle. Basic arithmetic and some high school algebra should suffice for survival purposes. The student, Brian, appears uncertain whether those are resources that he can muster. "I'm not sure I can do those things," he confesses.

The next day, at the professor's office, Brian agrees to take a diagnostic test to find out what mathematical skills he actually has. The results are abysmal. The only section of the test on which he is able to consistently give correct answers deals with addition of whole numbers. Everywhere else there are massive gaps in his understanding. And so Jim begins his semester faced with a student who lacks any desire to study this subject, has confessed his desire to be elsewhere, and has virtually none of the mental furniture needed for success in the course. Put yourself in Jim's place. What would you have done?

Brian strikes Jim as bright and articulate — there must be some reason why things came to this crisis. Jim asks Brian what happened. How could he have progressed through elementary school and high school with so many gaps in his understanding? When did this begin? Brian pauses, then tells a story. "When I was in first grade, one day my teacher held my arithmetic homework up in front of the class as an example to the rest of the class of how not to do the assignment. I was so angry at her that I vowed that I would never learn mathematics for the rest of my life." What about tests later in school? "I just memorized skills long enough to get through the tests, and then I forgot them."

Now Jim's pauses in turn. His response comes from an unexpected angle. Strange as it might sound, he tells Brian, "You will need to forgive your elementary school teacher if you want to make proper progress with learning statistics." Brian seems unconvinced — in Jim's words, "he looked at me like I was a creature from another planet." But Jim insists, and Brian agrees at least to think about it.

The two run into each other on campus that weekend. Has Brian done anything about forgiving his elementary school teacher, Jim wonders? "Nah, I haven't thought about it" is Brian's response. Jim stands his ground, in fact wonders later whether in his irritation he was a little too blunt. "If you don't forgive that teacher," he urges, "you won't be able to pass statistics. And if you don't pass statistics, you won't graduate. If you won't believe me, at least pray about it. See if God thinks this is important." Sheepishly, Brian says he'll do that.

On Monday morning Brian waits outside Jim's office with an update. "I did pray about what you said," he reports, "and I think you're right. But I also think I'm going to need a tutor." Jim arranges a tutor for him right away. As the semester continues, Brian's test scores begin to climb, until on the third test of the semester he scores 99%, the highest grade in the class. By the end of the semester, Brian's mathematical skills have increased in leaps and bounds, his grade is solid, and he completes his college graduation as an honors student.

What can we learn from Jim and Brian? A new technique for solving every learning difficulty through prayer and forgiveness in conjunction with tutoring? Hardly. But pause and ask: what happens to Brian if he does not encounter a mathematics professor who imagines that there could be a connection between forgiveness, prayer, and the ability to make headway in learning statistics in college? Does he quickly memorize enough skills to barely pass the tests and then abandon mathematics for good? Does his professor go back to the faculty lounge and grumble about apathetic students, wishing they could be weeded out? Might it be that the shaping of soul and spirit and the dynamics of the classroom intertwine on the trellis of learning?

ARE YOU TENDING YOUR TREE?

And so persist with attending to paradise. As the *Epistle to Diognetus* proceeds with its meditations on gardens and learning, we meet in paradise the fateful two trees, the tree of life and the tree of the knowledge of good and evil:

> For in that garden are planted both the Tree of Knowledge and the Tree of Life — for it is not the Tree of Knowledge that causes death — the deadly thing is disobedience. Scripture clearly says, *In the beginning God planted in the midst of the garden the tree of knowledge and the tree of life*; thereby showing that the way to life lies through knowledge. It is only because the first created couple used it improperly that, through the wiles of the serpent, they were stripped of all they had. Without knowledge there can be no life, and without life there can be no trustworthy knowledge; which is why the two trees were planted side by side.

The "deadly thing," the writer urges, is disobedience, not knowledge, for knowledge and life in its fullness need each other. Without true knowledge, no true life; without true life, no true knowledge.

Again, this Epistle is not alone. Irenaeus, for instance, discusses true and false wisdom in connection with God's assurance that "you may eat from every tree of the garden." We should "eat . . . from every Scripture of the Lord," but not with a proud mind that sets itself above God and ends up cast out of the Garden. There is a right and a wrong way of knowing. The details of interpretations of the two trees of Eden vary, but they agree on this: amid the allure of gardens and fruit there are choices for good or evil to be made. Discernment is necessary, and not all learning leads to life. Our Epistle goes on:

> The Apostle saw the force of this when he told us, *knowledge makes a windbag, but love is a builder*; that was his rebuke to the knowledge which is exercised without regard to the life-giving precepts of the truth. For a man who claims

to know, but is without the knowledge which is real and attested by life, knows nothing; the serpent has tricked him, because his heart is not set on life.

Knowledge itself is not evil. The problem is more that there are different kinds of appetite for learning, just as there are different kinds of appetite for food and sex. Bread is not bad, but there is gluttony. Bodies are not bad, but there is lust. Knowledge is not bad, but there is a kind of hunger for knowing that is rooted in pride, ambition, cynicism, the quest for status, or lack of faith. In place of loving attentiveness, discernment, and seeking to know for the good of others, this kind of hunger tries to make knowledge something to be controlled and exploited for personal gain. The Christian response is not to avoid knowledge, but to sanctify the appetite. Love, humility, and reverence can root knowledge properly:

> he who possesses knowledge coupled with reverence, and whose quest for life is earnest, may plant in hope and look for fruit.
>
> Let the heart of you, then, be knowledge, and let your life be true inward reception of the Word. Tending your tree in this way, and gathering its fruits, you will at all times enjoy a harvest that is pleasing to God, and one which no serpent can touch and no deceit penetrate.

Tend your tree, the Epistle urges, an admonition that might surprise our students. Pay attention to the shape of your appetite. Heed what will nourish your character and make you a reverent lover of truth. Weed out the motives and vices that tug the other way.

This Epistle, rescued from a fishmonger, offers one example of how thinking about learning as gardening became a part of the Christian imagination. Garden talk, with Eden as the backdrop, helped Christians to insist that learning, virtue, and faith must remain intimately connected. To separate intellectual growth from spiritual and moral growth, to separate knowledge from faith and goodness, to separate learning from the kind of person we are becoming, courts vanity. But the dominant tone was lush possibility — the chance to become part of a new paradise, planted by the river of life, bearing fruit in season, a well-watered garden rather than a windbag.

THE WALLED GARDEN REVISITED

Frankfurter Paradiesgärtlein

It's time to revisit the little garden of paradise. Recall what we saw there. The walled garden, separated from the wilderness of the world, is offered to us as a garden of the soul, a place where we can grow spiritually and be nourished and healed. Imagine painting your own classroom as a garden, we suggested — what would be in the picture? Let's try reversing the question. What might we glimpse if we shifted our head to one side and looked at the garden in the painting as a classroom?

Notice how this garden is rather well populated. Imagine how sterile the picture might look without the greenery — the beauty and vitality of flowers and birds and natural growth are far from background features. But a great deal of space is taken up by colorful people. This garden/classroom is not a place to get away from people and commune alone with nature. It is a place for fellowship, for community, even for communion. The relationships here are not defined or harried by the pressing transactions of everyday life. The people here are active in various ways, but none of them are scurrying. The carefully crafted space provides an environment in which we might willingly linger (of how many classrooms is that true?). The deepest patterns in the picture emerge not from each individual's activity, but from their right relationship to one another. Are our classrooms crafted as spaces for patiently growing together, rather than rushing from task to task? What patterns of relationship do they foster?

Of course the people in the picture are not just any people. They are not our next door neighbors and workplace colleagues. They are all holy figures, part of the communion of saints. If you are going to linger in the garden, the picture suggests, then consider your company. Here you will be spending time not just with the student sitting next to you, but in the company of folk from beyond your peer group, folk from other times and places. You will want to know more than when they were born and when they died. You want to know how they have lived and what truths they have to share. What can you learn from them that might bring healing to the wilderness of your own soul? As we enter, we are invited into a gathering that began long before we came on the scene, one that could help us to grow nearer its stature. Which guests loom large in our classrooms and curricula? With which conversation partners, in our curriculum and in the flesh, are our students taught to linger? Are students helped not only to learn about folk from other times and places, but to learn truth *from* them?

The garden is walled off along the rear, but open to the viewer in the foreground, gently inviting us in. The scene implies that we too should join the assembled company, but no one stands frowning with a finger pointed at our chests and a caption reading "I want you!" No one leans imperiously towards us over a lectern. Gardens rarely shout their invitations. In fact, the figures here seem more preoccupied with their activities than with our presence; they invite us as learners to join in, not to take center stage. And yet most of them are turned towards us, and there is space in their company for us to join. Community does not mean conformity — different folk are engaged in different activities, even faced in different directions. Yet the echoes of color and posture suggest an underlying harmony, a rightness to things. Can our classrooms echo this ethos of winsome invitation and welcome? Do our students gain a sense of joining in with something larger than their own immediate goals? Can we create spaces for students to seek truth differently while sustaining purposeful communion?

The spirit of this space is both playful and contemplative. The chuckle of delight and the absorbed gaze dwell together. The picture whispers to us that spending time here might change how we see. Taking time to attend carefully to the garden, to really notice its detail, we will gradually uncover new meanings in fruit, birds, and flowers, new relationships between the people present. And we will learn to look with hopeful eyes. We will see evil brought down to size and denied the final word. Healing and growth become real possibilities. We turn to face the world at our back with new eyes, having learned to see the "beauty deep down things" and to face the evils of life with fresh hope that they are neither ultimate nor permanent. Do our classrooms foster attentiveness to the world's beauty? Do they invite us to look and then look again, to move beyond the superficial glance? Do they inspire our students to face evil with hope?

LINGERING, LEARNING, HOPING

When I teach the past tense in second-year German classes, the available textbooks commonly offer me practice exercises in which fictional people bought things, caught trains, sold shares, and went on vacation. Searching for a way to extend the scope of our learning, I have come to rely on Adaline for help with this part of the syllabus.

Adaline was born to a German-speaking farming family living near Kiev in 1903. That made her 11 years old when World War I started, and part of her teenage years were spent as a refugee. The family trekked thousands of kilometers to Omsk and back, finding refuge where they could. After her marriage, Adaline and her husband took over the family farm, but here too history interrupted. The revolution of 1917 made it no longer such a good thing to be a landowner, and eventually the farm was confiscated, Adaline's husband was imprisoned, and the local official suggested she could live with her children under a nearby tree. She camped with relatives for a while, then following her husband's release the couple moved around the region working on collective farms. Crop failures and further brushes with the authorities kept them on the move; for a time her husband hid in the forest during the day to avoid arrest after a problem with paperwork. In 1933, Adolf Hitler had come to power in Germany, and as World War II progressed the German army eventually headed east. As they retreated after the defeat at Stalingrad, the German forces passed through Adaline's village. Since the family were German-speakers, they were picked up and taken along. Adaline was put on a train to Germany, while her husband and sons were conscripted. She spent the final phase of the war in Hamburg, living in a school sports hall and writing letters to the Red Cross to try to trace her family. After the war, her husband and one son made it to Hamburg, and they decided to settle there. They were still living there when my colleague, who was a family friend, made recordings of Adaline, then 93, telling her life story. He also obtained permission to use various family photos. Now she tells her story each year through word and image to my German students as they try to master the past tense.

Her photographs offer plenty of reminders to slow down and really see. We look at a picture of a room in her Hamburg house and talk about all the details that suggest the room of an elderly person. We consider how the array of photographs on the shelf suggests that at this stage of her life people are more important than things. We look at the outdoor, open-casket picture of her mother's funeral, and at the family headed to church in the horse-drawn cart. We are constrained to listen carefully as she narrates with hesitations and self-corrections what she did, what she ate, where she went, where she lived. We linger over some episodes, and consider how they challenge our choices and values. After listening to her story, students are assigned to find a local elderly person and interview them for an hour, then bring that story into class and re-narrate it in German. I want them to practice lingering by listening to others, writing about someone other than themselves, and expanding their personal cloud of witnesses.

On several occasions I have been struck by students' reaction to one of her closing comments. Towards the end of her description of her life's events, Adaline notes that

> when we were fleeing, we always still had trust that there is One there who cares for all our cares. And then we had also learned a lot of Bible verses by heart, and when it was still so dark, there was always some spark there, that gave us comfort and new courage.

Adaline's life strikes many of my students as one of unusual hardship. Her multiple experiences of life as a refugee, the repeated displacements, and the repeated threats to her most central relationships, seem like a litany of hardship. To hear her conclude her story with such an affirmation of hope impresses them. "I hope I am like Adaline when I am old" wrote one in an email after class. "She is my hero."

CAN YOU START A FIRE WITH TWO DRY STICKS?

Gardens are alluring. But classrooms can seem more like the wilderness. Sometimes *wilderness* is not a bad metaphor for the place of learning.

This was no particular surprise to Jesus, who was raised on Scriptures that explore the formation that takes place in the wilderness or desert. He was himself "driven by the Spirit into the wilderness," the Judean desert, at the beginning of his public ministry, there to be tempted and formed. And he repeatedly took his close disciples "away to a lonely place" as part of their formation.

Consider Jesus' classic teaching on prayer, recorded in Matthew 6:9-13 (with parallel in Luke 11):

> Our Father in heaven, hallowed be your name,
>> Your kingdom come, your will be done on earth as it is in heaven,
>>> Give us today our daily bread,
>>> And forgive us our debts, as we also have forgiven our debtors,
>> And lead us not into temptation,
> but deliver us from the evil one. (TNIV)

Jesus teaches his prayer in a lonely place. In Luke he has gone out to pray, and his disciples then gather to be taught; in Matthew he is in the wilderness on a mountain-top giving the "sermon on the mount." Both places evoke Jesus as the new Moses, the lawgiver who leads God's people through wilderness wandering into their promised land. The prayer is saturated with images from Israel's experiences after the Exodus: the daily bread of manna, the irreverent trespassing that caused immediate judgment, the leading of the people by fire and cloud, the temptation concerning water at Marah after being led there by Moses, the deliverance from evil at the crossing of the Red Sea when the pursuing armies were cut off.

Rooted in these images of Exodus, the twelve disciples frequently come across in the Gospels as people who expect their discipleship to result in taking command and receiving public respect. Jesus is the new Moses, and they expect to be installed in his post-conquest cabinet as rulers of the twelve tribes. He responds by communicating, again and again, that following him will for the time being be more like wandering in the wilderness than taking conquest of the land. It was Pharaoh, not the Israelites, who may have proudly strolled in a palace garden. Israel had to learn obedience in the desert.

How should a teacher respond when, despite the best intentions and noblest visions, the classroom is not a lush place of growth but an arid wasteland? The structure of Jesus' prayer provides one answer. It is a chiasm: A B C B' A'. The central fulcrum — give us this day our daily manna — is surrounded by petitions concerning obedience and forgiveness, which are in turn surrounded by petitions concerning God's sovereignty and care in heaven and on earth. The chiastic form normally emphasizes the central point — in this case dependence for daily provision. At the heart of the prayer is sharing abundance (as opposed to greedy hording). We are invited to focus on grateful pleasure, on the sustenance found in the good gifts we find before us. We are invited to live faithfully in hope that the dry place can become fruitful and God can provide in the wilderness. We could learn these things in a lush garden, but we usually don't. The garden of delight is a vision of redemption not yet fully worked out in the world; it calls for hope and trust when we see more desert than roses, not for sentimentality and complacency.

Can You Teach in the Desert?

There are times, too, when the garden is Gethsemane. It's Good Friday, and class is underway at a state university. The course is Literature of Western Civilization, which is not every student's favorite way to spend an hour. Today's text is the Gospel of Mark. Chris Anderson, a professor of English, is attempting to teach the crucifixion narrative, and finds himself gasping for air amid a cloying cloud of indifference. "All I see when I see the cross is oppression and hypocrisy," declares one student. Others joke about Christians knocking at their doors asking if Jesus is their personal savior. It's Good Friday, the meaning of the cross is the topic for discussion, and the teacher is filled with sincere desire for engagement. But the atmosphere in the room is anything but engaged.

A ripple of laughter.

Someone in the back is reading the student newspaper.

Another student walks in late, carrying a skateboard.

Anderson perseveres. He has precious things to teach, and knows that he needs to rise above his students' unresponsiveness. Set aside your assumptions for a moment, he urges. Yes, Christians have done bad things, and knowing that is part of your baggage. But don't let that baggage stop you from seeing what's there! Read the scene afresh. Don't let your judgments drown out what it is saying. He lays bare his own investment in the story and desire that his students engage:

> What's so moving for me in the scene is how it forces us into acts of interpretation, whatever they are. Here's the mystery, here's the cross. . . . We are all related to that mystery, whatever our stories, whatever our names for it.

The response to his moment of vulnerability is blunt.

"I'm not related to mystery," Tina says. "I'm not related at all."

Anderson records his reaction to this exchange with refreshing honesty:

> And that's it. The floor drops away. My mouth is dry, my knees are weak, the moment becomes among other things a moment of public shame — irrationally, since that handful of students is simply being casual and small. But I have been worked up, I have been identifying with the material in very personal ways, and in the face of the class's amused indifference I can't help but feel that maybe I have lost control. The mechanisms of shame are deep and mysterious. For whatever reason the period becomes one of those that Palmer in *The Courage to Teach* encourages us to describe, a day that I wish I had never been born. The floor drops away, my emotions rise, and all I do the rest of the fifty minutes is talk, lecturing on the history of interpretation.

And so the hoped for garden becomes a wasteland, a dry and barren place, searing and without water. Those who have written most eloquently about the garden of delight have always known this. Eschatological yearning for gardens of delight arises precisely in the waste places of the world, where things are not as they ought to be. There is Gethsemane as well as Eden, the hard path of suffering and obedience in hope that healing can arise. Biblical garden talk speaks to hope, not romanticism.

There are, of course, alternatives to hope. Despair can be all too tempting. Why not retreat from engagement and settle for handing out information? Settle for a dispassionate presentation of what's on the test and let students do with it what they will. Let teaching technique override relationship and truth. If I invest less of myself, there is less chance of hurt. If I minimize expectations and go through the motions, at least I will reduce the chances of being wounded by disappointment. Or perhaps the pressures are from outside myself, institutional chaos, poisoned relationships, decaying facilities — is there really hope of resisting?

Look at Anderson's words again, especially the connection between his hurt and his choice of teaching strategy. The floor drops away, and he lectures. Other lectures on other days may be moved by different forces, but on this particular day lecturing arises from shame, from the need to disengage and conceal. On days like this, Anderson says, the teacher comes home "beaten and drained, feeling like a fool." As the *Epistle to Diognetus* noted centuries ago, "life" and "knowledge" are connected, and sin, shame, and pedagogy can belong in the same breath. The spiritual and moral states of teacher and learner are part of what is at stake in classrooms; they might even be steering the pedagogical choices made. Are our own classroom choices molded by insecurity and fear of failure, or resentment of students for not sharing our passions and fulfilling our dreams, or the desire to perform, to puff ourselves up, or overweening delight in our own favorite sayings? Anderson implicitly invites us to join him in honest self-examination. Classrooms are deserts, places where thorns grow to choke the seedlings. Some days, gardens of delight can seem cruelly distant.

But there are alternatives to despair. Gethsemane was also a garden, and there Jesus accepted betrayal without violence or retaliation. The cross was embraced, its shame endured. An hour after his disastrous class, Anderson served as a deacon at a Good Friday service. Here the frame shifts. He writes:

> I'm too busy holding up this cross to judge anyone else, I'm too occupied with
> praying and with the joy I so seldom feel and never feel for very long but am

feeling here and now, the joy that comes through the pain of the crucifixion, the triumph that comes after the jeering, that joy comes flooding through me as it so seldom does but is now, here in this place.

Resentment relinquished, shame set aside, love and grace embraced as the normal shape of things, in spite of apparent signs to the contrary, in spite of a world where crucifixions happen. A fragile yet powerful moment of connection sows the seedling possibility of having *these* realities, *this* hope shape the next day's pedagogical choices, the next day's responses to students, in hope that the desert might yet bloom.

The Just Community

BIBLICAL GARDENS, WITH THEIR LIFE-GIVING water and fragrant growth, offer beauty and shade in the midst of the desert. The garden of delight can became the garden of the soul, calling us to tend our tree and pursue spiritual growth together, even amid shame and suffering. But gardens also compel us to look outward, to seek the flourishing of others and to build a just community.

YOU WILL BE LIKE A WELL-WATERED GARDEN

Is not this the kind of fasting I have chosen:
to loose the chains of injustice
    and untie the cords of the yoke,
to set the oppressed free
    and break every yoke?
Is it not to share your food with the hungry
    and to provide the poor wanderer with shelter —
when you see the naked, to clothe them,
    and not to turn away from your own flesh and blood?
Then your light will break forth like the dawn,
    and your healing will quickly appear;
then your righteousness will go before you,
    and the glory of the LORD will be your rear guard.
Then you will call, and the LORD will answer;
    you will cry for help, and he will say: Here am I.

If you do away with the yoke of oppression,
    with the pointing finger and malicious talk,
and if you spend yourselves in behalf of the hungry
    and satisfy the needs of the oppressed,
then your light will rise in the darkness,
    and your night will become like the noonday.
The LORD will guide you always;
    he will satisfy your needs in a sun-scorched land
    and will strengthen your frame.
You will be like a well-watered garden,
    like a spring whose waters never fail.
Your people will rebuild the ancient ruins
    and will raise up the age-old foundations;
you will be called Repairer of Broken Walls,
    Restorer of Streets with Dwellings.

                              (Isaiah 58:6-12, TNIV)

Are You Growing Wild Grapes?

Before Christians allowed Eden to fertilize their imagination, the Hebrew prophets beat them to it. For them the garden is not just a garden of the soul or a place of inward spiritual growth. The Garden of Eden serves the prophets as an image of flourishing community and just relationships.

Joel writes of a day of darkness and gloom about to break upon Israel. It will be a day when a vast invading army "like dawn spreading across the mountains" will lay waste to the land, leaving death and destruction in its wake. The orderly business of daily living will be given over to chaos; the healthy rhythms of life will yield to death. "The land is as the garden of Eden before them, and behind them a desolate wilderness" (Joel 2:3). The garden will become a wasteland.

Ezekiel writes from the other side of judgment, offering hope for restoration, but with the same image. Defeat and disaster have come and passed, and a remnant still clings to hope in the old promises. "On the day I cleanse you from all your sins, I will resettle your towns, and the ruins will be rebuilt. The desolate land will be cultivated instead of lying desolate in the sight of all who pass through it. They will say, 'This land that was laid waste has become like the Garden of Eden;

the cities that were lying in ruins, desolate and destroyed, are now fortified and inhabited'" (Ezekiel 36:33-35, TNIV). The wasteland will become a garden.

Notice that the picture here is not of some romantic yearning for a simple life among the trees before the advent of corrupt civilization. The garden doesn't stand for unspoiled nature, but for a healthy society. Where land is caringly cultivated to sustain human community, where homes are built and lived in without fear, where neighborhoods experience everyday wellbeing — that is like the Garden of Eden. It is sometimes said that the Bible begins in a garden and ends in a city. The prophets seem to have little difficulty imagining the city *as* a garden.

Notice as well that like all gardens, this one grows through tending. The judgments and promises of God are worked out in human actions in these passages, some ravaging the fields, others digging furrows and restoring walls. The land becomes like the Garden of Eden as people work together out of hope to rebuild wholeness, believing that even when things are badly broken, future healing is possible because generosity and beauty once were, and God is still faithful.

This becomes especially clear in Isaiah. "The LORD will surely comfort Zion," Isaiah writes, "and will look with compassion on all her ruins; he will make her deserts like Eden, her wastelands like the gardens of the LORD. Joy and gladness will be found in her, thanksgiving and the sound of singing." (Isaiah 51:3) The LORD will turn wastelands into gardens. But not the LORD alone. A few chapters later Isaiah writes:

> The LORD will guide you always;
> he will satisfy your needs in a sun-scorched land
> and will strengthen your frame.
> You will be like a well-watered garden,
> like a spring whose waters never fail.
> Your people will rebuild the ancient ruins
> and will raise up the age-old foundations;
> you will be called Repairer of Broken Walls,
> Restorer of Streets with Dwellings.
> (Isaiah 58:11-12, TNIV)

The image has shifted — we have moved from being the gardeners to being the garden, not as individuals but as a community. Those who seek justice, compassion, and healing become like a well-watered garden, and being a garden makes them builders of streets and walls, restorers of communities where all can thrive. If we zoom out a little from this passage and look at its context in Isaiah 58, we find that it comes amid a powerful plea for true fasting. Such fasting involves breaking the chains of wickedness, removing yokes of servitude, setting the oppressed free, sharing bread with the hungry, welcoming the poor and homeless into houses, and clothing the naked (Isaiah 58:6-7). When this kind of fasting occurs, we will be like a well-watered garden, repairers of walls.

The same connections are made much earlier in the book of Isaiah. In chapter 5 we meet a parable about "the one I love," who had a vineyard in a fertile spot on a hillside. "He dug it up and cleared it of stones," we are told, "and planted it with the choicest vines. He built a watchtower in it and cut out a winepress as well." He labored to make it flourish, preparing the ground and tending the vines. Then came that peculiar disappointment that follows when long, careful, hopeful labor all comes to naught. "Then he looked for a crop of good grapes, but it yielded only bad fruit."

The owner's reaction is decisive. "I will take away its hedge, and it will be destroyed; I will break down its wall, and it will be trampled," God declares. "I will make it a wasteland, neither pruned nor cultivated, and briers and thorns will grow there." The vineyard will become a wasteland. The interpretation of the parable follows immediately:

> The vineyard of the Lord Almighty
> > is the house of Israel,
> and the people of Judah
> > are the vines he delighted in.
> And he looked for justice, but saw bloodshed;
> > for righteousness, but heard cries of distress. (v. 7, TNIV)

In Isaiah 58 we are the garden; here we are the vineyard. In both, the focus is on actions that build or tear down justice. The kind of growth in view here is the growth of persons whose way of being in the world causes distress or wellbeing among those around them. Gardens of delight are communities of justice, places of shalom.

Describing shalom, and arguing that we should see it as the goal of learning, Nicholas Wolterstorff writes:

In shalom each person enjoys justice. . . . Shalom goes beyond justice, however. Shalom incorporates right relationships in general, whether or not those are required by justice: right relationships to God, to one's fellow human beings, to nature, and to oneself. The shalom community is not merely the just community but is the responsible community, in which God's laws for our multifaceted existence are obeyed. It is more even than that. We may all have acted justly and responsibly, and yet shalom may be missing: for the community may be lacking delight . . . shalom incorporates delight in one's relationships. To dwell in shalom is to find delight in living rightly before God, to find delight in living rightly in one's physical surroundings, to find delight in living rightly with one's fellow human beings, to find delight even in living rightly with oneself.

This unpacks nicely what is bound up in Isaiah's appeal for us to become a well-watered garden, and in his parable of God as the gardener planting a vine and finding only bad fruit.

The New Testament too has a tale of a divine gardener who planted a vine, went looking for fruit, and was prepared for drastic pruning if he didn't find it. "I am the true vine, and my Father is the gardener," said Jesus, taking upon himself Israel's calling to be a pleasing vine, a garden of delight for God. "He cuts off every branch in me that bears no fruit, while every branch that does bear fruit he prunes, so that it will be even more fruitful" (John 15:1-2, TNIV). He goes on to stress that his disciples must remain "in" him — we are to be part of God's planting, the vines he delights in. We, too, are called to be part of the garden being restored from out of the wastelands of the world, those who dare and hope to work for healing and wholeness amidst distress and decay. We, too, are to work with God to nurture shalom within and among us, so that beauty can flourish in the desert.

THE THREE-MINUTE GARDEN TOUR

I am sitting in a secondary school, at a parent-teacher conference, the teacher equivalent of speed dating. Each teacher gets three or four minutes to make introductions, establish common ground, and communicate something meaningful about my son's learning. Management of the relentless flow of parents is down to a fine art, and in quick succession, over in the scientific corner of the gymnasium, I sit down opposite two different science teachers. The two conversations are an exercise in contrasts.

The first teacher smiles, shakes hands, and gathers himself into a business-like posture. He studies the open grade book on his table, running his finger down the list of names until he finds the relevant entry. His finger then moves to the right as he reads aloud each score obtained by my son for work in his class, accompanying each with a word or two to identify the assignment. Once this data gathering is achieved, he looks up and smiles expectantly, offering us the chance to ask questions.

The second teacher, upon learning our names, sits back in his chair looks thoughtful for a moment. "Yes," he says, "I've appreciated having your son in my science class. The learning is going well, and I've also been impressed with his other contributions to class. The student sitting behind him has some learning difficulties, and sometimes has trouble staying on track with what we are do-ing. I've noticed that your son finds appropriate moments, moments that don't disrupt anyone else, to turn around and help this student navigate the learning tasks and stay on task. That chimes right in with what I've been aiming for in this class — I think we need to create a learning community in which we serve one another and look out for one another's needs as we learn science together."

Two conversations, two choices about what to name and what to leave unexplored, two implied visions of learning. One of them thinks it important to talk about learning in a way that connects it with creating communities where shalom is experienced. I find myself wondering if either teacher has explicitly discussed with their students the kinds of growth that might take place in their classroom, and what they have to do with the communities we build. Has either discussed their vision of learning with my son?

It's likely he has gleaned it anyway.

A GARDEN OF DELIGHTS FOR OUR GOD

Suppose you were sitting down to write a book about teaching, one that pulls together your hopes, your convictions, your dissatisfactions with how schools operate, your visions for how things could be different. You hope that this book will lead to far-reaching reforms, improving the lot of teachers and students everywhere. You don't know yet that your hopes will not be in vain — that this book will turn out to be one of the most important Western writings on education. You don't know that it will stand as a turning point in the history of schooling and will still be studied centuries after you have finished writing. You are staring at the blank sheet of paper on which your impassioned plea for improvement will take shape. You want to seize your readers' imaginations, give them a vision for how things could be, find words that will give them the hope and determination that might sustain change. What words would you want on the opening page?

That was the question facing a young Moravian pastor in the mid-seventeenth century. When the *Great Didactic* by John Amos Comenius was published, it opened with a dedicatory letter that began as follows:

> God, having created man out of dust, placed him in a Paradise of desire, which he had planted in the East, not only that man might tend it and care for it, but also that he might be a garden of delight for his God.

This is by now a familiar pair of images — we were created to work *in* a garden (Genesis) and to *be* a garden (Isaiah). Delight is again to the fore:

> For as Paradise was the pleasantest part of the world, so also was man the most perfect of things created. In Paradise each tree was delightful to look at, and more pleasant to enjoy than those which grew throughout the earth. In man the whole material of the world, all the forms and the varieties of forms were, as it were, brought together into one in order to display the whole skill and wisdom of God. Paradise contained the tree of the knowledge of good and evil; man had the intellect to distinguish, and the will to choose between the good and the bad.

There are more echoes here of familiar themes. There is beauty and abundance, care and celebration, the delights of creation put on display. Amid the delight, fateful choices await, with grave spiritual and moral consequences at stake. Yet we are not left alone to choose; just as rivers watered paradise, so the Holy Spirit irrigates us:

> In Paradise was the tree of life. In man was the tree of Immortality itself; that is to say, the wisdom of God, which had planted its eternal roots in man

(Ecclesiasticus 1.14). Rivers went out from the place of delight to irrigate Paradise, thence dividing into four heads (Genesis 2.10). Into man's heart flowed various gifts of the Holy Spirit, to irrigate him, and in turn living waters flowed out from his belly (John 7.38), that is, in man and through man is poured forth the manifold wisdom of God, just as if rivers divided in every direction . . .

As long as we are watered and nurtured, we become gardens tended and cultivated by God for his enjoyment and the display of his wisdom:

> And so each man is, in truth, a Garden of Delights for his God, as long as he remains in the spot where he has been placed. The Church too, which is a collection of men devoted to God, is often in Holy Writ likened to a Paradise, to a garden, to a vineyard of God.

This all sounds wonderful, but what of that ominous passing reference to good and evil? What about the fact that we often fail to experience our lives as gardens of delight? How many of our words and actions are really gurgling outpourings of wisdom? There is indeed a rather large "but" just around the corner, and it will begin to further enlarge our picture of gardens and learning:

> But alas for our misfortune! We have at the same time lost the Paradise of bodily delight in which we were, and that of spiritual delight, which we were ourselves. We have been cast out into the deserts of the earth, and have ourselves become wild and horrible wastelands.

We were meant to be gardens within a garden, irrigated with wisdom. We find ourselves cast out from paradise, yet unable to lay all the blame on our surroundings. We too have become less than delightful; we are desiccated, tangled, thorny, a haven for wild things. We will have to deal not only with the state of our souls, but with a world that has fallen and our role within it.

The letter to the reader insists, however, that despair is premature and cynicism is ignoble. God has not abandoned the world. There is also salvation, healing, and the promise of renewal. By God's grace we are to set about gardening again in hope; "it is inglorious to despair of progress." There are still tasks at which we can labor.

These images of gardens of delight degenerating into or emerging out of wastelands echo throughout Comenius's writing about education. We need, he writes, "an imitation of the School of Paradise, where God revealed the whole choir of His creatures for man to behold." Schools, too, can be wastelands or gardens of delight. Comenius proposed a series of textbook names like "The Seed Bed" and "The Rose Bed," and thought that each school should have an actual garden, a space where learners could take rest from their studies and gain a first-hand love for the natural world. Yet when he mentions gardens he is usually evoking not just the view from his window but the spiritual and moral drama of Genesis, Isaiah's yearning for good grapes of justice, and the long Christian tradition of picturing the growth of our souls in terms of gardening. Thinking of schools as gardens didn't just mean planting a shrubbery. It also meant orienting learning to spiritual and moral growth, to joy, and to *justice*, restoring right relationships with God, neighbor and creation.

The purpose of life, says Comenius, is service and joy. We are here "that we may serve God, his creatures and ourselves, and that we may enjoy the pleasure to be derived from God, from his creatures and from ourselves." He seems to be riffing on Proverbs 8, where God's Wisdom speaks of being present as the world was formed:

> I was there when he set the heavens in place,
> when he marked out the horizon on the face of the deep,
> when he established the clouds above
> and fixed securely the fountains of the deep,
> when he gave the sea its boundary
> so the waters would not overstep his command,
> and when he marked out the foundations of the earth.
> Then I was constantly at his side.
> I was filled with delight day after day,
> rejoicing always in his presence,
> rejoicing in his whole world
> and delighting in humankind. (v. 27-31, TNIV)

If Wisdom rejoices in God, in creation, and in people then we would be wise to do likewise. Schooling, Comenius insists, needs to find ways to foster this threefold rejoicing — how else could schools become gardens of delight, irrigated by wisdom?

It follows for Comenius that it would be wrong to try to separate intellect, virtue, and piety. Learning is always and inescapably spiritual, moral, and intellectual. Piety means grasping theology, seeking God, and obeying God, with the ultimate goal of *enjoying* God, "so acquiescing in His love and favor that nothing on earth appears to us more to be desired than God himself." This should in turn lead us to attentive and caring service towards the creatures that surround us. Comenius urges us to cultivate a growing taste for careful, disciplined absorption in the intricacies of what God has made. This is not just for the deepening of our own joy in creation, but also a path to seeking the delight of other creatures. We should teach students, Comenius argues, to treat creation well, so that "all creatures should have cause to join us in praising God."

What about the notion that we should take pleasure in and serve ourselves? Isn't that — quite literally — self-serving? Comenius says not — he is quite clear that we have to teach the young "that we are born not for ourselves alone, but for God and for our neighbour, that is to say, for the human race." He also distinguished delight from "mere amusement." What he has in mind is not entertainment. Rather we should seek "that very sweet delight which arises when a person who is given over to virtue rejoices in his own honest disposition, since he sees himself prompt to all things which the order of justice requires." As we give ourselves to the pursuit of virtue, we begin to discover joys that can only come from within that pursuit. We turn and catch ourselves doing something right, something healing, something just. A "very sweet delight" follows as we glimpse a little more garden than desert. Comenius yearns for a kind of education that will draw us to seek *this* kind of pleasure in self, a discovery of joy in the pursuit of justice.

The ultimate aim of such learning is that "the entire world will be a garden of delight for God, for people and for things." It's a gloriously impractical yet stubbornly hopeful aim, dared because of the conviction that it is also God's aim. It foregrounds the connections between what we delight in, how we treat one another, and how we treat the world around us. The test of educational success is not individual economic gain or intellectual achievement so much as growing evidence of holiness within us, justice among us, and healing in creation, all rooted in a deep and serious joy.

Comenius drew some practical consequences that were not commonplace in the mid-seventeenth century. Education must be provided without favoritism to rich and poor, to those of both greater and lesser intellectual ability, and to both male and female, lest false distinctions of worth should lead to pride. Comenius says in his educational writings:

> *Firstly,* the expressed wish is for full power of development into full humanity not of one particular person, but of *every single individual,* young and old, rich and poor, noble and ignoble, men and women — in a word, every being born on earth, with the ultimate aim of providing education to the entire human race regardless of age, class, sex and nationality.

This passage sounds curiously recent, in part because Comenius left his mark on modern schooling. Tellingly, the idea of education for all leads him straight back to gardening:

> I had this consideration in mind when I put the symbol of the art of the tree pruner in the frontispiece to this Deliberation, showing gardeners grafting freshly-plucked shoots from the tree of *Pansophia* [universal wisdom] into rooted layers in the hope of filling God's whole garden, which is the human race, with saplings of a similar nature.

The garden is a nursery in which we tend to fruitful young trees before planting them out into the world.

If this should sound naively optimistic, too glowing for the realities of the classroom, bear in mind that Comenius was well aware of the harsh realities of life. In 1618, when Comenius was 26, the Thirty Years War broke out. As a leader in a small, persecuted denomination he suffered life as a refugee and repeated personal loss. His plans for reforming schools were not always welcomed. When he traveled to England to contribute to the development of higher education there, the English Civil War promptly broke out and he was sidelined. When he was 63, war between Poland and Sweden resulted in the burning of his house and destruction of most of his possessions, including manuscripts over which he had labored for decades. Comenius was vividly aware that the world is not a garden of delight. It should be a garden, but it is all too often a "wild and horrible wasteland."

Comenius nevertheless insisted that God's intent was the renewal of the world, and that to give up cultivating the garden and despair of delight is to lay down our calling. He insisted that teaching and learning could more closely echo wisdom's fragrant chuckle, and that perhaps one day, if we are faithful, "schools will . . . be planned to such pleasant effect that they all become gardens of delight." When he was 77 and finally able to labor no more, his last writings took the form of a heartfelt plea:

> I have done what I could. If the weakness due to old age and overwork or the misfortunes and distractions of a busy life have prevented me from doing much more, I trust that I shall be forgiven. . . . behold! I am now ceasing from unraveling my life's work. Let this be the final fabric for the use of any who may desire it. But those who long for a better one (being now awakened to its importance) must be free to weave it.

In other words, go do some gardening of your own.

INVITING STUDENTS INTO THE GARDEN

Imagine a course in literature entitled "The Garden of 19th Century Chinese Literature." Or a course in economics or history entitled "The Ecology of Economies in the Industrial Age." Or a course in biology entitled "Nurturing Healthy Ecologies." What if the metaphor in the course's title were then allowed to shape the course's pedagogy, and the shared imagination developed among teacher and students as the course progresses? Imagine a syllabus that reads something like this:

Dear students,

This *course* is not a factory for learning, but a garden. It is a place to savor beauty, and cultivate delight. Part of our attention will be on the beauty of what we study. We will certainly aim to be critically engaged, but there will also be moments when we will intentionally cultivate the kind of gaze that takes in a glorious sunset reflecting on a calm lake. We'll try to attend to the multiple layers of beauty in the worlds we inhabit. I hope that we experience aesthetic delight together, seeing the beauty both of what we learn and of each other learning.

Gardens are places where wind and sun, flowers and animals interact. We too will need to focus on a variety of factors interacting, a wealth of local details. Some of us may be particularly attracted to one or another, but each is indispensable. We will need to listen to a variety of voices to build up a compelling picture. We are not aiming primarily at efficiency, but at deepening our insight and enhancing our appreciation for the beauty of what is.

Part of what happens in a garden involves attention to each other in new ways made possible because the garden is beautiful, provocative, or quiet. The Bible uses the image of gardens to talk about healthy communities where there is justice and flourishing and where cries of distress are met with care. Along the way, there will be days in which we don't focus on analyzing subject matter, but instead take the time to attend to each other, or to invited visitors, exploring how this course gives us the space for new conversations, and finding out what others wish we would hear. We may be provoked to have different conversations than we have ever had before about topics like race or politics or economics.

This is a place where we seek to cultivate fruitfulness. That means both planting and pruning, both nurturing and weeding. Many of our course assignments will involve a two-fold dynamic: nurturing seedling ideas and practices, and pruning away weed-like ideas and practices. We need to affirm and critique, celebrate and resist — any one alone will not suffice. We will also need to be patient as partly formed ideas slowly unfold into something more fascinating than their first appearance suggested. Dig up the seedling for its failure to impress and you'll never see the oak tree; let the weeds grow and fruit will be lacking. We will need to learn discernment together to know the difference.

Any ecology is threatened by toxins. Cynicism, indifference, and arrogance are three of the largest pollutants in our classroom ecology. We will engage over the course of the semester in practices designed to identify and then rid ourselves of these pollutants. We will be seeking to grow intellectually, but also in broader ways that draw in the shape of our souls. This goal will help structure how we go about learning together.

Make no mistake: a walk in the park is not necessarily frivolous or benign. It's where you go to mull over a life-changing decision or to gain perspective on a perplexing moral dilemma.

When we conclude our class together, the final exam will include one major question that will ask you explore this garden metaphor in light of our time together. As the course unfolds, I want you to reflect on how the content of the course, its pedagogy, and the patterns of interactions among us fit this metaphor — or not.

Now pause and ponder these questions: What expectations will have been evoked in the minds of the students? Are any of them different from average course expectations? In what ways have students been invited to imagine their learning differently? How will this course now need to be taught in order to make this introduction an honest description rather than a pious flight of fancy?

ARE YOU PLANTING SAPLINGS?

Isaiah declared that we can become gardens of delight as we build communities of justice and shalom and attend to cries of distress. Comenius urged that as schools refuse to separate intellect, virtue, and piety and seek to restore right relationships with God, neighbor and creation, they can become gardens of delight and plant saplings out into the wasteland of the world. Those saplings are of course our students, and the seeking and building involve the small choices that we make as we teach them.

I decided one day to offer my freshman students a different picture of what they were doing by learning German. At the start of class I had them read Deuteronomy 6:4-5 in German, a passage that defines the identity of Israel as the people of God:

Hear, O Israel, the LORD our God, the LORD is one. Love the LORD your God with all your heart, and with all your soul, and with all your strength. (TNIV)

I commented briefly that hearing involves laying down your agenda and waiting on someone else's words. Jesus combined this text with the call to love your neighbor from Leviticus — hearing God leads to hearing others. I said that one of my aims for my German students was that they should learn to *hear* others who do not speak their language. Language classes often emphasize speaking and finding ways of getting your message across. We often talk about learning to speak a foreign language and almost never about learning to hear a foreign language. But we don't learn languages just so that we can bless more of the world with our opinions. Through our learning we are becoming able to hear people we could not previously understand. I invited the students' reactions.

It was a brief conversation, but fit with the pattern of practice that we had been cultivating. I was conscious that while we were learning the words and structures of a second language, our spiritual and moral identities were not on vacation. We were learning to become faithful language users, sensitive to the humanity of strangers. I kept this in mind as I designed learning activities, putting emphasis on hearing the stories of German speakers (from biographies of the famous to oral history from ordinary elderly folk like Adaline) and practicing attentiveness to what others were saying.

Over a year after the Deuteronomy conversation, now a faded memory, I received a phone call from Germany. It was Matthew, a student who had been in that class and was now in Marburg. He was bursting with excitement.

That morning, he told me, he had boarded a bus and noticed that the German sitting next to him seemed dejected. He started a conversation and discovered that the man had just lost his job. Matthew interrupted his narrative at this point. "I remembered what you said in class," he said (what did I say in class, I wondered?). "You know, about hearing people instead of just speaking, and so I just listened to him talk. By the end he seemed really relieved to have been able to talk to someone about it. I offered some words of encouragement and he thanked me for listening. I just got home and I had to call you."

I don't know of a teaching technique that can reliably cause young Americans to engage compassionately with unemployed Germans. But I do think it matters how I teach, what kind of imagination I foster, how I focus our learning. There was a thread running from our approach to learning languages to the choices made by this student on a bus in Germany. We had approached the learning of German as if it, too, is caught up in the wounding and healing of the world. As I listened over the phone it seemed that a sapling had been planted. It felt like a fleeting glimpse of the garden of delight.

"In the Cool of the Evening"

Among lilies I am Jehovah,
the Lord God walking in the cool of the evening,
delighting in every green that grows, sorrowing
for those that fail. I am Christ the healer:
I spray for black spot and white fly, pluck aphids,
and when the leaves turn crisp I pluck them too
and drop them in the dirt to soften and return.
The Lord God walking in the cool of the evening.

With books I am merely the student,
saying why, why, why — exasperating myself
and even the long-dead with my questions.
But among dianthus, I am the decider:
Not here, but there. Not you, but something else.
The Lord God walking in the cool of the evening.

Beside bellflower, poppy, phlox, I keep the deathwatch.
Among lilies I am the slow mourner for the soft bulb
rotting in damp clay, the quiet griever
over fire blight in the pyracantha — fire blight,
canker, scale — and when I fail as Christ, I succeed
as the adversary, root-digger, extirpator —
the Lord God walking in the cool of the evening.

Beyond branch tips, where they scrape the sky,
I see the sheets are white, starched, and my skin is yellow,
yellow and going gray. Down the row,
the Lord God walks in the cool of the evening,
delighting, sorrowing, healing, failing to heal.
I am very calm, I am almost not afraid.
I look neither toward him nor away from him,
the Lord God walking in the cool of the evening.

— Andrew Hudgins

PART THREE

Buildings and Walls

IN THIS THIRD AND FINAL section, we are going to look at images that cluster around the enduring notion of education as building. We take for granted that educational *foundations* are laid and that we can *build upon* what we learned last week, without ever wondering aloud what ideas and bricks actually have in common. The thought of education as a *building* pictures learning as broken down into convenient individual pieces laid on top of each other, one by one. The resulting edifice might be stable or it might lean dangerously because of the lack of care and proper sequence with which the bricks were stacked — disciplined structure is required. Once laid, each brick should stay in place and retain the shape it had when placed there, extending what is below and supporting what is above.

Buildings are meant to stay put. Building images encourage us to see some things as more basic than others, as necessary foundations if the whole is to stand, or as boundary walls, or as windows that open into new rooms. They focus our attention on learning as an interlocking structure within a fixed and carefully planned space, and imply moving by methodical, pre-planned steps towards some larger monument to our efforts. The invitation in this section is to consider how we build, and what it is that we are building.

Drawing the Blueprints

CONSIDER THE WORD "SCHOOL." LET your mind wander. What images do you see?

Perhaps you conjured up a picture of a teacher and some students, or a pile of books, or even a principal walking down a long hallway. But you may have also thought of a room — perhaps your first-grade classroom, the one with tall windows and the low bookcase on the back wall and the guinea pigs making their little snuffling noises in a cage that always smelled faintly musty. Or you may have recalled the looming brick building that housed your middle-school classrooms or the science lab where you spent your afternoons, or the main hall on your college campus. Or perhaps a clip-art icon for "school" popped into your head:

The word "school" and images of buildings seem naturally to go together. But it isn't simply that education often takes place in iconic structures that we remember with wry affection. We also often associate teaching and learning — what goes on inside a school — with the activities of building or construction. In fact, metaphors involving buildings may be one of the most common ways that we think about what we do as teachers. Here is one young teacher's response to the prompt: What is your teaching metaphor?

> *Teaching is like building a house.* You start with a plan, a blueprint or an outline. From that plan, you gather your supplies. Maybe your supplies are ones you have created yourself or ones you have seen others use before. After gathering your supplies, you begin to lay the foundation. In building a house, it's a foundation of bricks; in teaching it is the foundation of knowledge. Each house you build requires a different, unique foundation. . . . It is your job as the builder to determine what kind of foundation your house needs. As you lay each brick, sometimes you find some do not fit, and you need to re-think your plan or blueprint. "Back to the drawing board."
>
> Once the house is built, your work is not over. That house, or foundation of knowledge in teaching, needs constant maintenance, repair and up-keep. Once you figure out what works, your job as a teacher or a builder still is ever changing. You must monitor the house and all its parts. One part may need more up-keep than the other, such as a window or a leaky faucet. One student may be gifted in science, but struggle in reading. You need to determine which part of the house and consequently which part of the student needs most of your attention. If you are a well-respected, organized and successful builder, other consumers may request your services. As you become a more seasoned builder, you will acquire more knowledge on which strategies in building a house are effective and which are not. Once you have established what works with one student, it cannot be applied to all others. One blueprint or plan for a house cannot be used again for every subsequent project. Collaborating with other builders and sharing approaches will also be a part of your job. Each house you build is unique in its own way, and no two houses are the same. You can learn from the mistakes you make on one house and apply it to your next project, but no secret ingredient will exist that works for all houses. This is the key to teaching.

In this reflection, the teacher links each part of the builder's craft to a particular teaching task — from designing blueprints, to gathering materials, construction, and maintenance. Students, in this version of the metaphor, are somewhat passive, individual houses that grow under the builder's touch. It is an image that feels both familiar and comforting. Although we don't always get it right and we are constantly learning to do a better job, we can lay a good foundation, build up a student's knowledge brick by brick, fix the leaky spots, and become known as effective teachers. This story assures us of worthwhile effort and orderly outcomes. It tells us that if we work hard and well, we'll eventually be able to gaze with a well-earned sense of satisfaction over a whole neighborhood of interesting, well-constructed homes and say, "I helped build these."

This story is just one way of unveiling the images of building that already live in the ways we think and talk about teaching and learning. Even when we don't think allegorically about teaching as the act of building, we do employ the metaphor, consciously or unconsciously, whenever we *construct* a syllabus, *build in* assessment goals, *build on* what we did last week, explain *foundational* ideas, or *scaffold* a set of skills. What if we explored this metaphor more consciously, trying out other ways of raising edifices in our teaching imagination?

Apprentice Builders

Although construction metaphors often lead to thinking about the teacher as the builder, they can also activate images of students as apprentice builders. I've imagined beginning a syllabus with this letter:

Dear Students,

This course — entitled "The Philosophical Case against Foundationalism" — is counter-intuitively and ironically designed to "build" or "construct" a case against foundationalism, a prominent approach to Christian philosophy. Foundationalism argues that the first principles on which we build a theory of knowledge are self-evident to all logical thinkers. We will use a famous text to help us make the case against foundationalism, Alvin Plantinga's *Warranted Christian Belief*.

Just as a building is constructed out of building blocks, so our case is built up out of many individual arguments. We'll spend eight or nine weeks working on these various arguments.

A building needs to be firm, but not overly rigid; similarly, as we go along we'll describe the places where there is some flexibility in the argumentation.

Buildings need a lightning rod and the capacity for draining excess water; our building will also need protection against typical external threats. We'll spend at least three weeks protecting our case against various possible attacks and threats.

Like any building worth inhabiting, our building involves both engineering and design, both technical and aesthetic concerns. So half-way through the class, we will pause to note and analyze the aesthetic features of some rhetorical strategies in favor of our arguments.

Context matters for all buildings — the materials close at hand, how people will interpret the building, what it will be used for. We will also pause part-way through the class to ask about the particular context that called forth Professor Plantinga's book, observe which resources the author drew upon (and which ones he did not draw upon), and observe how this book has been used in various contexts.

I should tell you that there is irony to the design of this class. And once we get to the end, we'll have the capacity to see why. [Students will come to understand that many of the critiques of foundationalism are themselves built on foundationalist or at least rationalist assumptions.] So the final exam questions will be "What would be a non-foundationalist case against foundationalism?" and "What would a non-foundationalist pedagogy for such a course look like?"

This letter lays out in some detail the architectural plans for an entire class by engaging the students' imaginations and enlisting them as apprentices in the construction of the course. What might become a rather dry recital of arguments and counter-arguments, for instance, is transformed into a storm of lightning bolts and lightning rods. The building metaphor itself suggests certain materials, such as concentrating on the need for flexibility in arguments or attending to both logical and rhetorical strategies.

If you were to employ a building metaphor in your own course, you could imagine other possibilities. Perhaps a conversation about homes damaged by earthquakes could lead to discussion of the importance of structural integrity in buildings — might such a beginning draw students' attention away from their worry over surface errors in their writing to the much more difficult but necessary task of constructing strong arguments? Might a consideration of the ethical responsibilities a writer has to her readers resemble the ethical responsibilities a contractor has to construct a safe and energy-efficient house? The analogy of an apartment building may help students understand how various theoretical models do not necessarily compete with one another, but instead "inhabit" an academic discipline differently, some more hospitable and some more edgy? The apartment building analogy itself can be compared to different models of parts and wholes — say the body made of many members, in which each of the parts is necessary to the whole.

What if we began to think about recasting the building metaphor in explicitly biblical terms? Let's move from a philosophy course to a music course, and replace the letter to students with a conversation. Perhaps it would go something like this:

Teacher: I'd like to begin class this morning with a verse from 1 Corinthians: "For we are co-workers in God's service; you are God's field, God's building" (1 Corinthians 3:9). According to the Apostle Paul, you are God's field, God's building. So as we start this new semester, let's think about this statement: "You are God's building." What do you think this means?

(After some awkward silence a few tentative hands begin to appear.)

Student 1: I think we'd have to look at the statement in context before we can understand what Paul means.

Teacher: What do you mean by "context?"

Student 2: Well, this is in the letter to the Corinthians, right? The Corinthians weren't exactly perfect Christians, were they?

Teacher: Not quite. In fact, Paul was scolding them for the deep divisions within their fellowship. They seemed to want to choose heroes and take sides. But what difference does that make to us?

Student 1: Paul talks about laying a foundation — which means his preaching, right? — and that there are good and bad ways to build on it . . . gold and silver vs. wood and hay, and so on.

Teacher: Right. What sort of building are we talking about?

Student 3: It's like when Jesus talks about building on the rock or on the sand — you know, the "wise and foolish builders." There it's a house.

Student 1: So the point is, we have to build on the right foundation — a solid one so it doesn't wash away — and we need to use good materials, and in the end what gets built will either stand or get burned up. Either way, it matters that something is built well.

Teacher: So . . .

Student 1 (continuing): So we need to study hard, get our homework done, and come to class, right?

(Some laughs; the students relax a little. By now most of the students think they understand the point; they get the joke. I'm trying to get them to think about how they learn and using a biblical illustration because that's what Christian teachers do. I pursue the image a bit further.)

Teacher: I agree that you should do all those things. But let's come at it from a different angle. You are thinking about how you as individual students should build your educational house well, that you should work hard to build on the foundation that we lay in this class. But this verse actually doesn't talk about you as an individual builder. It says that you are *God's* building. What about that? And the "you" is plural, not singular, right?

(One of the students in the back row leans in.)

Student 4: It means we're owned.

(General laughter as the allusion to the loser of a computer game sinks in.)

Student 4 (continuing): No. What I mean is, we are the building, and we belong to God, okay? And that means we are the ones being built. So whoever does the building had better get it right.

Teacher: Do you mean me?

(Cautious silence. Some nods of agreement. A few smiles.)

Teacher: It's an awesome business, teaching is. Since some of you are thinking about becoming teachers, now is as good a time as any to recognize the tremendous responsibility you are taking on. A few verses back Paul was using gardening images and said that whoever plants or waters, God causes the growth (3:7). Now the same applies to buildings. I'm called to be a builder of God's building — which is you — and I cannot build on any more secure foundation than what was laid by the master builder (in this case, Paul). What's more, in the end, it will be God's work in you that matters. Even though my hands are the ones that you see, it is His work in you that will endure.

Student 1: But isn't that sort of a cop out? I mean, if God's the one ultimately who's doing the building, who needs you? Let's say you're a bad teacher. Won't that leave us worse off than if we hadn't taken your class in the first place? You can't hide bad teaching behind piety, you know, just saying that you are doing God's work or praying before class or something.

Teacher: Exactly. But where does that leave you? Are you completely passive in this? Is learning something that just happens to you?

(To me we're making real progress. At this point in the conversation we've allowed ourselves to envision teaching and learning as a kind of contract, or perhaps better a covenant, between teacher and student, with rights and responsibilities on both ends. And I am increasingly interested in the way "you are God's building" is leading us to think about both process and product, both means and ends. One more exchange seems called for.)

Teacher (continuing): This is a course in music theory, and each of you has a certain level of basic competence in the subject already or you wouldn't be here. If you are God's building, how might we approach your ongoing work in this subject?

Student 4: I think we need to know whether or not our foundation is secure. Without getting all proof-texty, it seems to me that some of us are built of pretty weak stuff — and maybe that's our own fault. But we've got to know where the weak parts are before we build some more, don't we?

Student 2: Yeah, like what if I slept through most of last semester? I've looked at the textbook readings assigned for this week, and it's all just so confusing. I mean, why do we have to do this anyway? Not one bit of theory ever helped me to play my trombone better. And it certainly won't help me get a job.

(Sympathetic laughter.)

Student 1: The problem is, we're required to do this stuff, but none of us likes it.

Teacher: Does that matter?

Student 1: I think it does. But if I get the point about being "God's building" and all, maybe we need to believe that God knows what he's doing, and that, since he's the main builder, somehow or other it's all going to make sense. Or, at least, I can be open to wondering how it might make sense?

Over the course of the semester, we'll be drawn back into conversations about being God's building — especially at those high points when we suddenly "get it." We'll need to ask further questions — such as whether the teacher is the only one who gets to "build" and how the students share responsibility for what gets "built" in one another. In this opening discussion, we look at some basic motives for learning, think about the roles we might fill in the class, and examine attitudes we need to have to meet the challenges of teaching and learning. For now, the larger picture, still shrouded and incomplete, offers an image that we share and continue to construct together. It frames a space for us to work in together.

Deliberately establishing a single image to start a semester and then deepening it over time can help students make sense of the whole course. Students become more active and constructive learners. In particular, the concrete, tactile quality of building imagery answers to our deep human desire to make things. Constructing conversation around this can elicit a curiosity about becoming apprentice builders.

Laying the Foundations

THE FOUNDATIONS OF THE EARTH

The LORD created me at the beginning of his work,
    the first of his acts of old.
Ages ago I was set up,
    at the first, before the beginning of the earth.
When there were no depths I was brought forth,
    when there were no springs abounding with water.
Before the mountains had been shaped,
    before the hills, I was brought forth;
before he had made the earth with its fields,
    or the first of the dust of the world.
When he established the heavens, I was there,
    when he drew a circle on the face of the deep,
when he made firm the skies above,
    when he established the fountains of the deep,
when he assigned to the sea its limit,
    so that the waters might not transgress his command,
when he marked out the foundations of the earth,
    then I was beside him, like a master workman;
and I was daily his delight,
    rejoicing before him always,
rejoicing in his inhabited world
    and delighting in the sons of men.
                 (Proverbs 8:22-31, RSV)

PART THREE ❧ BUILDINGS AND WALLS

THE DIVINE ARCHITECT

What do foundations make you think of? Stolid, immovable masses, resistant to time and tide? A sense of security and permanence, of having a firm place to stand? A bulwark against frailty and change? If so, the Bible's use of building and foundation imagery might surprise you.

Our urge to build mirrors God's own creative work, and that work resounds with newness and joy. The grand poem of creation in the book of Job begins with this picture of an immense building:

> Where were you when I laid the earth's foundation?
>> Tell me, if you understand.
> Who marked off its dimensions? Surely you know!
>> Who stretched a measuring line across it?
> On what were its footings set,
>> or who laid its cornerstone —
> while the morning stars sang together
>> and all the angels shouted for joy? (Job 38:4-7, TNIV)

There is sheer delight among stars and angels as they watch the world under construction. God is at work, and it is good. The psalmists echo this joy as they imagine the divine architect creating his world:

> In the beginning you laid the foundations of the earth,
>> and the heavens are the work of your hands. (Psalm 102:25, TNIV)

> He set the earth on its foundations;
>> it can never be moved. (Psalm 104:5, TNIV)

The selection from Proverbs 8, quoted above, invokes the delight of Wisdom constructing the world with circles, boundaries, and foundations. Such biblical passages undergird this spacious medieval icon of God as the divine architect.

We see the precision of a master geometer inscribing the circle of the earth with his compass. We also glimpse the loving care of a parent cradling the world as it comes into being, a world that bears an uncanny resem-

blance to a child in the womb. These two images of creation — the design
of a building and the birth of a child — are combined with good reason.
Scripture often moves from images of construction to images of birth and
swaddling cloths.

Almost as soon as God has given Job the picture of a sturdy, secure foundation, he shifts to the messy, warm, painful, glorious moment of birth, before
returning to his image of creation as a house. Listen to the shifting word pictures in these verses:

> Who shut up the sea behind doors
>> when it burst forth from the womb,
> when I made the clouds its garment
>> and wrapped it in thick darkness,

> when I fixed limits for it
> > and set its doors and bars in place,
> when I said, "This far you may come and no farther;
> > here is where your proud waves halt"? (Job 38:8-11, TNIV)

God looks upon creation as a newborn baby, lovingly swaddled in thick, warm clouds, and as a newly completed house, doors and windows secured against intruders. Psalm 104 also invokes the image of a newborn earth swaddled with the waters of the sea:

> He set the earth on its foundations;
> > it can never be moved.

> You covered it with the watery depths as with a garment;
> > the waters stood above the mountains. (Psalm 104:5-6, TNIV)

And Psalm 102 chimes in with images that move from birth to death, reminding us that the world is not permanent; in fact, it is as fragile as a threadbare piece of clothing.

> In the beginning you laid the foundations of the earth,
> > and the heavens are the work of your hands.

> They will perish, but you remain;
> > they will all wear out like a garment.
> Like clothing you will change them
> > and they will be discarded. (Psalm 102:25-26, TNIV)

These quicksilver changes from buildings to newborns to raggedy clothes and back again to buildings are not by chance. The Bible often uses multiple images, even within a single text, to teach us about God. God is rock and mother hen and shepherd and living water and lamb and door, and many more besides. The sheer variety of these images destabilizes the tidy mental images of God we too easily construct. We cannot nail God down to a single master metaphor; we cannot fit God neatly into our minds.

Here in Job and the Psalms, the cascading word-pictures persistently make us look away from the buildings themselves and toward the person who builds and gives birth and swaddles and sets limits: "This far you may come and no farther." It is not the strong foundations or sturdy buildings that in themselves offer stability; stability only comes from their creator. God can just as easily wobble the foundations of the earth as set them in place. And that, in fact, is just what we are told God will do when he comes in judgment:

> For a fire will be kindled by my wrath,
>> one that burns down to the realm of the dead below.
> It will devour the earth and its harvests
>> and set afire the foundations of the mountains.
>>>> (Deuteronomy 32:22, NIV)

> The earth trembled and quaked,
>> and the foundations of the mountains shook;
>> they trembled because he was angry. (Psalm 18:7, NIV)

These biblical texts don't settle for picturing well-planned and well-executed structures that stand ever pristine and secure, even when God himself is the builder. The foundations of the earth itself will wobble and crack. And indeed, many central and iconic buildings in the Bible, designed or commanded by God himself, are insubstantial and temporary.

Noah's ark, Abraham and Sarah's tent, the "ark" carrying baby Moses down the Nile, the tabernacle, and the plant that shades Jonah, are all fragile, flimsy, contingent structures. They are not made to last; we should not look to them for our security. When King David wants to replace the tabernacle with a permanent building, God allows his son Solomon to construct the temple, but only after wrenching David's attention away from sticks and stones to the "house" that God has already started building, a house made of people whose cornerstone is Jesus Christ. God does allow the construction of the temple, but he also approves its destruction at the hands of the Babylonians (Jeremiah 25:8-9).

In the New Testament, Jesus provocatively announces that Herod's temple will be destroyed and points to his own body as the new temple: "I will destroy this temple made with human hands and in three days will build another, not made with hands" (Mark 14:58, TNIV). This temple is Christ and his church, constructed with living stones, with Jesus as the chief cornerstone. Peter and Paul both echo the image:

> As you come to him, the living Stone — rejected by humans but chosen by God and precious to him — you also, like living stones, are being built into a spiritual house to be a holy priesthood, offering spiritual sacrifices acceptable to God through Jesus Christ. (1 Peter 2:4-5, TNIV)

> Consequently, you are no longer foreigners and strangers, but fellow citizens with God's people and also members of his household, built on the foundation of the apostles and prophets, with Christ Jesus himself as the chief cornerstone. In him the whole building is joined together and rises to become a holy temple in the Lord. (Ephesians 2:19-21, TNIV)

In both the Old and New Testaments, we see that buildings and building are central images, but also that they are more dynamic and fragile than we might expect. Buildings rise and fall, the very foundations of the world will be shaken, the earth will be folded up like a worn-out dress. Even the church, built on the cornerstone of Christ himself and constructed of living stones, moves and breathes and grows.

Joining together building and birth, firm foundations and worn-out clothes, sturdy temples and living stones can revive the somewhat tired metaphor, "teaching is like building." What if some of the sturdy curricular edifices that we have constructed are ready for collapse or demolition? How might we imagine our vocation as teachers if we think of ourselves as midwives who "bring forth" rather than construct a building? What if we imagine ourselves not as the builders, let alone the architects, of our syllabi, lesson plans, and even students, but rather as living stones who, with our students, are being built up into a spiritual house? How, like God in the ancient icon, do we cradle our students as we mark out the span of the day's learning?

TEACHING LIVING STONES TO TALK

In her essay "Teaching a Stone to Talk" Annie Dillard describes a neighbor who has dedicated himself to teaching a palm-size rock to speak. It is a task that requires perseverance and precision: "Larry removes the cover [a square of untanned leather] for the stone's lessons," Dillard tells us, "or more accurately, I should say, for the ritual or rituals which they perform together several times a day". As Dillard watches her neighbor devote himself to the rock, she muses about the significance of such work, and the dedication it takes to commit to what is clearly a meaningless, hopeless task. After all, the only response — the only possible reply to this man's effort — is silence. For Dillard, such silence is not so much emptiness as a refusal. Nature simply refuses to communicate, to respond, to give any indication that the great vastness of the universe expresses anything at all. And yet the silence itself demands our attention: "There is a vibrancy to the silence, a suppression, as if someone were gagging the world. But you wait, you give your life's length to listening, and nothing happens".

There are times when we may feel that our classrooms are filled with silent stones, that we are engaging in rituals with little chance of success, that nothing will ever happen. Despite the healthy, scrubbed, vigorous, youthfulness that crowds the space, we encounter blank stares and mute lips. Even more frighteningly, we find ourselves encumbered with our own stony hearts, stranded in a gagged world that seems increasingly meaningless.

While it is true that usually "nothing happens" when you attempt to teach a stone to talk, there was once a time when stones almost cried out. If it hadn't been for the hosannas of the multitudes who greeted Christ on that Palm Sunday as he rode the donkey into Jerusalem, the silence of the mute creation would have exploded into praise. "I tell you," Jesus said, responding to the Pharisees, "if these become silent, the stones will cry out!" (Luke 19:40).

I've often wondered what sort of stones Jesus was referring to. As a child, I imagined him pointing to some rocks along the well-worn path. Perhaps they were like Larry's stone pupil. But I tend now to picture his gesture as encompassing the whole scene: the rocky heights of the Mount of Olives and Mount Zion and all the surrounding hills and valleys. The noise would be deafening. But even more remarkable would be the fact that such stones cried out at all. "Nature's silence is its one remark," writes Dillard, "and every flake of world is a chip off that old mute and immutable block". Perhaps Jesus smiled as he rebuked his seemingly wise but faithless critics. After all, wouldn't we, as we were fleeing the scene, look back and laugh at such a spectacle?

If even silent rocks sing out their hosannas when Jesus passes by, how much more boisterous will be the praise of living stones. It was doubtless with a rueful glance back at his own name, as well as these silent rocks, that Peter writes: "And coming to Him as to a living stone, rejected by men, but choice and precious in the sight of God, you also, as living stones, are being built up as a spiritual house for a holy priesthood, to offer up spiritual sacrifices acceptable to God through Jesus Christ" (1 Peter 2:4-5, NASB).

Combine these pictures: silent stones gaining a voice, living stones being built into a spiritual house, and then consider the classroom. Whether we give a lecture, lead a discussion, assign group work, or use any other pedagogical technique, reminding ourselves that we are not handling lifeless bricks but rather living stones being built together keeps us from both despair and arrogance.

First, we are reminded that teaching requires patience and reliance on the Spirit of God. No amount of enthusiasm or professorial acrobatics, not even the most expert use of technology, will get us very far outside of God taking hearts of stone, both ours and those of our students, and turning them into hearts of flesh (Ezekiel 36:26). So we should neither be overly self-congratulatory when a lesson goes well nor self-recriminating when it seems to collapse.

Second, after all our own talking, arguing, correcting, and making of points, we are reminded that what matters most is that we wait and listen. We are not the neighbor talking to an inert rock; we are ourselves one of the living stones, being built together with others into something more beautiful. We *want* to hear these living stones speak, to be part of their conversation. We want to enable and to amplify their voices. We want the noise they make to shake the earth to its foundations. So we will take and make the time in both our preparations and our teaching to listen for God's voice speaking to and through our students.

Finally, I think we can learn from Dillard's assessment of her neighbor's posture towards his stone. She writes, "I assume that like any other meaningful effort, the ritual involves sacrifice, the suppression of self-consciousness, and a certain precise tilt of the will, so that the will becomes transparent and hollow, a channel for the work". As I prepare for the next class, I aspire to obtain that "certain precise tilt of the will" that allows God to work through me, enabling me to teach God's precious living stones to cry out and not be silenced. The "will" part of that phrase reminds me that I have responsibilities to study, work, and generally get ready to teach well; but the "tilt of the will" also reminds me that all that preparation will mean little unless I am oriented toward God, unless in my teaching, as in my life, I am aware of doing what I do *coram Deo*, before the face of God.

THE CRYSTAL CASTLE

Imagine this: A woman sits at a table, eyes smudged purple with weariness, face deepened into shadows by the flickering oil lamp. All day long she has counseled, taught, encouraged, and prayed with the younger women who live in her house; she has agonized over the fate of friends pressured to conform to church rules in which they no longer believe; she has worried over the progress of her students; she has noticed a growing tension between two strong-willed housemates. Now she sits staring at a sheaf of papers, pen in hand. She writes a curriculum, beginning in this way:

> While I was begging our Lord today to speak for me, since I knew not what to say nor how to commence this work which obedience has laid upon me, an idea occurred to me which I will explain, and which will serve as a foundation for that I am about to write. I thought of the soul as resembling a castle, formed of a single diamond or a very transparent crystal, and containing many rooms, just as in heaven there are many mansions.

The tired woman is St. Teresa of Avila and these are the opening words of *The Interior Castle*, written in 1577 for the instruction of sisters in the sixteen monasteries she had founded. St. Teresa herself had joined a Carmelite monastery when she was only nineteen and had quickly distinguished herself as both a spiritually sensitive Christian and a gifted leader. Grieved over the lack of discipline and spiritual integrity among her fellow nuns, she established the order of Discalced Carmelites, who observed strict rules of poverty and obedience. They lived in the simplest of houses, subsisted on a meager diet, and wore wooden sandals rather than shoes even in winter — hence the name "discalced" or "those without footwear." Yet when she sat down to write a manual of spiritual instruction — a curriculum — for her sisters, the image she drew of their souls was that of a splendid crystal castle, shimmering with spacious rooms, a miniature heaven on earth.

This castle of our souls must be beautiful, she insisted, because it is the very place where God himself lives. "We shall see that the soul of the just man is but a paradise," she says, "in which, God tells us, He takes His delight. What, do you imagine, must that dwelling be in which a King so mighty, so wise, and so pure, containing in Himself all good, can delight to rest?" What indeed but a splendid palace? In her curriculum of spiritual instruction, St. Teresa calls her students to look not downward at their sandaled feet or coarse clothes or the turnips on their plates, but rather both inward and upward, to imagine themselves as a beautiful diamond castle, fit to welcome God himself. *The Interior Castle* is thus a handbook for the curriculum of prayer, the central subject matter, practice, and vocation of the Discalced Carmelites.

In this handbook St. Teresa imagines her students as mysterious and lovely buildings, whose splendor can never be fully described or understood:

> Nothing can be compared to the great beauty and capabilities of a soul; how-ever keen our intellects may be, they are as unable to comprehend them as to comprehend God, for, as He has told us, He created us in His own image and likeness. As this is so, we need not tire ourselves by trying to realize all the beauty of this castle, although, being His creature, there is all the difference between the soul and God that there is between the creature and the Creator; the fact that it is made in God's image teaches us how great are its dignity and loveliness.

St. Teresa's description of the human person as a beautiful building recalls the descriptions of the lovers in the Song of Songs: her neck is an ivory tower (4:4; 7:4); his legs are "pillars of marble set on bases of pure gold" (5:15). She develops this image, imagining the "many rooms in this castle, of which some are above, some below, others at the side" through which the Christian soul progresses in order to come at last to the central, seventh room, "the principal chamber in which God and the soul hold their most secret intercourse."

St. Teresa's vision of her students is remarkable for its sheer beauty. Your soul, she says, is not just a building, but a castle. Not just a castle, but a crystal castle, as bright and enduring as a diamond. Not just a crystal castle, but a crystal castle with many rooms, a castle where God resides.

To see the beauty in another's soul protects against intellectual and spiritual jealousy. The many rooms in the castle of our souls St. Teresa takes to be the "different kinds of graces God is pleased to bestow upon the soul." And because there are so many rooms, "no one can know all about them," least of all, she says, "a person so ignorant as I am." So when we see the gifts and graces God has given to someone else, when we glance around their spacious and well-appointed rooms, furnished with costly rugs, leather armchairs, and walnut bookcases full of first editions, and are tempted to compare them to our own apartments, decked out in garage-sale bargains, we will instead have our hearts turned to "praise Him for His great goodness in bestowing [these favors] on others."

St Teresa's cascading vision of a breathtakingly beautiful castle counteracts our tendency to employ the building metaphor in more utilitarian terms: first we lay the foundation, then we set up the scaffolding, then we mortar in the bricks, then we shingle the roof. The crystal castle displaces the image we may have of ourselves as the master teacher-builders. Our students are already gorgeous crystal castles, built and lovingly inhabited by God himself. What we — and they — most need is to open our eyes to see the beauty that is already there, to see them as God's work, God's building, God's delight. This, of course, is the language of Paul in Ephesians 2:10: "For we are his workmanship, created in Christ Jesus for good works, which God prepared beforehand, that we should walk in them" (RSV).

What might be the effect on our teaching and in our classrooms if we imagined our students, particularly the ones we see as more challenging and recalcitrant, as beautiful, spacious castles through which God is making his patient way? How much more care might students take of themselves and each other if, as they looked at their jeans-and-sweatshirt-selves, they saw instead a crystal palace, a castle where God himself lives?

Building the Walls

The Garden and the City

The Bible begins in a garden and ends in a city.

Like many simple statements, this familiar summary of the biblical narrative, stretching from Genesis to Revelation, points to an important truth without telling the whole story. The Bible actually begins not in the Garden of Eden, but rather with the construction of an entire cosmos, understood as a grand and immense building. "For every house is built by someone," the writer of Hebrews reminds us, "but God is the builder of everything" (Hebrews 3:4, NIV). And while the Bible does conclude with the vision of a splendid city, it is a heavenly Jerusalem that is remarkably garden-like, with a flowing river and tree of life placed at its very center (Revelation 22:1-2). Cities and gardens, along with deserts and vineyards and pilgrim paths, intersect throughout the story of Scripture.

When the prophets encourage the people of Israel that God stands ready to redeem them, they often intertwine images of restored gardens and rebuilt cities:

> Thus says the Lord GOD: "On the day that I cleanse you from all your iniquities, I will cause the cities to be inhabited, and the waste places shall be rebuilt. And the land that was desolate shall be tilled, instead of being the desolation that it was in the sight of all who passed by. And they will say, 'This land that was desolate has become like the garden of Eden; and the waste and desolate and ruined cities are now inhabited and fortified.' Then the nations that are left round about you shall know that I, the LORD, have rebuilt the ruined places, and replanted that which was desolate; I, the LORD, have spoken, and I will do it." (Ezekiel 36:33-36, RSV)

The trajectory from garden to city, however, does draw our attention to the steady outward movement from the splendid intimacy of God, Adam, and Eve in the original garden to the vibrant congestion of worshippers gathered around the Lamb's throne in the heavenly Jerusalem. God the architect has big plans in mind: cities and their buildings are meant for people — lots and lots of people.

God's generous, expansive grace is perhaps nowhere better illustrated than in the crowded corridors of heaven imagined by the Apostle John in his apocalypse. In the beginning God makes a man and a woman; in the end he welcomes their progeny — as many as the stars in the heavens or the sand on the seashore — into his city. So to say that the Bible begins in a garden and ends in a city is to understand something of God's grand intentions for all that he has made. Perhaps the Apostle Paul is thinking of this creative-redemptive trajectory when he intertwines the two images of cultivation and architecture in his letter to the Corinthian church: you are God's field, he says, you are God's building (1 Corinthians 3:9).

Understanding the integral unity of this biblical trajectory from Eden to New Jerusalem helps us counter the still prevalent romantic notions that put images of gardens and buildings into opposition with one another. It is tempting, for instance, to think of gardens as free, innocent, natural spaces, unencumbered by design or toil and to consider buildings merely the result of human engineering, manipulation, and work. After all, it is Cain, following the murder of his brother Abel, who first builds a city (Genesis 4:17).

But a garden is not a wilderness untouched by human hands: God's command to tend Eden is given immediately after his creation of Adam and Eve. This command demands cultivation, the beginning of human culture. Nor are buildings inert objects devoid of creativity, beauty, and life. Gardens and buildings both require construction and are meant to be inhabited and maintained. When we think about gardens and buildings as complementary metaphors, we recognize that they often share one feature in common: they both have walls.

In the Bible, one of the surest signs of God withdrawing his favor is his removal of a protective wall from a garden or vineyard: "So now let Me tell you what I am going to do to My vineyard: I will remove its hedge and it will be consumed; I will break down its wall and it will become trampled ground" (Isaiah 5:5, NASB). A walled garden is emblematic of God's grace and his provision for spiritual growth and renewal. Similarly, a walled city signals that God is among his people, redeeming and protecting them. Before anyone can even think about constructing a new temple, the bedraggled band of returning exiles must gather around Nehemiah and rebuild the walls of Jerusalem. To build such walls, in the biblical narrative, is to participate in the very work of God himself.

THINKING ABOUT WALLS

Walls are important to traditional gardens, necessary to ancient cities, and often serve as positive images in Scripture; what might they might tell us about teaching and learning?

In our everyday conversation, we often associate walls with something negative. An athlete may talk about "hitting the wall" to explain the sudden loss of energy that occurs midway through a race. A similar feeling assails almost everyone who undertakes a long writing assignment. Students working on a research paper, whether they are first-years, seniors, or post-docs, commonly report the sensation of "hitting a wall" as they face mounds of information and no clear direction for sorting it all out.

Walls may hide, limit, and constrict in our common ways of speaking. We say that someone has "walled up his emotion" or that it's like "talking to a brick wall" when we feel frustrated at our inability to communicate with a friend, colleague, or lover. Walls keep secrets. "If only these walls could talk," we say longingly, as we look around the rooms of our great-aunt's house. But when we are afraid of being overheard, we warn each other: "Be careful; the walls have ears!" In educational circles, we talk about breaking down walls that divide students or keep them from learning.

In fact, most of our common expressions — our everyday metaphors about walls — are vaguely threatening. Walls are frustrating barriers or ominous enclosures. They prevent us from doing what we would like to do, or they cut us off from other people. When the man in Robert Frost's poem "Mending Wall" says that "good fences make good neighbors," we understand that "good" here means "not too close or intimate," and we mistrust the sentiment.

Of course, after a moment of reflection, we also recognize that real walls are often very good things, where "good" means helpful and even necessary. The walls of our homes and schools protect us from cold, heat, rain, snow, and (usually) insects. A retaining wall in our backyard keeps mud from sliding down into the rose garden or basement. The wall around a medieval city kept intruders and wild animals out and the citizens safe and secure inside.

Thinking of a medieval or ancient city may help us understand why walls are almost always positive images in the Bible. They speak not so much of confinement as of protection. Think, for instance, of Nehemiah supervising the construction of Jerusalem's walls — with men, women, and children all pitching in to haul stones, smear mortar, and watch out for enemies. Or the walls of a sheep cote that keep away thieves and robbers (John 10). Or Isaiah's vision of restoration: "In that day this song will be sung in the land of Judah: 'We have a strong city; He sets up walls and ramparts for security'" (Isaiah 26:1, NASB). The secure salvation of God's people in the new heavens is pictured by their dwelling in a great city whose walls are made of precious stones.

Conversely, think of the biblical image of a broken wall as the emblem of undisciplined and self-destructive behavior: "Like a city that is broken into and without walls is a man who has no control over his spirit" (Proverbs 25:28, NASB) or of God's judgment against wickedness as the breaking down of protective walls: "So now let Me tell you what I am going to do to My vineyard: I will remove its hedge and it will be consumed; I will break down its wall and it will become trampled ground" (Isaiah 5:5, NASB).

When we consider the positive roles that walls play in the biblical narrative, we realize that it may be time to reconsider our modern prejudice against them and let these biblical images reshape our "walled off" imagination.

THE WALLS WE CONSTRUCT

Consider how the different walls pictured below might activate your pedagogical imagination.

The walls on the right hand side of the page suggest some creative possibilities for teaching. In the top and bottom pictures they delineate spaces, but don't appear to be holding up their respective buildings. We might imagine using these images to evaluate different sorts of arguments as we think through key questions with our students: Is this argument a load-bearing wall? Will an entire theorem collapse if it is removed or modified? Does this argument function more aesthetically, to clarify rather than to convince? Is this argument — load-bearing or not — intriguing, persuasive, beautiful? Is it functional (as in the top picture) or eye-catching (as in the bottom picture)? We might also imagine helping students understand that some arguments are matters of taste and judgment rather than of truth and falsity. You may prefer the cool minimalism of the top wall, and I may prefer the bold lines of the bottom walls. But both of them serve to mark out one space from another.

The middle picture, however, suggests a different use for walls. Here a cement façade becomes the canvas for expressing dissenting opinions in artistic and graphically arresting ways. A utilitarian structure is transformed, via graffiti, into a public building.

Hmm. If I think about my classroom as not just a physical but an imaginary space surrounded by four walls, might I allow or even encourage my students to spray it with graffiti? Do the walls of my class provide a canvas on which students can work out their responses to the material I present, sometimes in unexpected and even rebellious ways? What would happen if I designed a "graffiti assignment" or just handed out cans of spray paint (metaphorical or literal) after a lecture? In what ways do the walls of my classroom open out onto the public square?

Although I haven't distributed aerosol cans of paint, I have asked students in literature classes to draw, as a way of jarring their words loose from conventional written responses. I think of this as my own version of creating graffiti. Recently, during a semester-long project in which students in an Environmental Literature class visited the same tree each week and described their experiences in a blog, I gave this prompt:

> Return this week to your tree, pen or pencil in hand. Look at it — see it, attend to it — with your hand. You need not be an expert artist to draw your tree; this is not actually an exercise in drawing, but rather an exercise in seeing. Draw continuously for 20 minutes — set a timer. In your blog, discuss these questions: What did you notice as you were drawing your tree? What did you see when you spent 20 minutes actively engaged in seeing with your hand? What did you learn about your tree? about yourself? about the very act of seeing?

Not unexpectedly, most students found the task difficult. Despite my caveat that "You need not be an expert artist to draw your tree," many concentrated more on their inability to draw than on using their pen as a way to see. They were also a bit disconcerted to be confronted with a drawing

assignment in a literature class. Some, however, found that the exercise yielded some unexpected insights.

> As I was sketching my tree I began to realize just HOW intricate trees are. First I started by just sketching a 1ft by 1ft section of the trunk of my tree that included the maple syrup tapping hole. That alone took me about 10 minutes and I know I didn't do it justice. Bark itself is so detailed! There are furrows, crevices, cracks, splits, layers, moss, stains, and shades of all sorts. Unless I had done some super awesome shading, it would be really hard to portray the detail in just bark. (Chris)
>
> What I learned about myself is that I am not a great artist, but I also learned that by simply trying to draw something you can see so much more. . . . Getting the right attitude about a task, I learned, is a key factor. I wasn't thinking I would get much out of this drawing beforehand because drawing isn't my thing. But then I changed my attitude about the assignment, and I think I learned a lot because of that. (Marlene)
>
> It's incredible how many more tiny details you can see if you're actually looking for the details. Of the many times that I have visited my tree, I never noticed some of the nooks and points on the trunk of the tree. This has showed me to actually *look* not only with my eyes, but with my whole self. (Dale)

For these students, moving outside the literal walls of the classrooms and the metaphorical walls of a literature course, as well as inscribing their encounters on the public walls of a blog, where they took responsibility for what other people might read, pushed them toward significant discoveries not just about their tree but about themselves. In addition, when expected pedagogical walls were broken down, or at least cracked, they were forced to build their own structures of learning. And since persistent, guided practice hones construction skills, we repeated the assignment after we had talked in class about its challenges and opportunities. This time the students were better prepared. One of them wrote:

> I revisited my tree tonight, and it went much better than the last time. I brought nothing with me but a notebook, pencil, and an open mind. I found that when I focused on just the tree itself, not the drawing, I had an easier time just being still. I had never really studied my tree, despite all the times I've gone to look

at it. My dad told me once that when you love someone, you study them. You want to drink in every detail about the way they move, talk, smile, the very way they breathe. You absorb yourself in what they like and don't like, what they dream about. Every inch of every facet of their being is waiting to be explored. . . . The branches of my tree are thin, so it sways in step with the wind, but its roots are strong, and keep it from flying away in the dance. The leaves rustle with the wind, in a sort of song that promises freedom and ultimate joy. How did I miss this before? How could a measly drawing even begin to capture how utterly breathtaking this tree is? When you love something, you stop looking at it, and you begin to really *see* it. (Angelica)

Another simply wrote: "It is one thing to read *about* being attentive; it is another to be forced to *be* attentive." What began as a "graffiti" assignment became a significant building block in learning, through experience, what it means to see and love the world.

In contrast to the walls on the right hand side of the page, the three on the left are more obviously utilitarian. But here, too, we can raise questions of beauty and taste: we see the rough texture of the brick, the solid bulk of the castle enclosure, the open glass expanse of a contemporary office. Noticing the aesthetic features of these walls may slow us down and keep us from moving too hastily to rigid conclusions: a brick wall can be the thing against which you beat your head, but it can also keep you warm, when it houses a fireplace. A castle can wall you off from the world or protect you while you contemplate new ideas. An office building can feel sterile or provide efficient, comfortable working spaces.

The multiplicity of walls and their functions, in the Scriptures as well as in our daily lives, reminds us again not to invest any one image with a single meaning. As you looked at the six walls in this teaching moment, your thoughts may have traveled along entirely different paths to particular classes or assignments or syllabi that you might construct. That's okay; in fact, it's good. When you activate an image, such as buildings or walls, it can help you evaluate old practices in new ways, see connections that you had overlooked, or develop new ways of teaching. But the expansiveness of imagistic thinking also points out a potential danger — its boundaries are virtually limitless. That is why once we've let our imaginations be sparked by a set of images — say of six walls — we also need to let them be disciplined in conversation with Scripture and the Christian tradition.

In the six pictures we've discussed, none include people. But in the Christian imagination, walls are not just pretty or useful structures; they are made for people. Walls allocate places; they protect; they make possible all those human activities that require a secure space. When used properly, walls promote human flourishing. The positive role walls play in the Scriptures supports a rethinking of our often too-ready impulse to dismantle barriers or to encourage freedom *from* without considering at the same time freedom *for what*. The building metaphor reminds us to consider what can be learned only within the security of clearly defined spaces, even while we think creatively about the kinds of walls that need demolishing.

Climbing the Steps

BUILDINGS HAVE ALWAYS SERVED NOT only as dwellings but as ways of gaining elevation, whether seeking a vantage point from which to survey the surroundings, pointing dramatically into the sky, or simply getting a little way above the damp earth. As well as walls and windows, buildings commonly come with steps and ladders, sometimes even with towers. We associate climbing with progress, we talk about *moving up* to the next class and about the *ivory towers* of *higher education*. What perspectives on teaching might towers provide?

TOWERS OF LEARNING

Towers and their winding, arduous staircases have stood as an image for learning for generations. In the woodcut on the following page we see a tower in the heart of a medieval city. The late gothic turrets, balustrades, and ornamentations remind us of a cathedral or a church, but the inscriptions tell us that we are looking at a place of learning.

The picture appears in Gregorius Reisch's *Margarita Philosophica* (1503), or philosophical pearl, an illustrated compendium of academic knowledge. It served as a textbook introducing students to the seven liberal arts, the *trivium* (grammar, logic, rhetoric) and the *quadrivium* (arithmetic, music, geometry, astronomy), which culminated in the study of theology.

A tall woman stands before the entrance to the tower. This is Nicostrata, held in Roman lore to be the inventor of the alphabet. In her right hand is a hornbook displaying the alphabet; in her left hand is the key that will open the door to the tower of knowledge. Nicostrata shows an eager freshman who has

learned to read and write the entrance to the ground floor where Donatus teaches the students elementary Latin.

One young scholar has put on his travelling attire and proceeds up the stairs to the next level, where Priscianus instructs students in intermediate and advanced Latin. (Donatus and Priscianus were the authors of the standard Latin textbooks in the Middle Ages). Here, too, one student is ready to move on; on the third level he will study logic with Aristotle, rhetoric with Cicero, and arithmetic with Boethius. At the fourth level, Pythagoras, Euclid, and Ptolemy wait to offer instruction in music, geometry, and astronomy. This fulfilled the requirements for the *magister artium* (MA).

The fifth and sixth stories of the tower have a new shape. Here advanced studies start with Aristotle's natural and Seneca's moral philosophy, and culminate at the top in scholastic theology or metaphysics, as developed in Petrus Lombardus' *Four Books of Sentences,* the most popular and influential book of systematic and biblical theology from the 13th to the 16th century. After years of study, the scholar can graduate with a degree in theology. He has dwelled faithfully in a house of learning, a house that echoes the Proverbs 9 house of Wisdom:

> Wisdom has built her house;
>> she has set up its seven pillars.
> She has prepared her meat and mixed her wine;
>> she has also set her table.
> She has sent out her servants, and she calls
>> from the highest point of the city,
> "Let all who are simple come to my house!"
>> (Proverbs 9:1-4, TNIV)

Reisch's tower of knowledge offers a vision of the purpose of learning. "All wisdom is from God" is a favorite motto from Sirach 1:1 (also known as Ecclesiasticus) that appears in many medieval illustrations of the curriculum. Ascending the tower of knowledge leads the student to divine wisdom.

The image on the next page shows another tower of wisdom (*turris sapientiae*), this time emphasizing the active role of the student, who must build up the sturdy tower brick by brick. The bricks are inscribed with admonitions and encouragements towards a virtuous life. The tower's foundation is *humility, the mother of all virtues.* The width of the building is *charity* and the height of the tower is *perseverance in the good.* The two lower levels indicate the general virtuous dispositions a believer seeks, such as *diligence, peace, truth, justice, stability, patience, devotion,* and *contemplation.* Seven spiritual disciplines (*prayer, awareness of sin, confession, penitence, reparation, giving of alms,* and *fasting*) form the steps leading to the entrance of the door of *obedience* and *patience.* The 120 building blocks of the upper part of the tower represent specific virtuous acts believers should put into action to show their love of God.

By practicing what each block teaches, the diligent learner will build up a tower of wisdom in his or her soul. As one writer put it:

> The true teacher does not show his students the finished building shaped by millennia, but instead instructs them in shaping the building blocks, erects with them the edifice and teaches them the craft of building.

This image served as a teaching chart in universities and appeared in pastoral handbooks for the clergy preparing sermons. It offered a mnemonic device, a way of organizing and remembering key points. But the tower also invited believers to meditate and examine their conscience and moral conduct.

Contemplating the building blocks served the edification of the soul, climbing toward lived wisdom and building an inner tower to protect against the onslaught of temptations and vice.

These two towers place their own questions on our educational horizon. As we move from "basic" to "higher" levels of educational activity, what are we actually climbing towards? What is the ultimate goal? What role does the teacher play in laying a foundation and arranging pedagogical exercises that will allow a student to progress up the tower of knowledge? What role does the student play in constructing her own tower of wisdom? What bricks and stones are essential? Which ones simply get in the way? What makes for a stable tower, offering secure progress? Building metaphors direct our attention toward both what is learned and how it is learned. And they also keep before us the question of the ultimate goal of teaching and learning. Does the education we offer prompt movement towards wisdom?

CLIMBING THE LADDER

Imagine yourself sitting in a large room in 1624. The whole student body at *Schulpforta*, a famous German Protestant boarding school in Saxony, is gathered with the faculty in the assembly hall to listen to the principal who is addressing you at the beginning of the school year. His speech goes something like this: First he reminds you that about 100 years ago, during the Reformation, Duke Moritz of Saxony founded the school for the education of future clergymen and administrators. Then the speaker urges you to honor not only the memory of the generous Duke, but above all the presence of God in this house of learning. As he elaborates this thought, he recalls Jacob's dream in Genesis.

While Jacob was dreaming about the ladder, the principal explains, he was schooled by God. Jacob was given a lesson, which Abraham and Isaac had received before him. It is obvious, the speaker suggests, that Jacob's divine instruction was not unlike the daily review lessons familiar to students at *Schulpforta*. When Jacob woke up he was thankful that God took him to school, and he praised the Lord and called the site "a holy place, a house of God (Bethel) and the gate to heaven" (Genesis 28:17). Now the principal comes to the crux of his speech: Our school is called *Schulpforta*, based on the Latin *porta*, that is, a gate that leads to heaven. Schools are holy sites, houses of God, where

God dwells and where young people are learning about the ways of the Lord. "Our school too," he summarizes, "is God's house because the Word of God is being studied by the young; God himself is present and fills everything with his blessings." The principal then closes his meditation with a short prayer and dismisses you along with the others.

Up to the end of the 18th century it was common in Europe to view pedagogical institutions as sites where students could not only become literate and educated, but also encounter the divine as Jacob did in his dream. In innumerable speeches, schools were likened to houses of God, to little churches (*ecclesiola*), to godly towers of knowledge or temples erected to the honor of the Lord where students learned about the world, about God and the Scriptures, and about how to live a God-fearing life. Jacob's reaction to his dream was a common point of reference when offering such a high view of educational institutions.

When we talk about education today, we still talk in terms of ladders. However, the ladder metaphor now usually implies upward social mobility, getting ahead in life, reaching more power and a higher standard of living. For Christian educators in the past, the image of Jacob's ladder served as a central metaphor for spiritual rather than social or economic advancement, for learning to draw close to God by leading a life of obedience, justice, humility, and piety. In the Rule of St. Benedict we read:

> We descend by haughtiness, pride and we ascend by humility. The ladder is our
> life on earth and if we humble our hearts the Lord will raise it to heaven. Our
> body and soul are the sides of the ladder, into which our divine vocation has
> inserted the various steps of humility and discipline as we ascend.

As we speak with students about the goals and challenges of learning, what kinds of ladders do we implicitly or explicitly invite them to climb?

CLIMBING THE LIGHTHOUSE

"215 . . . 216 . . . 217 . . . we made it!" My friend and I wheezed out the last number, stepped through the small door onto the wrought iron balcony, leaned against the parapet, and turned our faces into the fresh sea wind. Winded, but a bit smug, we looked down at our companions stretched out below on the grass at the base of "Old Barney," the Barnegat Lighthouse on the New Jersey shore. The temptation to crow over our accomplishment was one we didn't even try to resist. "Hey, guys, the view up here is great. You should pull your lazy bones up those spiral stairs!"

I was reminded of this ignoble triumph the last time I talked with my students about the power of metaphors to shape our moral imaginations. We had asked ourselves what images came to mind when we thought about achieving a hard-won goal and, interestingly enough, many if not most of these involved pictures of ascent: getting to the top of a mountain and looking back at the rocky path, climbing the ladder of success, moving upwards toward God. On a more mundane note, one student wrote that making progress in our class was like climbing a tree: at the moment she felt tired and prickly from all the branches scratching her legs — which she allegorically and pointedly ascribed to the daily written assignments — and she could only see a few feet in front of her face. But she hoped that soon she'd get high enough to catch her breath, rest, and look down at a landscape that would resolve itself into a unified picture. When that happened, she might just believe that the climb had been worth it. We all laughed ruefully at the picture she had drawn and agreed that she had captured both difficulty and promise in her ascent metaphor.

Another student said that her grandmother routinely asked her what habits she was building into her life, and that she had recently thought more seriously about that word "building." She had begun to imagine herself each day picking up tools to lay a foundation, to build walls, to craft her life as a house that she would be proud to live in.

There is something right about these images of construction and ascent, of course. They highlight the need for disciplined effort and perseverance, for planning and due diligence, for learning and acting in a logical, sequenced manner, and they celebrate genuine accomplishment. There is pleasure both in climbing a mountain and looking down at the valley; pleasure both in building a house and moving in. But images of construction and ascent bring with them temptations to pride, elitism, and smugness — as well as temptations to despair and apathy when tasks seem monumental and overwhelming. The "ivory towers" of the Academy are not usually invoked as a term of praise; rather they symbolize learning that is disconnected from the lives of ordinary folk and, at its worst, diverts valuable resources from the many to the few. The uncompleted Tower of Babel remains an emblem of grasping pride and overweening desire. Climbing comes with a powerful urge to look down on those who have yet to climb our ladder or to begin constructing their own towers.

Given the dual-sided nature of building images — the call to succeed and the temptation to gloat — how might we best use metaphors of steps and buildings in our classrooms? Construction images can encourage students to make steady progress — just take one step at a time, we tell them when they feel overwhelmed with a large task. Just place one brick at a time, persevere in your work; eventually you will be pleased with what you have built. At the same time, however, we need to remind them, and ourselves, that ascent is always an act of grace in the biblical narrative. Consider again Jacob's famous dream:

> And he dreamed that there was a ladder set up on the earth, and the top of it reached to heaven; and behold, the angels of God were ascending and descending on it! And behold, the LORD stood above it and said, "I am the LORD, the God of Abraham your father and the God of Isaac; the land on which you lie I will give to you and to your descendants; and your descendants shall be like the dust of the earth, and you shall spread abroad to the west and to the east and to the north and to the south; and by you and your descendants shall all the families of the earth bless themselves. Behold, I am with you and will keep you wherever you go, and will bring you back to this land; for I will not leave you until I have done that of which I have spoken to you." Then Jacob awoke from his sleep and said, "Surely the LORD is in this place; and I did not know it." And he was afraid, and said, "How awesome is this place! This is none other than the house of God, and this is the gate of heaven." (Genesis 28:12-17, RSV)

When Jacob dreams of the ladder stretching from earth to heaven, he does not see himself eagerly ascending it, pushing his way upwards toward God. Rather, as he lies with his head on a rock, God sends angels who graciously ascend and descend on a ladder, a gateway, a ziggurat, a transformed Tower of Babel. With its base on the promised land and its top reaching up into heaven, the ladder represents God's continued presence with his people. Greedy, grasping, ambitious Jacob — who doesn't deserve the blessing he has stolen from Esau — nevertheless hears God's words of grace: "I am the LORD; I am the God of your fathers; I will give this land to you; I am with you; I will keep you wherever you go; I will bring you back." Despite Jacob's efforts to construct his own future, God promises to build up his tiny family until, one day, guileful

Jacob will become covenant Israel, and all the families of the earth will bless themselves through him and his descendants.

John highlights this promise of grace in his retelling of the Jacob's ladder story.

> Jesus saw Nathanael coming to him, and said of him, "Behold, an Israelite indeed, in whom is no guile!" Nathanael said to him, "How do you know me?" Jesus answered him, "Before Philip called you, when you were under the fig tree, I saw you." Nathanael answered him, "Rabbi, you are the Son of God! You are the King of Israel!" Jesus answered him, "Because I said to you, I saw you under the fig tree, do you believe? You shall see greater things than these." And he said to him, "Truly, truly, I say to you, you will see heaven opened, and the angels of God ascending and descending upon the Son of man." (John 1:47-51, RSV)

Jesus is gathering his disciples when he meets a skeptical Nathanael, who has declared to his friend Philip that nothing good, and certainly not a Messiah, could come from Nazareth. Perhaps with a smile on his face, Jesus takes up Nathanael's challenge. He greets him with words drenched in covenantal and messianic promise: Nathanael, you are a converted Jacob without your famous ancestor's guile or falsehood, a true Israelite whose place is under the fig tree, a symbol of God's blessing to his people.

The story piles grace upon grace. Nathanael, like Jacob, is promised a vision of God's continued covenant faithfulness, but the ladder he will see is not set up simply on the promised land but rather on the greater promised Son. And its top will not disappear into the heavens; instead Nathanael will see heaven itself opened up, the blessings of God available, through Jesus, to the whole earth.

Grace is always good news, but it is especially good news for perfectionist students and teachers who gravitate too readily towards thinking of themselves as builders. We easily wear ourselves out trying to get each brick exactly into place, only to find that our walls are askew, our mortar is lumpy, and our plumb line sags. We must be gently reminded that God himself descends to us on the ladder of his promises and carries us up into his presence; that God himself is building us into a temple not made with hands; that the new Jerusalem has only one architect — and it is not us.

"Unless the Lord builds the house, those who build it labor in vain" (Psalm 127:1, RSV).

Entering the Sanctuary

FIAT LUX! THE CLASSROOM AS CATHEDRAL

Those who have taught in windowless classrooms will understand the mood that can descend when one fluorescent light bulb begins to flicker uncontrollably. Sometimes we are granted patience, a sense of humor, and good will toward the maintenance staff. Other times our frustration and rage are out of proportion to the problem. Why, we protest, are classrooms such wretched places for learning? The concrete-block walls and worn carpet; the uncomfortable chairs; the unpredictable and sometimes overabundant heating; and so the litany goes. The spaces in which we teach often seem less than inspiring, tempting us to imagine our task in stolidly utilitarian terms.

What if instead of a dimly-lit concrete building, my classroom were a gothic cathedral? What if my students and I stood in the midst of a grand nave, or walked among the radiating chapels in the ambulatory, or sat in the presbytery with the canons singing prayers? What if my stuffy, dull classroom were an ocean of light, endlessly refracted through the prism of colored glass, reflected in the pink glow of limestone and the flash of gold and silver from the altar vessels, illuminating my students' faces as it fills their minds?

The 12th-century Abbot Suger of Saint-Denis had something like this in mind when he had carved into the wall of the newly-finished east end of his abbey church an "inscription to the glory of Light":

> With the new chevet attached to the old façade
> The heart of the sanctuary glows in splendor.
> That which is united in splendor, radiates in splendor
> And the magnificent work inundated with a new light shines.

For Suger, such a light-filled space was fitting for the Royal Abbey of France. It was a place where the celestial harmonies resounded in flesh and stone and glass, where raising your eyes to the stained glass windows raised your heart to heaven. In such a place one could meet God.

Dying fluorescent lights hardly evoke celestial harmonies, and it may seem like the most romantic of fantasies to think of our concrete-block classrooms as graceful cathedrals. But our classrooms can and should be places where we encounter God. Cathedrals focus on the incarnation, death, resurrection, and ascension of Christ. They offer a framework for learning how to approach God, how to contemplate the mystery of salvation, and how to carry about in one's own body the paradigm of faith: to come, receive, and go. Perhaps there are things we can learn for our educational spaces. Let's take a closer look.

Though built of stone and wood, the cruciform shape of the gothic cathedral is also the image of a human body with outstretched arms. The east-west axis of the great gothic cathedrals focuses worship toward Jerusalem, and through the temple of Jerusalem to the tabernacle and Mount Sinai. It is Christ's body that lies along this axis, the body that he, as high priest (Hebrews 9), gave in sacrifice to mediate a new covenant. As we enter from the west we stand at the feet of Christ, the stone carvings reminding us that we are among a great multitude, witnesses of Jesus' coming.

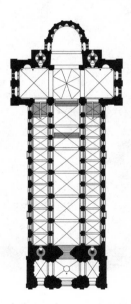

As we pass into the nave, we find ourselves engulfed in a vast space illuminated by windows that show Christ walking among us, teaching, healing, and ultimately dying, rising and ascending into heaven. Here we may come upon a great labyrinth and tread the bewildering pathways meditating on the reality of his death and burial, the harrowing of hell, and the miracle of his resurrection. We are in the very bowels of Christ, the core of his humanity. We participate in his human journey, following him as he clears a way for us through suffering toward redemption.

A little farther and we come to the transept, and then the entrance to the choir. There is a kind of embrace here, and acceptance. We are at Christ's mouth, where God speaks to us. The image is from Psalm 85:8-11.

> I will hear what God the LORD will say;
> For He will speak peace to His people, to His godly ones;
> But let them not turn back to folly.
> Surely His salvation is near to those who fear Him,
> That glory may dwell in our land.
> Lovingkindness and truth have met together;
> Righteousness and peace have kissed each other.
> Truth springs from the earth;
> And righteousness looks down from heaven. (NASB)

This is where the liturgy takes place, the psalms and prayers, the chants and responses, the reading of the Gospel, and the receiving of gifts. The prayers of the saints rise like incense to heaven, and the Word of God is heard in an endless dialogue in which the canons and choirboys are fused with the angelic host and the choir of the redeemed before the throne of the Lamb (Revelation 5).

Finally we arrive at the altar, the head of Christ, the sanctuary or Holy of Holies. It is crowned by the chevet (the radiating chapels that surround it), an image of Christ enthroned with the altar as his holy seat. Here the priest performs his sacred function under the illumination of the windows. Here we are, literally, face to face with God himself. And it is from here that we are sent out again. "Ite, missa est" ("Go forth, the Mass is ended") closes the divine office with an echo of Jesus' "Go therefore and make disciples of the nations, baptizing them in the name of the Father and the Son and the Holy Spirit, teaching them to observe all that I commanded you; and lo, I am with you always, even to the end of the age" (Matthew 28:19-20, NASB). The gothic cathedral becomes a mnemonic device as well as being a real place of encounter. It teaches that in his living body Jesus was God made flesh so that in our living bodies we might know him and worship him as our incarnate Lord.

Of course, the day-to-day reality of these vast structures was often less lofty. The cathedrals reflected the human beings who made them. Smoky with incense and candles, they bustled with all kinds of activity — even including the frequent intrusion of barking dogs — that had little or nothing to do with their intended purpose, and often functioned more as projections of the vanity of earthly rulers than images of the glory of the Savior. And they would no doubt make lousy classrooms. But for me, as I come back to the reality my students and I inhabit as learners in the 21st century, the image offers a suggestive metaphor.

What if my classroom is a cathedral? If I consciously think about my classroom in this way, I will construct the space, the syllabus, the assignments, and the daily rhythm in such a way that through all the smoke and dirt and barking dogs and fluctuating florescent lights, students encounter Christ in my course and grow in their understanding of what his life and death means for them. The Nicene Creed confesses that Christ "for us and for our salvation came down and was incarnate and was made man." For us. A cathedral-classroom points away from us toward Christ, but a Christ who became flesh for us. Christ comes to us in the dirt and flickering light of our own lives, but he also comes to lift us up.

Many students (and teachers) confine worship, the sacred space of the classroom, to an opening prayer or the recitation of a Bible verse or perhaps collective singing. Such moments can be precious and can turn students' faces toward God in ways that unconsciously shape what they are learning that day. But the point of progressing through a cathedral in worship is to be conscious of what we are doing and becoming at every moment of the day: to enter at the feet of Christ; to walk with Jesus as he ministers to both rich and poor, Jew and Gentile, the powerful and the outcast; to listen as God speaks to us and to utter our own responses; to be reminded of our sin and God's salvation; to be sent back into the world as witnesses to God's creating and redeeming power. Turning our classrooms into cathedrals unites the space of worship with the space of educational formation.

Seeing this unity can give rise to fresh practices. Cheryl teaches introduction to sociology and has collected a selection of Scripture texts that address questions of poverty, equity, justice, and charity. Each week, she integrates some of these texts, clustered around a theme, into the topic under discussion. She also, however, invites students to join her for twenty minutes every Thursday afternoon to read through these Scripture texts together. And every week students show up at her office, read the Bible aloud, and then quietly leave. They don't discuss the Scripture passages; they don't apply them; they just read them communally. Of course, during their class sessions they've also talked about the meaning and significance of the prophets inveighing against wealthy landowners or Jesus' blessing of a cup of cold water given in his name. Somewhat to their surprise, students find that the practice of reading aloud cements the texts into their lives and memories in ways that class discussion alone could not achieve. Class discussion informed by Scripture and the practice of slow, deliberate, communal reading draw worship and formation together in richly embodied ways. They have been learning, we might say, how to walk through the cathedral.

What if my classroom, fluorescent lights and all, were a gothic cathedral, an ocean of light, a place to learn to walk with Jesus, to come, receive, and be sent forth?

CATHEDRAL BUILDERS

Now far from the classroom, huddled out on the street in the midst of a cold German winter, I stand with a group of students on a bitterly cold New Year's Eve looking at what seems to be a large, abstract sculpture. Knobby florets of stone radiate out from a central cone, the whole object looming stolidly over us, almost ten meters high. I ask the students what they think it is. There are a few wild guesses. I explain that it is a life-size replica of one of the finials perched at the very tips of the twin spires of Köln cathedral, which towers just behind us. We turn and squint upward. Way up there, a hundred and fifty meters in the air, we can make out little angular protrusions atop each spire, tiny against the sky. We look back at the one hulking beside us, and start to grasp how high the cathedral actually is.

I talk some more about the building of the cathedral, how it started in 1238, came to a halt in 1473, and was eventually completed in 1880. How its spires are the second tallest in the world. How it was used as a warehouse for a time after the French Revolution, and survived fourteen bomb impacts during the Second World War. We have already wandered around inside, admiring the stained glass windows and the solemnity of the vast interior space. Now, as we stand looking back at the building, I invite them to imagine having the audacity to think one could build such a thing, especially without modern machinery.

What role does time play here? What would you have to believe about the world, I ask, how would you have to see your life to be able to labor at a building project that makes the notion of completion in your lifetime not just unrealistic but amusing? Could *we* muster the motivation, the sheer attention span, to work diligently at something that would not be completed until our great grandchildren are historical footnotes?

How about the carvings? Consider the people who carved the myriads of saints, kings, gargoyles, and small, decorative flourishes that bedeck the building from floor to finial. Suppose you worked on the roof, pouring your effort and skill into details invisible from the ground in an age devoid of helicopters. How would you have to understand the value of your labor to be able to work away for years at something that only you and God would ever see?

What about all the details? What would be precious enough to us that once we started ornamenting its house we would feel no impulse to stop at the point when we had done enough? Precious enough that we would want to pursue detail after detail until the details outstripped our ability to hold them all in our vision? Consider the doors, not just the impressive bronze doors that face the outside world but the many smaller doors inside, each hand-crafted, no two of them alike. How would you have to grasp the world for it to seem necessary to you that each new task be given special character and unique attention?

Even before we get to the specifically theological symbolism in the architecture, the building preaches to us, as the great churches were meant to do. It asks us about how we are building, the manner in which we grasp our own callings, the work we will leave behind us. It asks us what we might need to learn about ourselves, what kinds of persons we might need to become, in order to be capable of working at enduring things. It asks us about how we might need to grow if we are to build things that matter. If we were building a cathedral together, how then would we learn?

LABYRINTHS AND MAZES

We step back inside. On the floor in the nave of Chartres cathedral is the most famous labyrinth in the world. The labyrinth, or more properly the unicursal labyrinth, is not a maze, something good for an afternoon of fun in an English garden or an American cornfield but also charged with undertones of danger and fear. A maze incorporates dead ends and wrong turns. It may deceive you.

If you choose wrongly, you will seem to make progress for a while, but soon enough you'll find yourself at a dead end — or worse.

In classical mythology, what awaits you at the center of a maze, after all the hassle of retracing your steps and finally, finally finding the right path, is the raging Minotaur, part bull and part man, who fully intends to gore you to death. In a modern retelling of the Minotaur myth, the portkey at the center of the maze takes Harry Potter directly to Lord Voldemort.

It doesn't take much imagination to realize that for many students a new course often appears to them like a dreaded maze. This is particularly true of general education or required "core" courses that seem to lie entirely outside their natural interests or abilities. In such a course, a student may feel as if she is constantly making mistakes, constantly bumping up against dead ends, constantly faced with impossible choices, constantly in danger of being fed to the Minotaur or Lord Voldemort. In such a course, a student may feel overwhelmed with anxiety.

An anxious student cannot learn well, which is why it may help her to think of the course as a labyrinth. A labyrinth, unlike a maze, has no wrong turns and no dead ends.

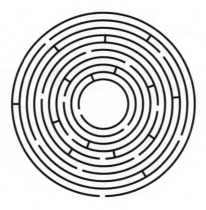

In a labyrinth you follow a single, designated path, designed with many twists and turns. Often you seem to be back-tracking; often you seem lost. From where you are standing at any given moment, you cannot see exactly how the path will take you to the center of labyrinth. But if you persevere, if you stay inside the labyrinth and refuse the temptations of abandoning the path or stepping outside the lines to look for a shortcut, eventually you will arrive at the center.

One of our colleagues uses the structure of the labyrinth to help non-science students navigate the demands of a required physics course. At the beginning of the semester, Matt talks with students about the famous labyrinth at Chartres Cathedral. He explains that its circular path, marked out in stone on the cathedral floor, welcomes worshippers into contemplative prayer as they make their way slowly along the designated path to the center of the labyrinth. He then gives each student the figure of a labyrinth printed on heavy card stock as part of their class packet and invites them to use it to trace their progress through the semester.

Some students develop the habit of using their labyrinth as a "worry stone," tracing a finger over the pattern when they become stressed or overwhelmed with a complicated assignment. Others write in key concepts as landmarks to show their progress through the class. The professor himself frequently refers to the labyrinth, particularly when a stretch of lessons seem to be moving in the wrong direction: "Trust me; soon we'll make a turn and you'll see how all of this material fits together."

Although the labyrinth metaphor can be reassuring to students, the maze metaphor too can speak of more than fear. Not all mazes harbor a Minotaur or Lord Voldemort at their centers, but mazes do present us with real choices, some of which lead to dead ends. Students like assignments that are linear, efficient, and closed-ended. But those are not always the assignments from which they learn the most.

There may be no better way to learn about the consequences of initial assumptions or framing questions, for instance, than to follow them out rigorously to their logical conclusions. In a classroom students can make bad, or at least less than optimal, choices without necessarily developing bad habits. The classroom offers an appropriate place to play "what if" games, to engage the puzzle of a maze, to make mistakes. We might occasionally say to students, "Today let's enter a maze. Here you are at X. What is the next step in this argument, and the next, and the next? Now evaluate where you are: are you at a dead end? Have you been gobbled up by the Minotaur? Can you retrace your steps, change an assumption or an argument, and make better progress?"

If the image of a labyrinth can reassure anxious students that they are on the right path, that all their effort and perseverance will eventually bring them safely home, then the image of the maze can encourage students to try out new ideas, to make mistakes, to venture into complicated arguments, to take risks. Both metaphors, used wisely, can be part of our pedagogical toolkit.

ABIDING IN THE ABBEYS

Cathedrals, with their naves, spires, and labyrinths, are not the only sacred places in the Christian landscape. Abbeys, as places of teaching and learning, are also marked off as sacred sites. Perhaps none is as well-known as Iona Abbey, off the West Coast of Scotland, one of the oldest sites of higher education in the English-speaking world.

Founded in the sixth century by St. Columba and his twelve companion monks, Iona Abbey served as a center of Christian learning, piety, and evangelism through the mid-sixteenth century. Its importance as a place of pilgrimage and worship was restored by the Iona Community in the 1930s. While it might be tempting to think of abbeys in general, and Iona Abbey in particular, merely as nostalgic remnants of medieval Christendom, for centuries they stood as the only houses of scholarship and learning, home to society's best educated men and women, nurseries for educating the young, the repository of the West's best libraries. Abbeys too can teach us, particularly about sustaining Christian educational institutions over the long haul.

The abbey was a community of persons bound together by promises to a common life. *Community* was not here a soft, unaccountable niceness toward one another, nor was it the ultimate goal of the institution — that would be a mark of groups that had lost sight of their vocation and had instead turned inward toward self-preservation. Rather "community" here meant *living a common life*, common in its schedule, its curriculum, its framework for decision making, its sense of ultimate reality, its fundamental priorities, even its literal ownership of resources. Community extended to leadership: abbeys were organized under the supervision of an abbot (from Aramaic, "father") or an abbess, usually elected by the members.

Public, voluntary, binding vows sealed a common life and common convictions, but these very vows allowed the community to be fearlessly open to learners, pilgrims, those in need of physical care, and even hostile visitors. The foundations of the common life were secured by these vows; the lineaments that bound the community together could not be severed, so abbeys could offer a radical hospitality. They were places of refuge as well as places of learning.

What would it mean today for the members of a school to imitate abbey life, to live a radically hospitable common life rather than simply living in proximity to one another on a college campus? What rituals would bind them into a community, and how might these rituals move them toward moral formation and maturity? If we look critically at the most powerful rituals that now bind our campuses together, do they promote maturity or do they prolong immaturity? What would a healthy and intentionally Christian set of rituals or common rhythms or even vows look like for 21st-century students?

Members of the abbey community also lived in partial seclusion. Today, schools and universities are under some pressure to be "engaged and relevant," especially for fundraising purposes. But traditionally the calling of scholars and students had some honored independence from the immediate, pragmatic concerns that constantly direct attention to the passing, the vulgar, and the remunerative. What would it mean for schools and colleges today to resist the urge to be relevant and transformative and engaged in "changing the world?" Might we assign more contemplative tasks outside class, or guide students to consider how their time is invested? Would we reward faculty for contemplative activities?

In addition, abbeys usually followed some "Rule" for common life. This rule called for an ordered communal life that followed a rhythm of physical work, scholarship, and prayer (which punctuated the work day at roughly three-hour intervals), though some orders incorporated "lay brothers" who specialized in physical labor as others concentrated on prayer and learning. Abbeys were thus places of both work and rest, of attention to body and spirit, of learning and teaching, of general revelation and special revelation, of prayer and action. Now rare, this seamless, holistic conception of life provides a context for intentional scholarship and learning. Would it be possible today to shape a school or college that functions as the organizing framework for the whole of one's learning and living?

Such holistic ordering was what abbeys envisioned for the novices they received and trained. What could Christian education learn from the apprenticeship model? Apprentices are built up, formed, molded after the likeness of a master teacher. These construction metaphors play readily into our current interest in foundational virtues, the formation of students, the development of spiritual and intellectual disciplines, and the cultivation of practices. This apprenticeship model intimately links heart and hand in the honored monastic tradition of *ora* and *labora*. But as Rebecca Konyndyk DeYoung points out in *Glittering Vices*, an emphasis on virtue formation can also all too easily displace the centrality of grace in our lives. "Work out your own salvation with fear and trembling," the Apostle Paul commands us, "for God is at work in you, both to will and to work for his good pleasure" (Philippians 2:12-13). This blessed balance of work and grace, modeled in the weekly Sabbath rhythm and the abbey's daily hours of prayer aptly sums up the whole of the Christian life and with it, the whole of Christian learning and teaching.

The monks and nuns lived out this balance of work and grace, and, as they did so, created beauty. Life, however frugal, was never ground down to ugliness. We probably pay too little attention today to the aesthetic dimensions of our syllabi, our assignments, our practices in the classroom. But beauty, says Simone Weil, is one of the few things in this world that pushes our clamoring self aside, decenters our ego, and stops us in our tracks. What do we do when we see something that we intuitively know to be beautiful? We catch our breath, then we look around for someone to share the moment. Beauty turns us away from ourselves and toward others; it inspires longing for God. Experiencing the beauty of the world, says Weil, creates in us a hunger to know the truest beauty of a human face, a hunger that can only ultimately be satisfied by Christ. God gives us beauties so that we may come to know Beauty. So what might it mean if we patterned our work after God's beautiful creation and asked of all our endeavors: "Is this beautiful? Is it ugly?" Might that simple question make us more skeptical of merely utilitarian assignments, of busyness, of checklists and boxed answers? Perhaps we could foster an alertness to those practices in the classroom that would lure our students away from their devices and entice them to lift up their heads and murmur — ah! If so, we might be closer to re-establishing an abbey in our own places of learning.

Setting Up House

WISDOM HAS BUILT HER HOUSE

One afternoon as we sat around a table drinking tea, munching cookies, and talking about metaphors and education, we made a disconcerting discovery. We were thinking that day about buildings and about how Christians have imagined the role of the liberal arts in higher education. We began by looking at this picture, which is found in the 12th century *Hortus Deliciarum*, the Garden of Delight, an encyclopedia or compendium of knowledge conceived for the instruction and spiritual edification of the Augustinian nuns in a convent in Alsace run by the abbess Herrad of Landsberg.

Wisdom, Lady Philosophy, sits serenely in the house she has constructed, a house that resembles the beautiful rose windows illuminating medieval cathedrals. Beneath her are Socrates and Plato, the acknowledged masters of secular learning, but the scroll in Wisdom's hands puts the work of these classical philosophers into its proper context. Quoting Sirach (Ecclesiasticus) 1:1, it reads, "All wisdom comes from God; only the wise can do whatever they desire." Around Wisdom are arrayed the seven liberal arts (beginning at the top and going clockwise: grammar, rhetoric, logic, music, arithmetic, geometry, astronomy). Each stands gracefully inside a pillared arcade, and these together visually depict Proverbs 9:1: "Wisdom has built her house; she has set up its seven pillars." Excluded from the rose window, but still included within the compendium of knowledge, are four representatives of the "impure poets" who invent fictitious tales.

The three heads in Lady Philosophy's crown represent the classical division of philosophy into ethics, logic, and metaphysics. Seven fountains of wisdom flow from her body. The inscription on her right reads, "The Holy Spirit is the inventor of the seven liberal arts," and is followed by a list of their names. This links the classical liberal arts with the seven gifts of the Holy Spirit as found in Isaiah 11:2-3: wisdom, understanding, right judgement, fortitude, knowledge, piety, and fear of the Lord.

The design itself tells the viewer that learning is both an integral part of God's house and a task that requires active discernment, particularly on the part of the teacher. The inscription in the outer ring of the rose window explains "the proper sequence of scholarly exercises: first to investigate, then to explain the investigation, to confirm it in writing, and finally to teach it to the pupils."

That afternoon, as we contemplated this illustration, we reflected on the kind of education it portrayed. The design is ordered and symmetrical, but not static or linear. It is inviting rather than forbidding, beckoning us into elegant, charming company. We, the learners, are invited to enter the picture through whichever archway most pleases us. We are promised that if we enter this house of learning and become wise, we can do "whatever we desire." We are invited to drink from, or perhaps play in, the fountains of wisdom that flow out from the central figure and to enter into conversation with the seven beautiful liberal arts. Even the excluded fictions, penned by the figures at the bottom, are still encompassed within the total design, suggesting that they can be redeemed. The evocation of the rose window lends a sense of the holy to the enterprise of learning, and a suggestion of a gentle light entering into our midst. The subjects themselves, however, are the things of this world, lit up rather than replaced by the light beyond the window. The text of the inner circle puts these words into the mouth of wisdom: "I the divine philosophy, wisely govern all things. Through the seven arts, which are subordinate to me, I study the underlying nature of all things."

We chatted happily for a while about this wisdom-centered curriculum, not oblivious to its limitations of time and place but charmed by its vision of all learning embedded within a sacred space and embodied in the disciplined practices of the seven liberal arts. Finally we sat back, refreshed and delighted with our vocation as teachers. Then we clicked to the next PowerPoint slide, to an image that has been used in the recent past to represent the curriculum of our own institution.

The contrast was shocking. An intricate rose window in a great cathedral had given way to a schematic drawing of what looks uncannily like a power turbine. The word "core" in this picture conjures up images of a nuclear reactor, or perhaps a magnetic coil, or a sample of rock drilled out of a geologic formation. The visual appeal is, however, negligible, and the image suggests rigidity more than dynamism, playfulness, or joy.

As we recovered from the abrupt aesthetic shift we gained some perspective. The rose window is not perfect. It could suggest a failure to honor the secular, a banishing to a less welcome outside space of those disciplines and aspects of learning not part of the "sacred" cluster in the middle. It may well be too arcane and allegorical to serve well as online guidance for students contemplating programs. And the core diagram has its virtues. It's clean and clear and efficient; the varied classes are connected to one another rather than simply segregated into a list; and there is a sense of progression from the Gateway to the Capstone. The design exudes a reassuring stability and solidity; at the same time we were confident that Calvin College's education is much more vibrant than the image might imply.

Our concern in the end was not that one image was in a straightforward sense better than the other. What troubled us was that the only sacred allusion with our more recent image is a disembodied tag line that references a God and a world neither of which are integral to the image. It concerned us that the image carried no human context, showed no tradition or company of saints into which the learner is being invited. Compared to the earlier image, this one was flat, impersonal, and pragmatic. We soberly wondered how generative this image might have become in our imagination and that of our students: did it encourage us to think of our core courses as mechanical and self-contained, with God and the world as framing references rather than central realities? Did it reinforce our students' tendency to want to "get core out of the way?"

Confronting these two pictures made us ask what kind of building we ought to imagine for our curriculum. What image would more creatively and accurately and evocatively answer these questions: What is the content of learning and how does one visualize this content? How should learning be ordered, divided and subdivided? How and by what is it held together? What illuminates it and brings it to life? Are there hierarchies? What do you put on the bottom and on the top? Does it show progression, a path of development that a learner must follow? Into what kind of company is the learner invited? What is the goal of the whole enterprise? What, in fact and not just in theory, makes our curriculum truly Christian?

CONSTRUCTING A PEDAGOGICAL HOUSE

Images of the house of wisdom challenge us think pedagogically about the literal, physical spaces in which learning happens. A fair amount of attention is being given these days to the ways in which we organize and arrange our classroom spaces. Particularly in elementary and secondary schooling, but increasingly in tertiary education as well, we have begun to think more about how the set-up of chairs, the amount of light, the aesthetics of wall displays, or the sounds that greet students as they enter the room either motivate or detract from the teaching and learning we hope to accomplish that day. The space constructed for learning can affect how learning unfolds in various ways. Might it help us to think in the same way about the plans that we make for organizing what is to be taught? What if we think about the kinds of spaces or buildings that our syllabi or curricula resemble?

When students come to our school, are they treated like customers in the marketplace of ideas? That might seem to be an entirely negative image, feeding directly into our consumerist culture, especially if we imagine the school as a mall where manipulated consumers restrict their attention to what immediately titillates. But there are other ways to play with the metaphor. As responsible consumers, do students find that Christian learning slows them down in important ways, helps them to examine the product labels, and thus make more discerning choices amidst all the products on offer? Do they begin to consider where products came from, the respect due to their makers, or the ripple effects of buying them? Imagine, for instance, a business or marketing class that uses the metaphor of "reading the labels" to help students interrogate the specific ingredients that go into certain accounting, or managing, or advertising practices. Such a class would not only critique shoddy practices, but would also take seriously its Christian calling to both consume and produce more healthy, just products.

Or consider the learning space as an exercise room. Again, we could dismiss this as sweaty, repetitive and mindless, or we could push in other directions. For what purposes and with what technologies do our students exercise their minds, bodies, and imaginations? Does it matter if we exercise our bodies primarily on indoor machines or out of doors? One of our colleagues, a kinesiology professor, insists that students learn to run outside in every sort of weather, because he wants running to be, among other things, an exercise in displacing our own comfort from the center of our lives. The goal is to embrace all that God has made — including (in many places) rain, sleet, and ice. What metaphorical ways of thinking about learning might exercise evoke?

Or change the image again to one of home: Do our students experience our classrooms as homey and welcoming? If so, why might "safe" and "home" be appropriate words to describe education? Is there a time and a place where it is appropriate to make unsafe and uncomfortable classrooms? And furthermore, if students experience their classroom as a home, is it a house in the suburb? An apartment in the city? A flat in another country? A hotel room? Do we encourage them to think of themselves as homeowners, renters, guests, or tourists? What specific practices are in place in the classroom that create home-like relationships and roles?

BUILDING STORY HOUSES

One way to think more richly about our classrooms, curricula, syllabi, and daily pedagogical decisions is to imagine that we are constructing with our students intricate story houses. Our teaching/learning encounters build a place that we inhabit together and a dynamic narrative that gives that place a particular kind of life. The shape of a class over a semester or a year takes on the dimensions of both place and story.

Sometimes we think of stories simply as pleasant, direct, and efficient means to an end — *exempla*, people in the medieval world would have called them. The plot begins here and ends there, and we walk away with a useful nugget of wisdom. A moment's reflection, however, reminds us that the stories we best love resemble more a house with fascinating hallways and odd little rooms and a kitchen with an old Aga stove, a house where you can hide from your mother's voice and curl up with another good book, a house that becomes its own little world. When we think of stories as houses we enter, recognizing how multi-layered and three-dimensional they are, they invite us to wander about. They surprise us, shaping our feelings and imagination as well as our ideas and beliefs. We are reminded, in other words, that stories are powerful precisely because they are neither efficient nor linear.

What if we thought of our classes as sacred story-houses, as narrative places that students inhabit for a semester and that shape not only their minds but also their moral imaginations? We might then ask ourselves how we lure students beyond the hallway to take up residence in our class, to linger and return. What texts, what assignments, what questions, what gestures and images might help students activate their moral imaginations? Or conversely, how is the architecture of our class already shaping their moral imaginations, perhaps in ways that we don't intend?

In this regard, I was drawn up short a few semesters after I began teaching when a student asked, "Why do we only read depressing stories in this class?"

"Because they're good literature," I sighed, without thinking.

Later that night, however, I reconsidered the question and my flippant answer. Why was I so confident that the literature I had studied and now taught was "good?" Good for whom? Good for what? Good for how long? I had fallen into the trap of believing that "good" was a self-defining category. Of course, I told myself, good literature was "difficult," "realistic," or at best "ambiguous"; my academic guild, not to mention dozens of anthologies, told me so. Consequently, I had not given much thought to whether the story-house I was constructing with my students that semester was safe and healthy, as well as challenging. Was the ongoing narrative of our class, shaped by our readings and discussions, actually good for students in any deep and lasting way?

Although the question "Why do we only read depressing stories in this class?" was, at one level, sophomoric (as befitted a second-year college student), it also named a real fear: "What kind of a person will I be at the end of this semester?" While I could argue that the richest stories and the most memorable houses are layered and suggestive — even a minimalist story or house gains power from the negative space it invokes — and that therefore we should read complex literature that could stimulate our moral imagination, I had no good reason to argue that complexity resides *only* in depressing stories. When I took a closer look at the architecture of my syllabi, I recognized how much of what I taught could be categorized as "smart" rather than "wise," "accepted in the Academy" rather than genuinely "good." It was time to repent, to look with a fresh eye at the stories I assigned, and change my syllabi.

BUILDING WELL

> Therefore everyone who hears these words of mine and puts them into practice is like a wise man who built his house on the rock. The rain came down, the streams rose, and the winds blew and beat against that house; yet it did not fall, because it had its foundation on the rock. But everyone who hears these words of mine and does not put them into practice is like a foolish man who built his house on sand. The rain came down, the streams rose, and the winds blew and beat against that house, and it fell with a great crash. (Matthew 7:24-27, TNIV)

Jesus' words about wise and foolish builders should ring in our ears when we imagine teaching as building. Bad building punctuates the Christian story, in this parable as in the Old Testament image of the Tower of Babel. This tower was erected not in a search for wisdom, but rather in a quest "to make a name for ourselves."

In this etching of the Tower of Babel, angels with trumpets from Revelation 14 bring apocalyptic destruction from heaven. Laborers and leaders alike try to flee and are smashed by falling debris. In the foreground the king lies half dead, hit by a column. The foolish tower turns out to have been erected on sand rather than on the rock of hearing and doing the word of God.

The cautionary tales of the wise and foolish builders and the Tower of Babel should unsettle any too-confident use we might make of the building metaphor. We talk about learning as laying a foundation, erecting a body of knowledge, and scaffolding student learning. We think of students as entering on the ground floor and climbing towards success; we encourage upward mobility as we award grades that lead to scholarships, letters of recommendation, and access to graduate school and jobs. The Bible, however, greets these ambitions with tales of warning.

Think for a moment about the building projects in the first few chapters of Genesis. In Genesis 4, Cain builds a city during his wife's first pregnancy; in Genesis 6 God commands Noah to build an ark; and in Genesis 11 the men of Shinar decide to build a city with a tower "that reaches to the heavens." In all three instances, buildings promise stability and safety, marking out a location that I can call "mine." Cain builds after being told by God that he will be a restless wanderer. The men of Shinar build "that we may make a name for ourselves and not be scattered over the face of the whole earth." Buildings make us feel secure, and buildings clustered together within a wall evoke both security and power. The ancient Near East epic of Gilgamesh is framed at beginning and end by such a boast: "Study the brickwork, study the fortification; climb the great ancient staircase to the terrace. . . . This is Uruk, the city of Gilgamesh, the Wild Ox."

But sandwiched between the cities of Cain and Shinar in the book of Genesis is another building, an ark. It is not a symbol of power, or even stability. It is merely a boat, a temporary shelter soon to be abandoned when the flood recedes. Yet this boat offers more security than Cain's city or the men of Shinar's tower or Gilgamesh's brick-bound Uruk. The ark anticipates the psalmist's praise, "God is my refuge and my strength," by pointing away from itself to the God who orders and designs it.

The ark is a building; Noah must cut down cypress wood, boil up tar, and construct a big boat on dry land. The ark offers Noah and his family a physical home for nearly a year. But the ark does not save Noah and his family; God's promise saves them. God promised Eve that one of her descendants would

crush the serpent's head. God promised Noah that he would be that descen-
dent through whom God's covenant would pass. The ark — that little building
bobbing on the flood waters — is merely the means to the future carried in
those promises.

This essential contrast between human building and God's building, the
human city and the city of God as Augustine would later call them, runs
throughout the biblical narrative. When God settles on the family of Abraham
to be those through whom he will bless all nations, he keeps them living in
tents for four generations and then sends them into exile in Egypt for another
four hundred years. No permanent buildings or cities for them.

Even when God's people finally enter the Promised Land, they hear the
repeated refrain that they will live in cities they did not build and houses they
did not construct. They will still need to depend upon God and be grateful
to him; God, not buildings or cities, remains their only refuge, fortress, and
strength. Immediately after the great Shema in the book of Deuteronomy,
"Hear, O Israel: The LORD our God, the LORD is one. Love the LORD your
God with all your heart and with all your soul and with all your strength," the
people are warned: "When the LORD your God brings you into the land he
swore to your fathers, to Abraham, Isaac and Jacob, to give you — a land with
large, flourishing cities you did not build, houses filled with all kinds of good
things you did not provide, wells you did not dig, and vineyards and olive
groves you did not plant — then when you eat and are satisfied, be careful that
you do not forget the LORD, who brought you out of Egypt, out of the land
of slavery" (Deuteronomy 6:4-5, 10-12). The Israelites — and we ourselves —
are asked to think about this question: Do we think of buildings as places that
solidify and protect our own interests or as places where we may dwell, open
to God's purposes?

We do need physical places to live, rest, find refuge, and worship, yet in
the biblical narrative these remain temporary, pragmatic, and insubstantial in
light of God's presence. We see this clearly in the biblical places of worship.
Even before the tabernacle is built, God reveals himself to Jacob in a dream,
through a ladder that connects heaven to earth. In contrast to the sturdiness of
Babel's tower, this ladder, which appears repeatedly in the Christian tradition,
is marked not as a monument but as a pathway. It pictures a dynamic link,
prefiguring both Christ as Way and the petition, "Your will be done, on earth
as it is in heaven."

The tabernacle itself — a tent that sits in the center of the tents housing the Israelites on their wilderness journey — speaks of God's presence but does not contain him. When David wants to build a permanent house for God — why should I live in a palace and my God dwell in a tent, he muses — God acquiesces, but turns David's attention from the house the king will build for God to the house God himself will build, the lineage of the Messiah. "House" here puns nicely on the concept of a building and a family dynasty; the latter will long outlast the former. And in one of the festive events of the Jewish liturgical year, Sukkot, it is tabernacles or temporary "booths" made of willows, palm trees, and thin sticks that are built to commemorate Israel's wilderness wanderings and God's guiding presence.

Old Testament images of impermanent buildings — ladders, tabernacles, temples, booths — tumble into the New Testament, finding their fulfillment in the incarnated God. Jesus, says the Gospel writer, is the Word who has tabernacled among us (John 1:14). Jesus is the ladder upon which the angels ascend and descend to God (John 1:51). Jesus' own body is the temple (John 2:19-21). He is the stone the builders rejected (Luke 20:17). On the mountain of transfiguration, Peter catches a glimpse of God's glory in Christ and cries out, "Let's build booths and stay here" (Luke 9:33), a classic misunderstanding of the Messiah's mission, although what it does get right is that Jesus is the culmination of tabernacle imagery. The Apostles Peter and Paul conjoin temple and body images to speak of Jews and Gentiles together as the living stones that God is using to build his own church.

The living stones image reminds us just how radically the biblical text shifts the metaphor of building from inert, powerful structure to dynamic process. Buildings themselves may serve as emblems of foolish pride — Babel, Nineveh, Babylon or even faithless Jerusalem — or as icons through which we experience the presence of God himself. When the temple functioned properly, it brought the Israelites face to face first with their own sin and then with God's gracious provision of salvation. When the temple became merely a place for nationalistic pride, Jesus quickly denounced it: "And as some spoke of the temple, how it was adorned with noble stones and offerings, he said, 'As for these things which you see, the days will come when there shall not be left here one stone upon another that will not be thrown down'" (Luke 21:5-6, RSV).

Human ingenuity and responsibility find their proper place within the larger context of God's providence: Noah builds the ark according to the

Lord's instruction; Bezalel builds the tabernacle according to the Lord's detailed plans; Ezekiel's cubed temple could never be built of human materials; and although the Apostle Paul calls himself an "expert builder," he says so in the context of building up the body of Christ (1 Corinthians 3:9-10). As the Psalm so well summarizes: "Unless the LORD builds the house, its builders labor in vain" (Psalm 127:1). Although this verse carries a warning to those of us who think of ourselves as teacher-builders, it also brings us encouragement and hope. We do work hard to be good teachers. We do want our students to grow strong and tall. But as we mix the mortar, and lay our stones, and drop the plumb line each day, we can be confident that God is building a better house than we can even imagine.

The Classroom as Household

We conclude, then, with a reflection on the house that the Lord builds and on the ancient structure of the *oikia.*

The Greek word *oikia* has several meanings. It can simply mean *house,* that is, a structure used as a dwelling place. It can also mean the social unit or *family* that lives in the house, the *estate* of a well-to-do or landed family, or the whole *clan,* including descendants, along with their house and property.

The New Testament repeatedly uses this word *oikia* to refer to God's new community, established by Christ. In fact, the New Testament is brimming with references to the "household of God," with comments about believers as "brothers and sisters" or "fellow heirs" in that household, and with stories about stewards of households *(oikonómos,* "household law," from which we get *economist).* The apostles present themselves as foundation stones or door-slaves for this new household, and talk about the church as the bride of the householder. The New Testament church is reported to have frequently met *en oíkois,* in household-churches. The epistles even contain several explicit "household codes" (e.g., Ephesians 5:21–6:11; Colossians 3:18–4:1; 1 Peter 2:13–3:33) that follow the outline of rulebooks for the ordering of households in the surrounding culture. In other words, for the early church *household* was a primary metaphor for the place and manner by which new persons and communities are formed, from which the world is changed. *Household* was the place where people were educated to become Christians.

What is particularly helpful for us to see, however, are the ways in which Christian households, and especially the household of the church, differed from the general conception of household in the Roman Empire. If you wanted to know how to run a household in the first century, you would turn to Aristotle's *Politics* (as redacted for Caesar Augustus by Arius Didymus), in which *oikia* is presented as the fundamental building-block of a rightly-ordered culture. For Aristotle, when the household is rightly organized it joins different parts into a creative tension: male and female, slave and free, child and parent. Individuals by themselves cannot form the basis for civilization, because no one person can adequately embody these creative tensions. And besides that, individuals are fundamentally unlike each other: free men are marked out from the moment of their birth to have deliberative and leadership capacities; other men are marked out from the start to be slaves by nature, and it would be unnatural if they were not the slaves of free men. Women too cannot function as free men do, because they lack the ability to deliberate.

Well-organized households then come together to form a larger unit, the *polis* or state, which is simply the community of these free households. The natural leaders of households and states are men, and their word is law. The *paterfamilias,* the estate father who rules an extended family may not be taken to court, because he is assumed to represent the *oikia* in court. Family members are considered extensions of his body; he may, for example, order a wife to abandon a newborn to die. Thus, in Aristotle's natural and well-functioning culture, husband rules wife and wife obeys husband; father rules child and child obeys father; master rules slave and slave obeys master.

But when the New Testament writers take over the idea of the household as their primary metaphor to describe Christians in community, they quietly subvert Aristotle's "natural" order. The explicit family codes, for example, are addressed not only to deliberation-capable free males (the audience of Aristotle's codes), but to each member of the household in turn — wives, slaves, husbands, children. The New Testament codes speak of mutual submission, and frequently begin each section with "in the same way . . ." as if a universal code beyond cultural household roles is being invoked. And, of course, the Apostles place themselves into this social order as the doorkeeper slaves, not as the ruling *paterfamilias,* whereas the brand new converts they are teaching are addressed not as young children or as slaves, but rather as full sons and heirs of the Father.

It is worth pondering these two conceptions of the formative *oikia* — Aristotle's top-down hierarchy and Scripture's model of service and adoption — when we think about our own classrooms. A "natural" Aristotelian model suggests that teachers are inherently different from students — not just that they have different roles, but that their very natures are alien to one another. A student is, by nature, inferior, an "empty vessel" who should unquestionably accept the designs of his superiors.

The New Testament, by contrast, presents a well-ordered household of formation not as a tyrant's dream, nor as a free-form unordered experiment, but as a place where authority is expressed through service, everyone is a deliberative and resourceful agent, the Spirit of God works in and through each, and the formation of the person takes precedence over nominal lines of power and honor.

Consider chapters 18-20 of Matthew's gospel. Chapter 18 opens with the disciples' question: Who gets to be the *paterfamilias* in Jesus' kingdom? Jesus answers by *calling a child* and naming that child as the model citizen in his kingdom. Everyone must emulate the child, particularly in the child's humility, and anyone who causes such a marginalized one to fall is subject to judgment. Chapter 19 is then organized as a household code — teaching on husband/wife, parent/child, and master/slave relationships — in which again children figure prominently: it is to such as these that the kingdom of heaven belongs. By the end of this section, however, the disciples appear to have learned nothing. They are still arguing about which of them will be *paterfamilias* (20:24-28), and Jesus' reply is telling: "You know that the rulers of the Gentiles lord it over them, but *it will not be so among you*; rather whoever wishes to be great among you must be your servant."

What does Matthew tell us about a gospel model for formation and teaching? We call learners together (18:2; 19:14; 20:25). We never look down on students (18:10; 19:14; 20:26-27). We serve learners extravagantly in a way that brings blessing (18:13; 19:15; 20:28). The householder expresses leadership by stooping to wash feet, touching the unclean, holding the door open for the newcomer. This sort of household can form persons to take their place in God's new community. This is the sort of household that our classrooms ought to become.

"Let Evening Come"

Let the light of late afternoon
shine through chinks in the barn, moving
up the bales as the sun moves down.

Let the cricket take up chafing
as a woman takes up her needles
and her yarn. Let evening come.

Let dew collect on the hoe abandoned
in long grass. Let the stars appear
and the moon disclose her silver horn.

Let the fox go back to its sandy den.
Let the wind die down. Let the shed
go black inside. Let evening come.

To the bottle in the ditch, to the scoop
In the oats, to air in the lung
let evening come.

Let it come, as it will, and don't
be afraid. God does not leave us
comfortless, so let evening come.

— Jane Kenyon

An Ending, An Invitation

WE'VE COME TO THE END of our journey together. We have sailed and galloped and driven and circled and rested and sung and trudged. We have no doubt found some parts of the journey tedious, best forgotten, and others more memorable. We have paused to break bread together and to pay attention to those with whom we travel. We have joined the communion of saints on their pilgrimages. As we progressed in hope through the wilderness; we have looked for signs of it becoming a garden of delight. We have kept an eye open for beauty, for signs of flourishing, for community and justice. We have looked for teaching to be more than foraging, and pondered what it is that we are actually building, what walls we need to put up or tear down and kind of community they will sustain. We have wondered how to move from trying to lay foundations impervious to the tremors of God in history to building pedagogy as worship, as a space where light might enter and bring alive stories of life abundant.

We have not exhausted the biblical and theological metaphors that have been married to teaching and learning across time or that might continue to vivify what we do. We have not sought to narrate a comprehensive history, but rather to spend time unfolding a few core images. We have wanted to make these metaphors less trite, less worn and faded, more resonant with possibility. Our wanting has, no doubt, exceeded our ability, but we hope that we have provided some fruitful starting points, some openings into which you have peered, some quiet corners where your own imagination can flourish.

In all of this we have been gloriously impractical — not once have we discussed how to grade homework or get students to take notes in lectures. At the same time, we have been constantly mindful of the classroom itself, of teachers and learners and the ways in which we shape our life together in the educational setting. We have entered the world of a biblically informed imagination not as a means of escape, but as an avenue to seeing with different eyes and therefore seeing new possibilities and perhaps beginning to grow into them. The end of this book is therefore not a conclusion, a set of established claims and guidelines now justified, summarized, and ready to take away. The work of imagination does not lead to a single prescription or a detailed blueprint; it opens worlds to live into.

The end of this book is therefore like its beginning, an invitation. An invitation to refuse the truncation of imagination and the erosion of hope that happen when we allow our vision of teaching and learning to be bounded only by the urgent, the countable, the standardized, the quick tip and the time-saving technique. An invitation to return, to loop back and dwell in some of the spaces opened up by the reflections that make up this book, to meditate and allow for the possibility of gradual change. An invitation to focus on what kind of person (and therefore what kind of teacher) we are gradually becoming and the place our vision of the world plays in that process. An invitation to wonder what teaching and learning might look like seen by those who know that they live in a world created by a God who has filled it with beauty and story and song and who walks with us through the vale of tears and draws us toward future glory.

At the end, then, we again offer this book as an invitation. We hope you will make it your own.

Notes

Notes to the Introduction

Why Read This Book?

"Now listen in to two psychologists debating" The discussion of whether the brain is a hydraulic system or an information system is quoted from page 46 of Jeffrey Kluger, "Getting to No: The Science of Building Willpower," *TIME*, March 5, 2012, pp. 44-47.

"they use quite different images — different metaphors — to make their points." There is a very large literature on metaphor, its role in thought and action, and its influence in education in particular. Our discussion here presupposes that literature, but it is not our purpose here to survey it. Some useful and/or influential starting points are: George Lakoff and Mark Johnson, *Metaphors We Live By* (University of Chicago Press, 1980); David Punter, *Metaphor* (New York: Routledge, 2007); Janet Martin Soskice, *Metaphor and Religious Language* (Oxford University Press, 1987); Andrew Ortony, ed., *Metaphor and Thought* (Cambridge University Press, 1993). A recent Christian exploration of metaphors in education is the volume edited by Ken Badley and Harro Van Brummelen, titled *Metaphors We Teach By: How Metaphors Shape What We Do in Classrooms* (Eugene, OR: Wipf & Stock, 2012). On the broader role of imagination in Christian formation, see e.g. James K. A. Smith, *Imagining the Kingdom: How Worship Works* (Grand Rapids: Baker Academic, 2013).

"for it to make sense to point to a spot on a foot-wide globe" This example is discussed by Etienne Wenger on p. 177 of his book *Communities of Practice: Learning, Meaning, and Identity* (Cambridge University Press, 1998). In that book,

Wenger discusses the important role that shared imagination plays in shaping and sustaining communities of practice, including schools and classrooms.

"A recent report from a medical forum discussing cancer treatment" The examples of battle metaphors in cancer treatment are taken from Richard T. Penson, Lidia Schapira, Kristy J. Daniels, Bruce A. Chabner, and Thomas J. Lynch Jr. "Cancer as Metaphor," *The Oncologist* 9 (2004): 708-16. The comment about bellicose metaphors is on page 709.

"He asks us to imagine encountering two stonecutters at work" Etienne Wenger's example of the two stonecutters is quoted from page 176 of *Communities of Practice*.

"The ideal garden has ranged from the walled enclosure" On the different kinds of gardening through history, see Elizabeth Barlow Rogers, *Landscape Design: A Cultural and Architectural History* (New York: Harry N. Abrams, 2001).

"can evoke a larger background narrative" Metalepsis is the technical term for an allusion to a prior text being used to evoke a larger portion of that text than just the words that are explicitly echoed, so that a particular background story is evoked in the mind of the reader. On metalepsis in relation to Scripture, see Richard B. Hays, *Echoes of Scripture in the Letters of St. Paul* (New Haven and London: Yale University Press, 1989) and *The Conversion of the Imagination: Paul as Interpreter of Israel's Scripture* (Grand Rapids: Eerdmans, 2005).

NOTES TO PART ONE

Setting Our Feet on the Road

"The notion that life is a journey" The network of expressions that make up the systematic metaphor "life is a journey" is discussed, for instance, in George Lakoff, "What is Metaphor?" in *Advances in Connectionist and Neural Computation Theory, Vol. 3: Analogical Connections,* ed. John Barnden and Keith Holyoak (Norwood, NJ: Ablex, 1994), pp. 203-58. Examples of talking about teaching and learning in terms of a systematic journey metaphor are listed, for instance, in Lynne Cameron, *Metaphor in Educational Discourse* (New York: Continuum, 2003) pp. 246-52. Some other educational metaphors seem to be

associated with more specific kinds of journeys; Dorn and Johanningmeier, for instance, trace the educational use of the term "dropout" to earlier usage to describe stepping out of the ranks during a military march. See Sherman Dorn and Erwin V. Johanningmeier, "Dropping out and the Military Metaphor for Schooling," *History of Education Quarterly* 39, no. 2 (1999): 193-98.

Pinned to the Ground
"At the center of the huddle is a large funnel" The image of the Nuremberg Funnel is from a broadsheet engraving by David Mannasser, ca. 1650. Germanisches Nationalmuseum Nürnberg. Graphische Sammlung Inv. HB24807/1294. Reproduced by permission. The book from which the term Nuremberg Funnel is derived is Georg Philipp Harsdörffer, *Poetischer Trichter. Die Teutsche Dicht- und Reimkunst/ ohne Behuf der Lateinischen Sprache in VI Stunden einzugiessen. Samt einem Anhang Von der Rechtschreibung und Schriftscheidung oder Distinction. Durch ein Mitglied der hochlöblichen Fruchtbringenden Gesellschaft. Zum zweiten Mal aufgelegt und an vielen Orten vermehret* (Nürnberg: Wolfgang Endter, 1648–1650).

Is There a Destination?
"an early modern satirist of education noted" For the comment about needing "buttocks of lead" see John Amos Comenius, *The Labyrinth of the World and the Paradise of the Heart*, trans. Howard Louthan and Andrea Sterk, (New York: Paulist, 1998), p. 94.

"As educational history has walked hand in hand" On the history of changing uses of the journey metaphor in education, see Alexandra Gutski, *Metaphern der Pädagogik: Metaphorische Konzepte von Schule, schulischem Lernen und Lehren in pädagogischen Texten von Comenius bis zur Gegenwart* (Bern: Peter Lang, 2007).

"talk of an educational superhighway" There is much current discussion and investment surrounding the idea of the internet providing an "education superhighway." The call to action at http://www.educationsuperhighway.org admonishes that "K-12 schools need learning-ready internet. Our students are being left behind" and promises that by "removing roadblocks" and "slow connection speeds" that have students "getting bogged down," we're "building the road to a better future for our students." Nothing concrete is said about

teaching and learning or about what is to be learned; the power of the journeying metaphor carries the appeal.

The First Step

"I" in this section is David Smith.

"Abram trusted in God." The extract from the story about Abram is from Barbara McMeekin, *Abraham's Big Family* (Stowmarket: Kevin Mayhew, 1983).

"To the just man, temporal comfort is like a bed" These words from Gregory the Great are from his *Moralia in Iob*, quoted here from Michael W. Twomey, "Homo Viator," in *Encyclopedia of Medieval Pilgrimage* (Brill Online, 2013). Retrieved January 30, 2013 from http://referenceworks.brillonline.com/entries/encyclopedia-of-medieval-pilgrimage/homo-viator-SIM_00303. This article also provides background on the medieval concept of *homo viator*.

Are We Tourists or Pilgrims?

In Whose Heart Are Highways

"These are the highways trodden by pilgrims in their annual journeys to the temple." Several translations therefore add "highways to Zion," while TNIV has: "whose hearts are set on pilgrimage."

"a celebration of God's rule over the entire land" See Gordon McConville, "Pilgrimage and 'Place': An Old Testament View," in *Explorations in a Christian Theology of Pilgrimage*, ed. Craig Bartholomew and Fred Hughes (Aldershot: Ashgate, 2004), pp. 17-28. Compare John Goldingay's comments (John Goldingay, *Psalms*, vol. 2: Psalms 42-89 [Grand Rapids: Baker Academic, 2009]):

> people who keep in their mind the fact that they will be going to Jerusalem for the festival are thereby reminded not only that Yhwh dwells there but also that the Yhwh who dwells there is the real God who is also a strength and protection to people who live far away. The fact that Yhwh dwells in Jerusalem does not mean that people who live in Hebron or Lachish are beyond Yhwh's sphere of influence. (p. 593)

"they make it a place of springs" On works of mercy and leaving springs, see

also Derek Tidball, "Bauman and the Postmodern Identity," in Bartholomew and Hughes, eds., *Explorations in a Christian Theology of Pilgrimage*, ed. Craig Bartholomew and Fred Hughes (Aldershot: Ashgate, 2004), p. 196.

Perils and Pitfalls of Pilgrimages

"Between the writing of the Psalms and our own day stretches a long history of people making pilgrimage." The discussion here of the historical patterns, motivations, and dangers of pilgrimage is indebted to various sources. Annie Shaver-Crandell, Paula Gerson, and Alison Stones, *The Pilgrim's Guide to Santiago De Compostela: A Gazetteer* (London: Harvey Miller Publishers, 1995) contains an English translation of the "Pilgrim's Guide" with many notes, illustrations, and the plan of Santiago de Compostela. Kathleen Ashley and Marilyn Deegan, *Being a Pilgrim: Art and Ritual on the Medieval Routes to Santiago* (Farnham: Lund Humphries, 2009) offers a collection of images with very fine introductory studies on the art and context of the pilgrimage. Edwin Mullins, *The Pilgrimage to Santiago* (London: Secker & Warburg, 1974, reprint Signal Books, 2000) is an art-historical travel guide, useful because it offers in effect a 20th century version of the "Pilgrim's Guide," on which it serves as a kind of contemporary commentary. On the historical practices of pilgrimage more generally, Larissa Juliet Taylor, ed., *Encyclopedia of Medieval Pilgrimage* (Brill Online, 2013; http://referenceworks.brillonline.com/browse/encyclopedia -of-medieval-pilgrimage) was invaluable, in particular the essays by Jessalynn Bird ("Opposition to Pilgrimage"), Andrew Holt ("Hazards of Pilgrimage"), and Diana Webb ("Motivations for Pilgrimage"). Craig Batholomew and Fred Hughes, eds., *Explorations in a Christian Theology of Pilgrimage* (Aldershot: Ashgate, 2004) offers theological evaluation of pilgrimage practices, with some historical discussion; see in the present context the essay by Dee Dyas, "Medieval Patterns of Pilgrimage: A Mirror for Today?" (p. 92-109).

A Journey into Learning

"I" in this section is Tim Steele.

The Rhythms of the Road

"I" in this section is David Smith. "Joe" is not the student's real name.

"We read of words that bring light out of chaos" The passages referred to here

included Genesis 1 and 2, 9–11; Leviticus 19; Psalm 12; Proverbs 10; Matthew 25; Luke 10; Acts 2; and Revelation 7.

"We mused over Babel and Pentecost" On hospitality, Babel, Pentecost, and language learning, see further David I. Smith and Barbara Carvill, *The Gift of the Stranger: Faith, Hospitality, and Foreign Language Learning* (Grand Rapids: Eerdmans, 2000).

Meekly Galloping Full-Tilt

"Who the Meek are Not" is found in Mary Karr's *Sinners Welcome* (New York: HarperCollins, 2006), p. 23.

Longing for a Better Country

"Jesus himself and the church that is to be his body" On the relationship of Jerusalem, the temple, and the renewal of creation, see G. K. Beale, *The Temple and the Church's Mission: A Biblical Theology of the Dwelling Place of God* (Downers Grove, IL: IVP Academic, 2004).

Walking the Path

Have You Chosen a Path?

"a German print from the early 15th century" For the source of the image see "Der Jüngling auf dem Lebensbaume," M. Haberditzl, Die Einblattdrucke des 15. Jahrhunderts. Bd. 1 Die Holzschnitte, Wien 1920. S. 34. Nr. 168, Tafel CVIII. Copyright: Kolorierter Einblattholzschnitt "Der Jüngling auf dem Lebensbaum" ca 1460. Albertina, Vienna, Inv. DG1930/204. Reproduced by permission. See also Reindert Falkenburg and Joachim Patinir, *Landscape as Image of the Pilgrimage of Life* (Amsterdam: John Benjamin, 1988), p. 77 and Wolfgang Harms, *Homo Viator in Bivio: Studien zur Bildlichkeit des Weges* (München: Fink 1970), p. 68.

"some early Christians embraced the tale" For the role of the Y and its use in art and literature from antiquity to early Christianity up to the 19th century, see Harms, *Homo Viator in Bivio*. Harms gives many examples of similar images in which the person represented is more conventionally standing before two paths. By equating the Y with a tree, artists could merge both the images of the narrow and the wide path and the tree and its fruit from Matthew 11–20. For

Hercules and the two paths, see Erwin Panofsky, *Hercules am Scheidewege und andere antike Bildstoffe in der neueren Kunst* (Berlin: Gebr. Mann Verlag, 1997), p. 63. The motif appears elsewhere; compare for instance: "It is said that the way of man's life resembles the letter Y because every man, when he reaches the threshold of manhood and therewith the place where the way forks, hesitates and ponders which direction it were best to take." Lactantius VI, 3 (ca 240 – ca 320), cited in Brigitte Scheer-Schäzler, "Heracles and Bunyan's Pilgrim," *Comparative Literature* 23, no. 3 (1971): 240-54 (p. 242). In the 4-5th century AD Prudentius describes the way of virtue as rocky and steep but leading into the golden mountains; the path of vice begins broad through green and pleasant meadows but ends in morass. (Scheer-Schäzler, "Heracles," fn. 16).

"inclined toward the way of darkness" The branch on the left is labeled "day" (tag), and the opposing branch is labeled "night" (nacht).

"You shall satisfy all the desires . . . money to own." The text on the picture reads (in archaic German), "Du salt deines leibes gelusten han/und mit der werlt in freuden stan/ wiltu nach meyme wiln leben/ so wil ich dir diz gelt czu eygen geben."

"You shall follow my teachings; you should always turn to God." "Du salt folgen meyner lere/allezeit solt dich czu gote keren."

"[Young] man, turn to me; I will give you the kingdom of heaven." "Mensche kere dich czu mir/ das hymmelreich daz gebe ich dir."

"I have [chosen] two paths [at odds with each other]; may God help me so that I'll be able to stand." "Ich habe zweyer hände wege/hilf got das ich des bestehn phlege."

"Day and night we are sneaking up to you; you cannot escape us." "Wir tag und nacht dich ersleichen/des kanstu uns nicht entweichen."

Harbors and Hazards

"For either God or nature or necessity" The various words from Augustine are cited from Augustine of Hippo, *Trilogy on Faith and Happiness*, trans. Roland J. Teske, SJ, (New York: New City Press, 2010), pp. 23-26. "The Happy Life" is one of Augustine's early works. The passage drawn upon here works with Neoplatonic themes of the soul's return to itself, but the imagery remains evocative

apart from the specific philosophical categories with which it is articulated. We are not concerned here with the particular theories of the soul and of memory that preoccupy Augustine.

Setting Out and Looking Out

"choosing the correct fork . . . God owns all the roads." These words are quoted from Craig Barnes, *Searching for Home: Spirituality of Restless People* (Grand Rapids: Brazos, 2003), p. 121, 127.

Driver Education

"Matt and Scott" The example is described at greater length in Matt Phelps and Scott Waalkes, "Educating Desire and Imagination in a 'Faith in the World' Seminar," *Journal of Education and Christian Belief* 16, no. 2 (2012): 195-214. The quotations from students in this section are all drawn from that article.

Walking in Circles

"I" in this section is Susan Felch.

"arrive where we started / And know the place for the first time." These words are from T. S. Eliot, "Little Gidding" V, *Four Quartets* (New York: Mariner Books, 1968).

What Stations Structure Your Journey?

"Heinrich Böll, in a remarkable short story" The original story discussed here is the title story of the following collection: Heinrich Böll, *Wanderer, kommst du nach Spa . . .: Erzählungen* (München: DTV, 1967) pp. 45-56. It can be read in translation as "Stranger, Bear Word to the Spartans, We..." in *The Stories of Heinrich Böll*, trans. Leila Vennewitz (Evanston, IL: Northwestern University Press, 1985).

"the famous epigram about the 300 Spartans" On the reception history of the Spartan epigram after which Böll's story is titled, see Lukas Thommen, "Wanderer, kommst du nach Sparta . . . : Rückblick auf einen Mythos," *NZZ Online*, February 21, 2004, http://www.nzz.ch/2004/02/21/li/article97RZO.html, retrieved Thursday, March 31, 2011; David J. Parent, "Böll's 'Wanderer, kommst du nach Spa'. A Reply to Schiller's 'Der Spaziergang'," *Essays in Literature* 1 (1974): 109-17.

"a sharp critique of Nazi propaganda" The relationship of the Sparta motif to Nazi wartime propaganda is described in Roderick H. Watt, "'Wanderer, kommst du nach Sparta': History through Propaganda into Literary Commonplace," *Modern Language Review* 80, no. 4 (1985): 871-83.

What Sustains the Journey?

Pilgrimage in the Desert

"I" in this section is Kurt Schaefer.

"Biblical imagery of paths and journeys is replete with talk of slipping feet" For slipping feet, see Deuteronomy 32:35; Psalms 38:16; 94:18; for crooked paths see e.g. Proverbs 2:15; Isaiah 59:8; Lamentations 3:9; Acts 13:10; for feet and stones, see Psalms 91:12; Matthew 4:6; for references to level paths see e.g. Psalms 27:11; 143:10; Proverbs 15:19; Isaiah 26:7; 42:16. Mention of robbers and weariness in the journey is very frequent — see e.g. 2 Samuel 16:14; 17:2; Job 12:6; Isaiah 42:24; Jeremiah 6:15, 18; 7:11; Hosea 6:9; Luke 10:30; 19:46; 2 Thessalonians 3:13; Hebrews 12:3.

"What breaks the pilgrim's stride and keeps her from making good on all of her first and best dreams?" In reviewing some of the professional literature on demoralization, I was surprised to find that the phenomenon is relatively understudied. "(Demoralization) is arguably the main reason people seek psychiatric treatment, yet is a concept largely ignored in psychiatry." David M. Clarke and David W. Kissane, "Demoralization: Its phenomenology and importance," *Australian and New Zealand Journal of Psychiatry*, 36, no. 6 (December 2002): 733.

"That would be too predictable." I use the word "predictable" deliberately. This counter-intuitive experience — that we might mess up soon after our circumstances improve — makes sense in the light of the theory of "affective forecasting errors," a topic that helped Kahneman and Tversky win the 2002 Nobel Prize in Economics. People tend to make systematic errors when forecasting the good feelings they will have after they buy something or complete an action. In particular, they overestimate both the duration and intensity of their emotional reactions to events, whether the events are positive or negative. So when one is having difficulties — say, running away from a pursuing Egyptian army — one may over-anticipate how wonderful things would be if that army

would just disappear. If the army actually does miraculously disappear, reality will not live up to our (inflated) expectations, and the resulting disappointment — demoralization — can lead people into behaving — contrary to what we might expect — more self-indulgently in good times than in bad times. See, for example, Timothy D. Wilson and Daniel T. Gilbert, "Affective Forecasting: Knowing What to Want," *Current Directions in Psychological Science*, 14, no. 3 (June 2005).

"If the forces of demoralization ignored such willing allies" "Visceral influences" like hunger, thirst, moods, and cravings have a predictable effect on behavior, often driving people to act against their own principles *in full knowledge that this is what they are doing.* They tend to crowd out all other goals, and cause us to ignore even the visceral damage that will result in the future. (See George Loewenstein, "Out of Control: Visceral Influences on Behavior," *Organizational Behavior and Human Decision Processes* 65, no. 3 [March 1996]: 272-92.) Combined with the affective forecasting errors referenced above, we now have a theory of why demoralization is always a danger, in good times and bad.

"some common non-negotiable needs" In *The Joy of the Gospel,* Pope Francis identifies a set of causes of demoralization and burnout among the Christian laity. His list might be thought of as complimentary to mine. He emphasizes the virtues and vices of the individual worker; I tend to emphasize the practical, social, and contextual realities that might precipitate or reinforce these personal vices. Francis lists unrealistic expectations, impatience, vanity, depersonalization of the work, and obsessive control, conspiring as things that elicit "the gray pragmatism of the daily life of the church," in which "a tomb psychology . . . slowly transforms Christians into mummies in a museum," disillusioned, melancholy, hopeless, dark, and weary. See *Evangelii Gaudium* (Vatican City: Libreria Editrece Vaticana, 2013), paragraph 82-83, available at http://www .vatican.va/holy_father/francesco/apost_exhortations/documents/papa -francesco_esortazione-ap_20131124_evangelii-gaudium_en.html. See also J. Ratzinger, *The Current Situation of Faith and Theology,* translated in *L'Osservatore Romano,* English edition, November 6, 1996.

"when they do not take good care of themselves" Unfortunately, not taking care of yourself is also one of the *symptoms* of burnout, which sets up a self-reinforcing negative cycle. This cycle seems especially prevalent in the service professions

like teaching that require high emotional involvement and a tenuous connection between effort and outcome. See S. Jackson, R. Schwab, and R. Schuler, "Toward an understanding of the burnout phenomenon," *Journal of Applied Psychology* 71, no. 4 (November 1986): 630-40; D. van Dierendonck, B. Garssen, and A. Visser, "Burnout prevention through personal growth," *International Journal of Stress Management* 12, no. 1 (February 2005): 62-77.

"Other needs develop on a slow simmer of unresolved internal conflicts" I am gently suggesting what some call a cognitive-behavioral approach to the problem. I am not the first to suggest that this may be the best strategy for individual burnout. See W. B. Schaufeli and D. Enzmann, *The Burnout Companion to Study and Practice: A Critical Analysis* (London: Taylor and Francis, 1998).

"And then there are the more purely external factors." The Mayo Clinic online staff analysis of burnout emphasizes these sources of the problem. See http:// www.mayoclinic.org/burnout/art-20046642

"Continue asking until you think you're getting close to the core issue." This approach to analysis — the Five Whys — was popularized by Toyota in the 1970s, and it seems to have worked out pretty well for them.

"Many pilgrims throughout history have kept such a record of their pilgrimage" Records of pilgrimage in India over the last eight centuries have been widespread enough to now serve as a genealogical research tool.

"We thank you for setting us at tasks" This prayer is from the Prayers and Thanksgivings section of the Book of Common Prayer, see http://www .bcponline.org/

Hurrying to the Tent Entrance

"hospitality is an act of decentering in which the guest is honored" Compare Jesus' experience at the house of Simon the Pharisee in Luke 7:36-48.

"Hospitality requires that the host recognize" The words from Amy Oden are quoted from her book *And You Welcomed Me: A Sourcebook on Hospitality in Early Christianity* (Nashville: Abingdon Press, 2001), p. 26.

"Our duties in our monastery are those of hospitality." The words of Jerome (from

his *Apology in Answer to Rufinus*) are cited from Oden, *And You Welcomed Me*, p. 69.

"Have a room, to which Christ may come." The words of Chrysostom (from his 45th homily on the Acts of the Apostles) are cited from Oden, *And You Welcomed Me*, p. 62.

How Do You Host Your Students?

"What makes a classroom an inviting and hospitable hostel" The practice of hospitality has been explored in connection with theology and education by a number of writers. See, for example, on the theological side Christine D. Pohl, *Making Room: Recovering Hospitality as a Christian Tradition* (Grand Rapids: Eerdmans, 1999); Elizabeth Newman, *Untamed Hospitality: Welcoming God and Other Strangers* (Grand Rapids: Brazos, 2007); and Miroslav Volf, *Exclusion and Embrace: A Theological Exploration of Identity, Otherness, and Reconciliation* (Nashville: Abingdon Press, 1996). In relation to education, see the works by Nouwen and Palmer cited below, and also, for example, David W. Anderson, "Hospitable Classrooms: Biblical Hospitality and Inclusive Education," *Journal of Education and Christian Belief* 15, no. 1 (2011): 13-27; David I. Smith and Barbara Carvill, *The Gift of the Stranger: Faith, Hospitality, and Foreign Language Learning* (Grand Rapids: Eerdmans, 2000).

"The Rule of St. Benedict, which guided many medieval monasteries" The Rule of St. Benedict can be read at http://www.ccel.org/ccel/benedict/rule2/files/rule2.html

"Henri Nouwen sees the role of host" See Henri Nouwen, *Reaching Out: The Three Movements of the Spiritual Life* (New York: Doubleday, 1986), pp. 84-97.

"Parker Palmer similarly claims" The Parker Palmer quotations are from Parker Palmer, *To Know as We Are Known* (San Francisco: Harper, 1983), pp. 71, 74.

Teaching is Breaking Bread

"Teaching itself is breaking bread, so says Bernard of Clairvaux." The quotations from Bernard in this section are all drawn from Bernard of Clairvaux, *On the Song of Songs 1*, trans. Kilian Walsh (Spencer, MA: Cistercian Publications, 1971). The sections quoted are from the first sermon. The material in this section appears in different form in David I. Smith, "Teaching is breaking bread:

educational vision, biblical metaphor, and Bernard of Clairvaux," *Journal of Christian Education* 55, no. 1 (2012-2013): 29-36. A general introduction to Bernard's sermons on the Song of Songs can be found in William Loyd Allen, "Bernard of Clairvaux's Sermons on the Song of Songs: Why They Matter," *Review and Expositor* 105 (2008): 403-16. Bernard's first sermon on the Song of Songs, including the use of bread imagery, is helpfully discussed by Duncan Robertson in his article, "The Experience of Reading: Bernard of Clairvaux Sermons on the Song of Songs, I," *Religion and Literature* 19, no. 1 (1987): 1-20.

"inviting us into the intimacy of the chapter house" Whether and in what form Bernard delivered the sermons orally has been debated. See e.g. Robertson, "The Experience of Reading"; Jean Leclercq, "Les Sermons sur les Cantiques ont-ils été pronounces?" *Revue Benedictine* 65 (1955): 71-89; Jean LeClercq, "Introduction," in Bernard of Clairvaux, *On the Song of Songs*, vol 2, Cistercian Fathers series no. 7 (Spencer, MA: Cistercian Publications, 1976), pp. vii-xxx.
"He invites his learners to share an image" Luke Anderson ("The Rhetorical Epistemology in Saint Bernard's Super Cantica," in *Bernardus Magister: Papers Presented at the Nonacentenary Celebration of the Birth of Saint Bernard of Clairvaux*, ed. John R. Sommerfeldt [Spencer, MA: Cistercian Publications/Cîteaux: Commentarii Cistercienses, 1992], pp. 95-128) offers a helpful account of how Bernard understood his use of "figures"; while there is a place for the kind of rational knowing that aspires to objectivity, figurative language has another goal, which is to engage the affections in ways that lead to wisdom, which is a practical form of truth. This avenue of knowing honors the fact that humans naturally arrive at understanding through bodily experience of the world; "God surely understands that we are constituted rational not merely in virtue of the soul, but insofar as the soul inhabits a 'body'" (p. 117). This connection of sensory images with bodily experience and with practical wisdom links knowing to the meeting of human needs in a manner that further undergirds the connection of learning with bread.

Into the Labyrinth

"published his own pilgrim tale" This section draws from John Amos Comenius, *The Labyrinth of the World and the Paradise of the Heart*, trans. Andrea Sterk (Mahwah, NJ: Paulist Press, 1997). The direct quotations in this section are from chapter 10 in the Sterk translation, as follows:

"I saw some people who behaved very greedily" (p. 96)

"shape more carefully and artistically the boxes," (p. 98)

"I saw some who merely took from the vessels of others" (p. 98)

"relegated to dusty shelves and back corners." (p. 99)

"they spared neither the wounded nor the dead" (p. 100)

Traveling Companions

"I" in this section is David Smith.

Singing Our Journey

"Pilgrimages are not just traveled, but sung." This section is adapted from an unpublished paper by Jeff Bouman of Calvin College (the "Jeff" of the story), titled "Seeds of Mercy and Seeds of Justice: Building the Universe with Focused Readings and Songs." The words quoted from students in this section are drawn from this paper.

"The act of singing together" The quotation is from Don Saliers, "Singing Our Lives," in Dorothy C. Bass, *Practicing Our Faith: A Way of Life for a Searching People* (San Francisco: Jossey-Bass, 1997), pp. 179-93, p. 180.

"a seamless coat of learning" See Alfred North Whitehead, *The Aims of Education* (New York: MacMillan, 1929), p. 11.

A Rhythm of Work and Rest

"Imagine a teacher who becomes passionate" This section is based on Kurt Schaefer's experiments in his own classroom.

"it involves a shared story, a shared imagination" On the relationship between practices, narrative, and imagination, see further Alasdair MacIntyre, *After Virtue*, 3rd ed. (University of Notre Dame Press, 2007); David I. Smith and James K. A. Smith, *Teaching and Christian Practices: Reshaping Faith and Learning* (Grand Rapids: Eerdmans, 2011); Etienne Wenger, *Communities of Practice: Learning, Meaning, and Identity* (Cambridge University Press, 1998).

"Sabbaths 1979: X" Copyright © 1998 by Wendell Berry, from *A Timbered Choir* ([Berkeley: Counterpoint, 1998], p. 18). Reprinted by permission of Counterpoint.

NOTES TO PART TWO

Clearing the Ground

"man meddles with them and they become evil." The passage is quoted from Jean-Jacques Rousseau, *Émile*, trans. Barbara Foxley (London: Dent, 1911), p. 5.

"A garden is not, except in so far as it contains plants" The quotation is from Robin Alexander, *Versions of Primary Education* (London: Routledge, 1995), p. 13.

Generous Beauty: Is Your Classroom a Royal Garden

Planted by Streams of Water

"Why would kings boast about gardens?" William Brown notes (p. 67) that "in addition to their prowess on the battlefield, kings excelled in horticultural skill. It was altogether common practice among ancient Near Eastern despots . . . to cultivate their gardens with plants taken from foreign lands." William P. Brown, *Seeing the Psalms: A Theology of Metaphor* (Louisville: Westminster John Knox), pp. 67-71.

"Cisterns were important sources of life and health." For biblical passages reflecting the importance of cisterns, see e.g. Genesis 37:20-29; 2 Chronicles 26:10; Proverbs 5:15; Jeremiah 2:13; 38:1-13.

"Psalm 1 applies the thought to people" For discussion of the "channels" of water in Psalm 1 and their relationship to royal gardens, see Brown, *Seeing the Psalms*, pp. 55-79.

"the human story begins in a garden within God's cosmic temple." For a detailed exploration of the relationship between garden, temple, cosmos, and God's presence in creation see G. K. Beale, *The Temple and the Church's Mission: A Biblical Theology of the Dwelling Place of God* (Downers Grove, IL: IVP Academic, 2004).

"This is language reserved for royalty" On the relationship of *imago dei* language to royal power and identity, see J. Richard Middleton, *The Liberating Image: The* Imago Dei *in Genesis 1* (Grand Rapids: Brazos, 2005).

Does it Snow in Your Classroom?

"Doug is a scientist." Thanks to Douglas Vander Griend for the snowflakes example.

"Josh teaches science in a secondary school." The salt example is drawn from http://www.whatiflearning.com/examples/76-chemistry-and-wonder — the site at www.whatiflearning.com has many more examples of teaching and learning informed by Christian faith, hope, and love drawn particularly from elementary and secondary education.

"Sue teaches mathematics" The mathematics example is based on Unit 6 of John Shortt and John Westwell, eds., *Charis Mathematics Units 1-9* (St Albans: Association of Christian Teachers, 1996), available at http://www.johnshortt.org/Documents/Math-Unit06-Fractals.pdf. Image of the Koch snowflake by Wxs from https://commons.wikimedia.org/wiki/File:KochFlake.png, licensed under the Creative Commons Attribution-Share Alike 3.0 Unported license. Image on p. 100 is based on "Sierpinski Triangle" by Beojan Stanislaus uploaded by Perhelion to https://en.wikipedia.org/wiki/Sierpinski_triangle#/media/File:Sierpinski_triangle.svg, licensed under the Creative Commons Attribution-Share Alike 3.0 Unported license. Both images retrieved 2 July 2015.

Painting Your Classroom

The painting is from *Meister des Frankfurter Paradiesgärtleins* (ca 1410) 23.3 cm × 33.4 cm, Städelsches Kunstinstitut, Frankfurt am Main. Retrieved 6 June 2014 from https://en.wikipedia.org/wiki/Paradiesg%C3%A4rtlein#/media/File:Meister_des_Frankfurter_Paradiesg%C3%A4rtleins_001.jpg. A good introduction to paintings of this kind is Reindert L. Falkenburg, *The Fruit of Devotion Mysticism and the Imagery of Love in Flemish Paintings of the Virgin and Child 1540-1550.* (Amsterdam: John Benjamins, 1994). Also helpful is Heimo Reinitzer, *Der verschlossene Garten. Der Garten Marias im Mittelalter.* (Wolfenbüttel: Herzog August Bibliothek, 1982 [=Wolfenbüttler Hefte 12]). The purpose of this painting as an invitation to contemplate the life of faith is discussed in Ewald M. Vetter, "Das Frankfurter Paradiesgärtlein," *Heidelberger Jahrbücher* 9 (1965): 102-46. Vetter identifies the saint with the water ladle as Saint Barbara, whose earthly remains had supposedly been successfully used to find water so that dry parched land became fertile again, echoing Psalm 107:35. In the picture, the well is placed on a small piece of infertile soil. Cf. Vetter, "Paradies-gärtlein," p. 110. The identity of the warrior saint by the tree is not definitely established. Vetter interprets this figure as Saint Oswald, because of the black raven at his feet. "Paradiesgärtlein," pp. 115-21. The symbolism of the various plants is discussed in E. Wolfhardt, "Beiträge zur Pflanzensymbolik. Über die Pflanzen des Frankfurter Paradiesgärtleins." *Zeitschrift für Kunstwissenschaft* 8 (1954): 177-96, and in Werner Ernst Loeckle, *Das Frankfurter Paradiesgärtlein als Meditationsbild* (Freiburg: Verlag Die Kommenden, 1969). The Lily of the Valley, for instance, speaks of Mary's virtue of chastity and humility, because the corolla of this white flower hangs down. The red petals of the anemone point to Christ's blood shed at his crucifixion.

Do Students Know They Are Gardeners?

"Then Elisabeth spoke up . . ." Elisabeth is a pseudonym. I do not recollect which individual teacher shared the story. "I" in this section is David Smith.

Shaping the Soul

Do You Tend the Garden of the Soul?

"Once these truths have been brought before you" The passage from the *Epistle of Diognetus* is for the most part quoted from the Staniforth translation in *Early Christian Writings: The Apostolic Fathers*, trans. Maxwell Staniforth/Andrew Louth (St. Ives: Penguin Classics, 1987 [1968]); the passage discussed here is from p.150. Some phrases have, however, been substituted from the translation in Cyril C. Richardson, *Early Christian Fathers* (Philadelphia: Westminster Press, 1953) (available online at http://www.ccel.org/ccel/richardson/fathers .html); in particular, Staniforth's "they make a grove to spring up and flourish within themselves" has been replaced by Richardson's "cultivating in them-selves a flourishing tree," and Staniforth's "knowledge coupled with fear" has been amended to "with reverence," again following Richardson. For discus-sion of the various city — and kingdom — related terms used by a number of early Christian writers to describe membership in the community of faith, and their relationship to the question of Greek versus Christian paideia, see Michael Azkoul, "The Greek Fathers: Polis and Paideia," *St Vladimir's Theo-logical Quarterly* 23, no. 2 (1979): 67-86. For detailed discussion of the use of

paradise and wilderness imagery in the early church, including the idea of the church as a provisional paradise, see George H. Williams, *Wilderness and Paradise in Christian Thought: The Biblical Experience of the Desert in the History of Christianity & the Paradise Theme in the Theological Idea of the University* (New York: Harper & Brothers, 1962); see especially chapter 2. The comments from Irenaeus are drawn from *Against Heresies* V, xx, 2, in *The Ante-Nicene Fathers; Translations of the Writings of the Fathers Down to AD 325,* ed. Alexander Roberts and James Donaldson (Grand Rapids: Eerdmans, 1950-1951). The story of the *Epistle to Diognetus* manuscript and how it came down to us can be found in the introduction to the epistle in the same volume (pp. 139-140), and in Paul Foster, "The Epistle to Diognetus," *Expository Times* 118, no.4 (2007): 162-68. Foster's article provides a helpful overview of the epistle. The final two chapters of the epistle, which include the section discussed here, are thought to be from a different author than the preceding chapters, perhaps from the early third century. On the history of the idea of paradise and its role in the Western imagination, see Jean Delumeau, *A History of Paradise: The Garden of Eden in Myth and Tradition* (University of Illinois Press, 2000).

"Lovelessness, indifference, will never be able to generate sufficient attention" The quotation is from Mikhail M. Bakhtin, *Toward a Philosophy of the Act,* trans. Liapunov (Austin, TX: University of Texas Press, 1993) p. 64.

"A while later Saint Ambrose" For Saint Ambrose's allegorical take on Eden, see Ambrose and John S. Savage, *Hexameron, Paradise, and Cain and Abel,* Fathers of the Church, vol. 42 (New York: Catholic University of America Press, 1961) pp. 329, 351. Augustine's variant on Genesis 2:15 is found in his commentary on Genesis: Augustine, *The Literal Meaning of Genesis,* trans. John Hammond Taylor, Ancient Christian Writers, vol. 2 (New York: Newman Press, 1982), p. 52. The association of the serpent with false teachers that can be found in 2 Corinthians 11:2-3, where Paul worries that false preachers and apostles will deceive the Corinthian Christians "as the serpent deceived Eve by his cunning," and in 1 Timothy 2:12-14, where Paul says that women are not to teach since "the woman was deceived," was noted by patristic commentators and helped cement the idea of the Garden of Eden as a place of instruction; The story of how the early church came to adopt the image of the garden of Eden as a place of instruction is told in Eric Jager, *The Tempter's Voice: Language and the Fall in Medieval Literature* (Ithaca: Cornell University Press, 1993).

On the garden of the heart see e.g. Bernard of Clairvaux, *On the Song of Songs,* trans. Kilian Walsh, Cistercian Fathers (Spencer, MA: Cistercian Publications, 1971). Herrad of Hohenbourg's quasi-encyclopedia can be found in R. Green, M. Evans, C. Bischoff, and M. Curschmann, *Herrad of Hohenbourg, Hortus Deliciarum,* 2 vols (London: Warburg Institute, 1977). For further discussion of how the motif unfolds in more recent history, see Williams, *Wilderness and Paradise,* pp. 130-31.

The Soul of Statistics

"Imagine this classroom" This story is retold from David Smith, John Shortt, and James Bradley, "Editorial: Reconciliation in the Classroom," *Journal of Education and Christian Belief* 10, no. 1 (2006): 3-5.

Are You Tending Your Tree?

"there are different kinds of appetite for learning." For a helpful summary of Augustine's account see Paul J. Griffiths, *The Vice of Curiosity: An Essay on Intellectual Appetite* (Winnipeg: CMU Press, 2006).

The Walled Garden Revisited

The painting is from *Meister des Frankfurter Paradiesgärtleins* (ca 1410) 23.3 cm × 33.4 cm, Städelsches Kunstinstitut, Frankfurt am Main. Retrieved 6 June 2014 from https://en.wikipedia.org/wiki/Paradiesg%C3%A4rtlein#/media/File :Meister_des_Frankfurter_Paradiesg%C3%A4rtleins_001.jpg.

Lingering, Learning, Hoping

"I" in this section is David Smith.

The learning materials based on Adaline's life story are found in David Baker, Helen Brammer, Cath Chapman, Shirley Dobson, Keith Heywood, and David Smith, *Charis Deutsch: Einheiten 1-5* (St. Albans: Association of Christian Teachers, 1996). They can be accessed online at http://www.johnshortt.org/ Pages/CharisDeutsch.aspx. This teaching unit is discussed in David I. Smith, Kate Avila, Sarah De Young, and Ashley Uyaguari, "Of Log Cabins, Fallen Bishops and Tenacious Parents: (Auto)biographical Narrative and the Spirituality of Language Learning," in *Spirituality, Social Justice and Language Learn-*

ing, ed. David I. Smith and Terry A. Osborn, (Greenwich, CT: Information Age Publishing, 2007), pp. 107-29.

Can You Teach in the Desert?

"Chris Anderson, a professor of English, is attempting to teach the crucifixion narrative" This incident is described by Chris Anderson in his book *Teaching as Believing: Faith in the University* (Waco: Baylor University Press, 2004).

The Just Community

Are You Growing Wild Grapes?

"The prophets seem to have little difficulty imagining the city as a garden." On the relationship between the garden, the cosmos conceived as a temple, and the eschatological city, see G. K. Beale, *The Temple and the Church's Mission: A Biblical Theology of the Dwelling Place of God* (Downers Grove, IL: IVP, 2004).

"In shalom each person enjoys justice . . ." The quotation from Nicholas Wolterstorff is taken from his book, *Educating for Shalom: Essays on Christian Higher Education* (Grand Rapids: Eerdmans, 2004), p. 23.

The Three-Minute Garden Tour

"I" in this section is David Smith.

A Garden of Delights for Our God

"That was the question facing a young Moravian pastor . . ." John Amos Comenius is regarded as the father of modern Western education, and the secondary literature on him is large. For a concise and helpful overview of Comenius' life and times and his educational ideas, see Daniel Murphy, *Comenius: A Critical Reassessment of his Life and Work* (Dublin: Irish Academic Press, 1995). Comenius' own understanding of the role of metaphor and analogy in theorizing is discussed in Jan Janko, "Comenius' Syncrisis as the Means of Man and World Knowledge," *Acta Comeniana* 9 (1991): 43-55. Previous work on his use of garden metaphors and their relationship to theology and to Christian education can be found in John Shortt, David Smith, and Trevor Cooling, "Metaphor, Scripture and Education," *Journal of Christian Education* 43, no. 1 (2000): 22-28; and David I. Smith, "Biblical Imagery and Educational Imagination: Come-

nius and the Garden of Delight" in *The Bible and the University,* ed. David Lyle
Jeffrey and C. Stephen Evans (Grand Rapids: Zondervan, 2007), pp. 188-215.

"God, having created man out of dust . . ." Comenius, *Great Didactic,* Dedicatory
Letter. The quotations from the Great Didactic in this section are translated from
the Latin text found in Klaus Schaller, ed., *Johann Amos Comenius: Ausgewählte
Werke,* vol. 1 (Hildesheim/New York: Georg Olms Verlag, 1973). There is an
English translation by M. W. Keatinge still in print (M. W. Keatinge, *The Great
Didactic of John Amos Comenius,* 2nd ed. [New York: Russell & Russell, 1967]),
but it is dated and abridges the dedicatory letter, so we have here used our own
translation. Translations of the other works by Comenius cited here are found in
Vladimir Jelinek, *The Analytical Didactic of Comenius* (Chicago, IL: University of
Chicago Press, 1953); A. M. O. Dobbie, *Comenius' Pampaedia or Universal Educa-
tion* (Dover: Buckland, 1986); and John Amos Comenius, *Pannuthesia or Universal
Warning,* trans. A. M. O. Dobbie (Shipston-on-Stour: Peter I. Drinkwater, 1991).

"placed him in a Paradise of desire" The phrase "Paradise of desire" at the start
of the dedicatory letter translates "paradiso voluptatis," which corresponds
to what modern English translations of Genesis render as "garden of Eden."

"wild and horrible wastelands." Keatinge translates here as "wilderness"; however, in a modern western context "wilderness" has taken on an attractive ring,
associated with the unspoiled and the adventurous rather than with unkempt,
dangerous places where the unwary traveler may meet an unpleasant end.
"Wasteland" better captures the sense of unfruitfulness and desolation.

"an imitation of the School of Paradise," Comenius, *Pampaedia,* p. 29.

"that we may serve God, his creatures and ourselves" Comenius, *Great Didactic,*
p. 72.

"so acquiescing in His love and favor" Comenius, *Great Didactic,* Keatinge, p. 218.

"all creatures should have cause to join us" Comenius, *Pampaedia,* p. 26.

"that we are born not for ourselves alone, but for God" Comenius, *Great Didactic,*
p. 214.

"that very sweet delight which arises" Comenius, *Great Didactic,* p. 73.

"the entire world will be a garden of delight for God" Comenius, *Pampaedia,* p. 29.

"Firstly, the expressed wish is for full power of development" Comenius, *Pampaedia*, p. 19.

"I had this consideration in mind" Comenius, *Pampaedia*, p. 21.

"schools will then be planned to such pleasant effect" Comenius, *Pampaedia*, p. 56.

"I have done what I could" Comenius, *Pannuthesia*, pp. 17-19.

Inviting Students into the Garden

"This course *is not a factory for learning"* Rebecca Oxford and her colleagues note the prevalence of factory metaphors in the talk of teachers and students about schooling. "Unlike the image of a craftsperson, a sculptor or an artist, schooling governed by the manufacturing metaphor reduces the teacher to an instrument of an overarching bureaucratic authority, which seeks to manage every atom of the process through standardized scientific practices. Central to the factory system, and of course the entire market economy in general, is the use of rivalry and extrinsic rewards and punishment as the essential motivators." Rebecca L. Oxford, Stephen Tomlinson, Ana Barcelos, Cassandra Harrington, Roberta Z. Lavine, Amany Saleh, and Ana Longhini, "Clashing metaphors about classroom teachers: toward a systematic typology for the language teaching field," *System* 26, no. 1 (1998): 3-50, p. 13.

Are You Planting Saplings?

"I" in this section is David Smith.

"In the Cool of the Evening" From *Ecstatic in the Poison: New Poems* (p. 59) by Andrew Hudgins. Copyright © 2003 by Andrew Hudgins. Published in 2003 by Overlook Duckworth, Peter Mayer Publishers, Inc. New York, NY. www .overlookpress.com. All rights reserved.

NOTES TO PART THREE

Drawing the Blueprints

The schoolhouse image is from Clipart.com, item: # 21188865. Retrieved 14 August 2013 from http://www.clipart.com/en/close-up?o=3869617&memlevel

=A&a=a&q=school&k_mode=all&s=361&e=378&show=&c=&cid=&
findincat=&g=&cc=&page=21&k_exc=&pubid=

"Teaching is like building a house . . ." This description was written by Melissa Cohen while she was working toward her master's degree at The College of New Jersey and may be found at http://portfolio.project.tcnj.edu/summer2004/ Cohen/My%20Teaching%20Metaphor.htm

Apprentice Builders

"I" in this section is first John Witvliet and then Tim Steele. The text referred to is Alvin Plantinga, *Warranted Christian Belief* (Oxford University Press, 1999).

Laying the Foundations

The Divine Architect

"this spacious medieval icon of God" This illumination of the God as the divine architect comes from the Bible moralisée, c. 1250. Österreichische Nationalbibliothek, Codex Vindobonensis 2554, fol lv. Reproduced by permission.

Teaching Living Stones to Talk

The "I" in this section is Tim Steele.

"In her essay 'Teaching a Stone to Talk'" This essay by Annie Dillard appears in her collection, *Teaching a Stone to Talk* (New York: Harper Perennial, 1992), pp. 85-94.

"Larry removes the cover" (p. 86)

"There is a vibrancy to the silence" (p. 90)

"Nature's silence is its one remark" (p. 87)

"I assume that like any other meaningful effort, the ritual involves sacrifice" (p. 86)

The Crystal Castle

"While I was begging our Lord today to speak for me" St. Teresa of Avila writes these words in *El Castillo Interior*, translated as *The Interior Castle*, 1.1, which may be accessed at http://www.ccel.org/ccel/teresa/castle2.v.i.html.

"We shall see that the soul of the just man is but a paradise" 1.2

"Nothing can be compared" 1.2

"many rooms in this castle" 1.4

"praise Him for His great goodness" 1.4

Building the Walls

The Walls We Construct

The "I" in this section is Susan Felch.

The images of walls are sourced moving clockwise from the top left as follows:

Clipart.com, item: # 10028922. Retrieved 2 July 2015 from http://www.clipart
.com/en/close-up?o=2835999&a=p&q=10028901&k_mode=all&s=1&e=1&
show=&c=&cid=&findincat=&g=&cc=&page=&k_exc=&pubid=&color=
&b=i&date=

Clipart.com, item: # 24684712. Retrieved 2 July 2015 from http://www.clipart
.com/en/close-up?o=4281457&a=p&q=24684714&k_mode=all&s=1&e=1&
show=&c=&cid=&findincat=&g=&cc=&page=&k_exc=&pubid=&color=
&b=i&date=

Mehta, Kunal, Graffiti Fist, Image ID: 146645084 Retrieved 6 July 2015 from
http://www.shutterstock.com/pic.mhtml?id=146645084&src=id

Johnson, Jodie, Front of a two storey contemporary architect designed town-
house home, Image ID: 85178257, Retrieved 6 July 2015 from http://www
.shutterstock.com/pic.mhtml?id=85178257&src=id

Chaoshu, Li, Modern Office, Image ID: 111398168, Retrieved 6 July 2015 from
http://www.shutterstock.com/pic.mhtml?id=111398168&src=id

Clipart.com, item: #79301386. Retrieved 2 July 2015 from http://www.clipart
.com/en/close-up?o=11554154&a=p&q=79301383&k_mode=all&s=1&e=1&
show=&c=&cid=&findincat=&g=&cc=&page=&k_exc=&pubid=&color=
&b=i&date=

Climbing the Steps

Towers of Learning

"Gregorius Reisch's Margarita Philosophica". The discussion here is based on
Frank Büttner: *Die Illustrationen der Margarita Philosophica des Gregor Reisch*
in *Sammeln–Ordnen–Veranschaulichen. Zur Wissenskompilatorik in der Frühen
Neuzeit*, ed. Frank Büttner, Markus Friedrich, Helmut Zedelmaier (Münster:
LIT, 2003), pp. 269-300; Lutz Geldsetzer, ed., *Margarita philosophica. Mit einem
Vorwort, einer Einleitung und einem neuen Inhaltsverzeichnis von Lutz Geldsetzer*
(Düsseldorf: Stern, 1973).

"which culminated in the study of theology" A detailed and comprehensive introduction to the medieval curriculum is provided by Paul Abelson, *The Seven
Liberal Arts: A Study in Mediaeval Culture 1906* (New York: Russell & Russell, 1906; reprinted 1965), also available online https://archive.org/details/
sevenliberalarto2abelgoog. Also informative and helpful is Adolf Katzenel-
lenbogen's introduction to the iconography of the Seven Liberal Arts in "The
Representation of the Seven Liberal Arts," in *Twelfth-Century Europe and the
Foundations of Modern Society*, ed. Marshall Clagett, Gaines Post, and Robert
Reynolds (Madison: The University of Wisconsin Press 1961), pp. 39-58. The
most extensive study of the use of visuals in medieval schooling, with over 50
illustrations, is offered by Karl-August Wirth in "Von Mittelalterlichen Bildern
und Lehrfiguren im Dienste der Schule und des Unterrichts," in *Studien zum
städtischen Bildungswesen des Späten Mittelalters und der Frühen Neuzeit*, ed.
Bernd Moeller, Hans Patze, and Karl Stackmann (Göttingen: Vandenhoeck &
Ruprecht, 1983), pp. 256-370.

Image of Reisch's tower of knowledge retrieved 6 June 2014 from https://
commons.wikimedia.org/wiki/File:Gregor_Reisch_-_Margarita_
philosophica_-_4th_ed._Basel_1517_-_p._VI_-_Typus_grammaticae_
-_1000ppi.png.

"tower of wisdom (turris sapientiae)" Kevin Gœuriot gives a thourough analysis
of 15 of 30 extant manuscripts containing the Tower of Wisdom in "La Tour
de la Sagesse: Etude Historique d'un exemple d'image 'edificatrice' a la fin du
Moyen Age," *Revue d'Histoire Ecclesiastique* 103, no. 2 (2008): 363-403.

"The true teacher does not show his students" The quotation is B. Carvill's transla-

tion of *"Der Wahre Lehrer zeigt seinem Schüler nicht das fertige Gebäude..."* from the famous pedagogical treatise by Adolph Diesterweg, *Wegweiser zur Bildung für deutsche Lehrer* (Essen: Bädeker, 1844), p. 177, cited by Alexandra Guski, *Metaphern der Pädagogik,* Explorationen 53 (Bern: Peter Lang, 2007), p. 336.

Image of the Tower of Wisdom, Woodcut, ca 1475. Copyright: Germanisches Nationalmuseum Nürnberg, Inv. Nr. HB 24559 Kaps 1335. Reproduced by permission.

Climbing the Ladder

"'Our school too,' he summarizes, 'is God's house'" This is quoted from Gisela Brühl, *Die Schule im Urteil ihrer Lehrer vom ausgehenden 16. bis zum ausgehenden 19. Jahrhundert* (Wiesbaden: Deutscher Fachschriften Verlag, 1969), p. 19. The author gives many examples of school sermons and studies their use of metaphors for the school such as temple, workshop of the Holy Spirit, daughter of the Church, seedling nursery, and garden of paradise. Further building metaphors for schools, including schools as factories, diploma mills, supermarkets, or even prisons, are discussed in Alexandra Guski, *Metaphern der Pädagogik* (Bern: Peter Lang, 2007), p. 155. Using Lakoff's cognitive theory of metaphor, Guski explores the use of pedagogical metaphors in educational texts from Comenius to the present.

Climbing the Lighthouse

The "I" in this section is Susan Felch.

Entering the Sanctuary

Fiat Lux! The Classroom as Cathedral

The "I" in this section is Tim Steele.

The description of the cathedral in this section draws from various sources. The following are helpful sources: Margot Fassler, "Liturgy and Sacred History in the Twelfth-Century Tympana at Chartres," *The Art Bulletin* 75, no. 3 (Sept. 1993): 499-520; Margot Fassler, *The Virgin of Chartres: Making History through Liturgy and the Arts* (New Haven and London: Yale University Press, 2010); Jean Gimpel, *The Cathedral Builders,* trans. Teresa Waugh (New York: Grove Press, 1983; reprint HarperPerennial, 1992); Otto von Simson, *The Gothic Ca-*

thedral, 2nd ed. (Princeton: Princeton University Press, 1962; reprint 1974); Craig Wright, *The Maze and the Warrior: Symbols in Architecture, Theology, and Music* (Cambridge, MA: Harvard University Press, 2001).

The cathedral image is from Clipart.com, item: # 34821309. Retrieved 2 July 2015 from http://www.clipart.com/en/close-up?o=5079786&a=a&q= 34821306&k_mode=all&s=1&e=1&show=&c=&cid=&findincat=&g=&cc= &page=&k_exc=&pubid=&color=&b=i&date=

Lesniewski, Rainer, Cathedral Floor Plan, Image ID: 268782788, Retrieved 6 July 2015 from http://www.shutterstock.com/pic-268782788/stock-vector -cathedral-floor-plan.html?src=XDuvGHL5rtFz83zVMo9JMQ-1-26

"Cheryl teaches introduction to sociology" Cheryl Brandsen is professor of sociology and Provost at Calvin College.

Cathedral Builders

The "I" in this section is David Smith.

"the twin spires of Köln cathedral" An outline of the history of Cologne (Köln) Cathedral can be found at http://www.koelner-dom.de/index .php?id=18821&L=1.

Labyrinths and Mazes

"you'll find yourself at a dead end" Margaret Visser notes in *The Geometry of Love* that in a maze there is only one "correct route and there are many dead ends: every choice of direction is consequence-laden, and it is easy to travel a long way in error." Margaret Visser, *The Geometry of Love: Space, Time, Mystery, and Meaning in an Ordinary Church* (New York: North Point Press, 2002), pp. 60-61.

Stamatova, Maryna, Vector illustration of round maze. Image ID: 252555448 Retrieved 6 July 2015 from http://www.shutterstock.com/pic.mhtml?id= 252555448&src=id

"One of our colleagues uses the structure" For a more detailed discussion of the unicursal labyrinth in the classroom, see Matthew Walhout, "Thrill Rides and Labyrinths: The Pedagogical Logic of Freedom and Constraint," in *Teaching*

and Christian Practices: Reshaping Faith and Learning, ed. David I. Smith and James K. A. Smith (Grand Rapids: Eerdmans, 2011), pp. 177-93.

Abiding in the Abbeys

"Founded in the sixth century by St. Columba" A history of St. Columba and Iona Abbey can be found in Ian Finlay's *Columba* (London: Gollancz, 1979, reprinted by Kingfisher Books in 1990).

"The abbey was a community of persons" A useful introduction to abbeys is Trevor Yorke's *The English Abbey Explained* (Newbury: Countryside Books, 2004).

"But as Rebecca Konyndyk DeYoung points out" See *Glittering Vices: A New Look at the Seven Deadly Sins and Their Remedies* (Grand Rapids: Eerdmans, 2009).

"But beauty, says Simone Weil" See the essay "Love of the Order of the World," found in her collection *Waiting for God* (New York: Harper Perennial, 2009), p. 100.

"creates in us a hunger to know the truest beauty of a human face" Weil, *Waiting for God,* p. 109.

Setting Up House

Wisdom Has Built Her House

"Hortus Deliciarum, the Garden of Delight" www.plosin.com/work/Hortus .html. For a scholarly discussion and reconstruction of the manuscript, see Rosalie Green, Michael Evans, Christine Bischoff, and Michael Curschmann, eds., *The Hortus Deliciarum of Herrad of Hohenbourg (Landsberg, 1176-96): A Reconstruction* (Leiden: Warburg Institute/E. J. Brill, 1919).

The image from the *Hortus Deliciarum* is reproduced from Dnalor 01, *Philosophia et septem artes liberales* (Philosophy and the Seven Liberal Arts), as illustrated in *Hortus deliciarum*. Wikimedia commons, licence: license CC-BY-SA 3.0. Retrieved 6 July 2015 from https://en.wikipedia.org/wiki/Hortus _deliciarum#/media/File:Hortus_Deliciarum,_Die_Philosophie_mit_den _sieben_freien_K%C3%BCnsten.JPG.

The core curriculum image is reproduced courtesy of Calvin College.

Building Story Houses

"I" in this section is Susan Felch.

Building Well

Etching of the Tower of Babel by Cornelisz Anthonisz Teunissen, *Destruction de la Tour de Babel*, 1547. Photo: Joerg P. Anders. Kupferstichkabinett, Staatliche Museen, Berlin, Germany. Art Resource, NY Image Reference: ART186232. Reproduced by persmission.

"The ancient Near East epic of Gilgamesh" Quotations are taken from David Ferry's *Gilgamesh: A New Rendering in English Verse* (New York: Farrar, Straus and Giroux, 1993).

The Classroom as Household

"Let Evening Come" Jane Kenyson, "Let Evening Come" from *Collected Poems* (p. 176). Copyright © 2005 by The Estate of Jane Kenyon. Reprinted with the permission of The Permissions Company, Inc. on behalf of Graywolf Press, Minneapolis, Minnesota, www.graywolfpress.org.

General Index

Page numbers in bold refer to illustrations

Scripture Index

Index of Reflections